Introduction to Programming Concepts with Case Studies in Python

Göktürk Üçoluk · Sinan Kalkan

Introduction to Programming Concepts with Case Studies in Python

 Springer

Göktürk Üçoluk
Department of Computer Engineering
Middle East Technical University
Ankara, Turkey

Sinan Kalkan
Department of Computer Engineering
Middle East Technical University
Ankara, Turkey

ISBN 978-3-7091-1342-4   ISBN 978-3-7091-1343-1 (eBook)
DOI 10.1007/978-3-7091-1343-1
Springer Wien Heidelberg New York Dordrecht London

Library of Congress Control Number: 2012951836

Printed on acid-free paper

Springer is part of Springer Science+Business Media (www.springer.com)

Preface

Purpose

This is a book aiming to be an introduction to Computer Science concepts as far as programming is concerned. It is designed as the textbook of a freshman level CS course and provides the fundamental concepts and abstract notions for solving computational problems. The Python language serves as a medium for illustration/demonstration.

Approach

This book introduces concepts by starting with the Q/A 'WHY?' and proceeds by the Q/A 'HOW?'. Most other books start with the Q/A 'WHAT?' which is then followed by a 'HOW?'. So, this book introduces the concepts starting from the grass-roots of the 'needs'. Moreover, the answer to the question 'HOW?' is somewhat different in this book. The book gives pseudo-algorithms for the 'use' of some CS concepts (like recursion or iteration). To the best of our knowledge, there is no other book that gives a recipe, for example, for developing a recursive solution to a world problem. In other textbooks, recursion is explained by displaying several recursive solutions to well-known problems (the definition of the factorial function is the most famous one) and hoping for the student to discover the technique behind it. That is why students following such textbooks easily understand what 'recursion' is but get stunned when the time comes to construct a recursive definition on their own. This teaching technique is applied throughout the book while various CS concepts got introduced.

This book is authored in concordance with a multi-paradigm approach, which is first 'functional' followed by 'imperative' and then 'object oriented'.

The CS content of this book is not hijacked by a programming language. This is also unique to this book. All other books either do not use any PL at all or first introduce the concepts only by means of the PL they use. This entanglement causes a poor formation of the abstract CS concept, if it does at all. This book introduces the concepts 'theoretically' and then projects it onto the Python PL. If the Python parts (which are printed on light greenish background) would be removed, the book would still be intact and comprehensible but be purely theoretical.

Audience

This book is intended for freshman students and lecturers in Computer science or engineering as a text book of an introductory course frequently named as one of:

- Introduction to Programming
- Introduction to Programming Constructs
- Introduction to Computer Science
- Introduction to Computer Engineering

Acknowledgments

We would like to thank Faruk Polat and İ. Hakkı Toroslu from the Middle East Technical University's Department of Computer Engineering and Reda Alhajj from the Department of Computer Science of University of Calgary for their constant support. We would also like to thank Chris Taylor for her professional proofreading of the manuscript and our student Rowanne Kabalan for her valuable comments on the language usage. Moreover, we are very grateful to Aziz Türk for his key help in the official procedures of publishing the book.

   Last but not least, we thank our life partners Gülnur and Gökçe and our families: without their support, this book would not have been possible.

Department of Computer Engineering,   Göktürk Üçoluk
Middle East Technical University,   Sinan Kalkan
Ankara, Turkey

Contents

Chapter 1
The World of Programming

Leaving the television media context to one side, in its most general meaning, a 'program' can be defined as:

a series of steps to be carried out or goals to be accomplished,

and hence, 'programming' is the act of generating a program.

Logically, programming requires a medium, or an environment since 'a series of steps towards a goal' can be meaningful only if there are entities or events, *i.e.*, an environment; otherwise, there would no need for goals. This environment can be a classroom full of students and a lecturer, where the program can be defined as the set of lectures to teach students certain subjects; or, a kitchen where a chef *follows* a program (*i.e.*, a recipe) to *produce* a requested dish; or, a bridge table or a war scenario.

Our environment is a 'computer'. Actually, to be more specific, it is a 'Von Neumann' type computing machine. Although Von Neumann machines are generally referred to as computers because of their dominant existence, it is simply not correct to assume that there is a single type of computing machinery, or a so called 'computer'. Based on carbon chemistry, we have the 'connection machine', which is more commonly known as the 'brain'; based on silicon chemistry, we have the 'Harvard architecture computer', the 'associative computer', 'analog computers', 'cell processors', 'Artificial Neural nets', and more. Also in exists are computational structures defined by means of pencil and paper; *e.g.*, the 'Turing machine', the 'Oracle machine',[1] the 'non-deterministic Turing machine' or even the 'quantum computer', which, these days, has begun to have a physical existence.

A Von Neumann architecture looks like the block structure displayed in Fig. 1.1. Without going into details, let us summarize the properties of this architecture as follows:

---

[1] 'Oracle machine' has nothing to do with the world-wide known database company 'ORACLE'.

G. Üçoluk, S. Kalkan, *Introduction to Programming Concepts with Case Studies in Python*, DOI 10.1007/978-3-7091-1343-1_1, © Springer-Verlag Wien 2012

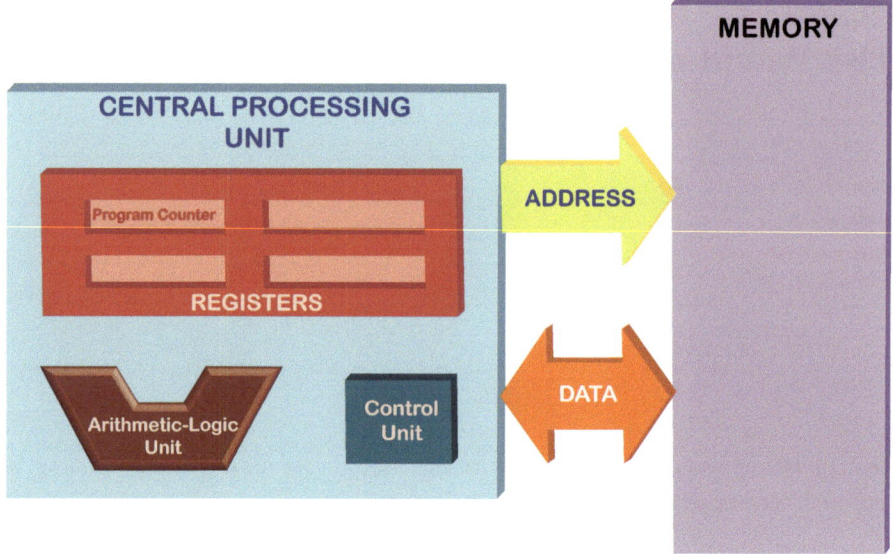

Fig. 1.1 Von Neumann Architecture

- It is an automatic digital computing system. It is based on binary representations. In such a system all information processed is in the form of binary digits.[2]
- It consists of two clearly distinct entities: The Central Processing Unit (CPU), and a Memory.
- The CPU is where all the 'brainy' (*i.e.*, control) actions are carried out. The processing of information (so called data) is performed here. The processing in a CPU involves simple arithmetical and logical operations or an access to a certain point in memory.

  The memory is nothing more than a very homogeneous but bulky electronic notebook. Each 'page' of this notebook, which has a number, can hold a *byte* (*i.e.*, eight bits) of information. Technically, the page number is called the *address* of that byte. It is possible to overwrite the content as many times as needed; however, the content that has been overwritten is gone forever and cannot be retrieved. Unless overwritten, the content remains there.

- The CPU and memory communicate through two sets of wires which we call the *address bus* and the *data bus*. In addition to these two buses, there is a single wire running from the CPU to the memory which carries a single bit of information depending on the desire of the CPU: will it store some data in the memory (*i.e.*, write to the memory) or fetch some data (*i.e.* read) from the memory. This single wire is called the R/W line.

---

[2] Actually 'digital' does not necessarily mean 'binary'. But to build binary logic electronic circuits is cheap and easy. So, in time, due to the technological course all digital circuits are built to support binary logic. Hence, 'digital' became a synonym for binary electronic circuitry.

Fig. 1.2 The continuous
Fetch-Decode-Execute cycle

A very important aspect of this architecture is that it is always the CPU that determines the address that is to be accessed in the memory. In other words, it is the CPU that generates and sends the address information via the address bus. There is no chance that the memory 'sends back' an address.

The CPU sets the address bus to carry a certain address and also sets the R/W line depending on whether the content at the given address will be read or written. If it is a write action, then the CPU also sets the data bus to the content that will be stored at the specific 'page' with that address. If it is a read action, this time it is the memory that sets the data bus to carry a copy of the content of the 'page' at the given address. Therefore, the address bus is unidirectional whereas the data bus is bidirectional.

- When the CPU is powered on or after the CPU has carried out a unit of action, it reads its next action, so called *instruction*, from the memory.[3] Depending on the outcome of last instruction, the CPU knows exactly, in the memory, where its next instruction is located. The CPU puts that address on the address bus, sets the R/W line to 'read' and the memory device, in response to this, sends back the instruction over the data bus. The CPU gets, decodes (understands, or interprets) and then performs the new instruction. Performing the action described by an instruction is called 'executing the instruction'. After this execution, the CPU will go and fetch the next instruction and execute it. This continuous circle is called the *Fetch-Decode-Execute cycle* (Fig. 1.2).
- The memory holds instructions and the information to be consumed directly by those instructions (see Fig. 1.3 for a simple example that illustrates this). This data is immediately fetched by the CPU (actually, if the data bus is large enough, α is fetched right along with the instruction byte) and used in that execute cycle.

---

[3]In the binary representation of instructions and data there exists some degree of freedom. Namely,
- what action will be represented by which binary sequence,
- what will be the binary representation for numbers (both floating points and integers)
is a design choice. This choice is made by the CPU manufacturer.

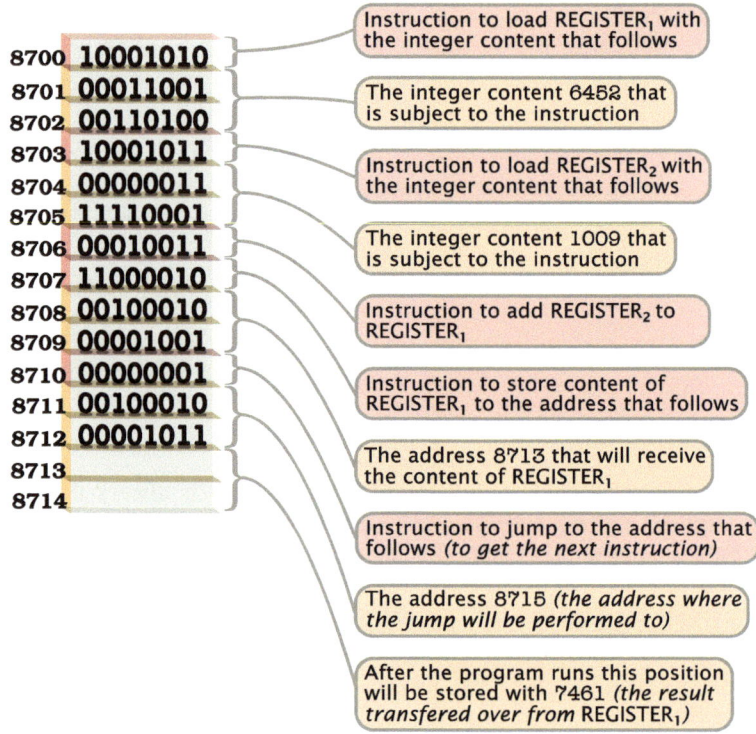

Fig. 1.3 The memory holds the instructions and the information to be consumed by the instructions. Also some results generated by the CPU are stored to the memory, for later use. In the figure you see a segment of the memory (the address range: [8700–8714]) holding a small machine code program. The program loads the first register with the integer 6452, the second with 1009 and then adds these leaving the result in the first. Then stores this integer result to the memory position that starts at 8713. Making use of a jump instruction the program 'steps over' this position that holds the result and continues its instruction fetch from the address 8715

However, it is not only the instructions and this adjunct information that fills the memory. Any data which is subject to be processed or used is stored in the memory, as well. Individual numbers, sequences of numbers that represent digitized images, sounds or any tabular numerical information are also stored in the memory. For example, when you open an text file in your favorite text editor, the memory contains sequences of words in the memory without an associated instruction.

It is essential to understand the Von Neumann architecture and how it functions since many aspects of 'programming' are directly based on it.

> Programming, in the context of the Von Neumann architecture, is generating the correct memory content that will achieve a given objective when executed by the CPU.

1.1 Programming Languages

Programming a Von Neumann machine by hand, *i.e.*, constructing the memory layout byte-by-byte is an extremely hard, if not impossible, task. The byte-by-byte memory layout corresponding to a program is called the *machine code*.

Interestingly, the first programming had to be done the most painful way: by producing machine code by hand. Now, for a second, consider yourself in the following position: You are given a set of instructions (encoded into a single byte), a schema to represent numbers (integers and real numbers) and characters (again all in bytes), and you are asked to perform the following tasks that a programmer is often confronted with:

- Find the average of a couple of thousand numbers,
- Multiply two 100×100 matrices,
- Determine the shortest itinerary from city A to city B,
- Find all the traffic signs in an image.

You will soon discover that, not to end up in a mental institution, you need to be able to program a Von Neumann machine using a more sophisticated set of instructions and data that are more understandable by humans, and you need a tool which will translate this human comprehensible form of the instructions and data (numbers and characters, at least), into that cumbersome, ugly looking, incomprehensible sequence of bytes; *i.e.*, machine code.

1.1.1 Low-Level Programming Languages

Here is such a sequence of bytes which multiplies two integer numbers sitting in two different locations in the memory and stores the result in another memory position:

```
01010101 01001000 10001001 11100101 10001011 00010101 10110010 00000011
00100000 00000000 10001011 00000101 10110000 00000011 00100000 00000000
00001111 10101111 11000010 10001001 00000101 10111011 00000011 00100000
00000000 10111000 00000000 00000000 00000000 00000000 11001001 11000011
...
11001000 00000001 00000000 00000000 00000000 00000000
```

And, the following is a human readable form, where the instructions have been given some short names, the numbers are readable, and some distinction between instructions, instruction related data, and pure data is recognizable:

```
main:
        pushq   %rbp
        movq    %rsp, %rbp
        movl    alice(%rip), %edx
        movl    bob(%rip), %eax
        imull   %edx, %eax
        movl    %eax, carol(%rip)
```

```
        movl      $0, %eax
        leave
        ret
alice:
        .long     123
bob:
        .long     456
```

This level of symbolization is a relief to some extent, and is called the *assembly* level. However, it still is a low level of programming, because the program does not get shorter actually: It only becomes more readable. Nonetheless, a programmer that has to generate machine code would certainly prefer writing in assembly then producing the machine code by hand, which requires a tool that will translate the instruction entered in the assembly language into machine code. Such tools are called *assemblers* and are programs themselves, which take another program (written in an assembly language) as input, and generate the corresponding machine code for it.

The assembler code displayed above is exactly the code that would produce the machine code for a Pentium CPU shown at the beginning of this section. Though it is a valuable aid to a programmer, a trained eye can look at the assembler code and can easily visualize what the corresponding machine code would look like. So, in a sense, the job of an assembler is nothing more than a dictionary for the instructions, and the very tedious translation from the human style denotation of numbers to the machine style binary representation. Therefore, assembly level programming, as well as machine code programming, is considered *low-level programming*.

It is certainly an interesting fact to note that the first assembler on Earth has been coded purely by hand, in machine code.

1.1.2 High-Level Programming Languages

Now, having the working example of an assembler in front of us, why not take the concept of 'translation' one step further? Knowing the abilities of a CPU at the instruction level and also having control over the whole space of the memory, why not construct a machine code producing program that 'understands' the needs of the programmer better, in a more intelligent way and generates the corresponding machine code, or even provides an environment in which it performs what it is asked for without translating it into a machine code at all. A more capable translator or a command interpreting program!

But, what are the boundaries of 'intelligence' here? Human intelligence? Certainly not! Even though this type of translator or command interpreter will have intelligence, it will not be able to cope with the ambiguities and heavy background information references of our daily languages; English, Turkish, French or Swazi. Therefore, we have to compromise and use a restricted language, which is much more mathematical and logical compared to natural languages. Actually, what we would like is a language in which we can express our algorithms without much pain. In particular, the pain about the specific brand of CPU and its specific set of instructions, register types and count *etc.* is unbearable. We have many other issues to worry about in the field of programming.

So, we have to create a set of rules that define a programming language both *syntax*- and *semantic*-wise, in a very rigorous manner. Just to refresh your vocabulary: syntax is the set of rules that govern what is allowed to write down, and semantics is the meaning of what is written down.

Such syntactic and semantic definitions have been made over the past 50 years, and now, we have around 700 programming languages of different complexities. There are about a couple of thousands more, created experimentally, as M.Sc. or Ph.D. theses *etc.*

Most of these languages implement high-level concepts (those which are not present at the machine level) such as

- human readable form of numbers and strings *(like decimal, octal, hexadecimal representations for numbers)*,
- containers *(automatic allocation for places in the memory to hold data and naming them)*,
- expressions *(calculation of formulas based on operators which have precedences the way we are used to from mathematics)*,
- constructs for repetitive execution *(conditional re-execution of code parts)*,
- functions,
- pointers *(a concept which fuses together the 'type of the data' and the 'address of the data')*,
- facilities for data organization *(ability to define new data types based on the primitive ones, organizing them in the memory in certain layouts)*.

Before diving into the variety of the programming languages, let us have a glimpse at the problem that we introduced above, *i.e.*, multiplication of two integers and storage of the result, now coded in a high level programming language, C:

```
int alice = 123;
int bob = 456;
int carol;
main(void)
{
    carol = alice*bob;
}
```

This is much more understandable and shorter, isn't it?

1.2 Programming Paradigms

During the course of the evolution of the programing languages, different strategies or world views about programming have also developed. These world views are reflected in the programming languages that have been designed by the programmers.

For example, one world view is regarding the programming task as transforming some initial data (the initial information that defines the problem) into a final form (the data that is the answer to that problem) by applying a sequence of functions. From this perspective, writing a program is defining some functions which then are used in a functional composition; a composition which, when applied to some initial data, yields the answer to the problem. The earliest realization of this approach was the LISP language, designed by John McCarthy in 1958 at MIT. After LISP, more programming languages have been developed, and more world views have emerged.

The Oxford dictionary defines the word paradigm as follows:

> **paradigm** |'parə,dïm|
> *noun*
> A world view underlying the theories and methodology of a particular scientific subject.

These world views in the world of programming are known as *programming paradigms*. Below is a list of some of the major paradigms:

- Imperative
- Functional
- Logical-declarative
- Object oriented
- Concurrent
- Event driven

1.2.1 The Imperative Programming Paradigm

In imperative programming, a problem is solved by writing down a sequence of action units which are called *statements*. Each statement performs either a change on the data environment (the parts of the memory that holds the data) of the program or alters the flow of execution. In this sense, imperative programs are easy to translate into machine code. If $statement_A$ is followed by $statement_B$, then in the machine code translations of these statements $machine\_code_A$ will also be followed by $machine\_code_B$.

1.2.2 The Functional Programming Paradigm

In this paradigm, the data environment is extremely restricted. There is a certain, common, data region where functions receive their parameters and return their results to. That is all, and with a deliberate intention no other data regions are created.

The programmer's task is to find a way of decomposing the problem into functions, so that, when a composition of those functions is constructed and applied to the initial data of the problem, the result gets computed.

1.2.3 The Logical-Declarative Programming Paradigm

In this paradigm, the programmer states the relations among the data as *facts* or *rules* (sometimes also referred to as *relations*).

For example, facts can be the information about who is whose mother and the rule can be a logical rule stating that X is the grandmother of Y if X is the mother of an intermediate person who is the mother Y. Below is such a program in Prolog a well-known logical programming language.

```
mother(matilda,ruth).
mother(trudi,peggy).
mother(eve,alice).
mother(zoe,sue).
mother(eve,trudi).
mother(matilda,eve).
mother(eve,carol).
grandma(X,Y) :- mother(X,Z), mother(Z,Y).
```

The mother() rule tells the computer about the existing motherhood relations in the data (*i.e.*, the people); for example, mother(mathilda,ruth) states that mathilda is the mother of ruth. Based on the mother() rule, a new rule grandma() is easily defined: grandma(X,Y) is valid if both mother(X,Z) and mother(Z,Y) are valid for an arbitrary person Z, which the computer tries to find among the rules that are given to it by the programmer.

Now, a question (technically a *query*) that asks for all grandmas and granddaughters:

```
?- grandma(G,T).
```

will yield an answer where all solutions are provided:

```
G=matilda, T=alice
G=matilda, T=trudi
G=matilda, T=carol
```

Contrary to other programming paradigms, we do not cook up the solution in the logical programming paradigm: We do not write functions nor do we imperatively give orders. We simply state rule(s) that define relations among the data, and ask for the data that satisfies the rules.

1.2.4 The Object-Oriented Programming Paradigm

Object Oriented paradigm is may be the most common paradigm in commercial circles. The separation of the 'data' and the 'action on the data', which actually steams from the Von Neumann architecture itself, is lost, and they are reunited in this paradigm. Of course, this unification is artificial, but still useful.

An object has some internal data and functions, so called *methods*. It is possible to create as many replicas (*instances*) of an object as desired. Each of these instances has its own data space, where the object keeps its 'private' information content. Some of the functions of the object can be called from the outside world. Here, the outside world is the parts of the program which do not belong to the object's definition. The outside word cannot access an object's data space since it is private. Instead, accessing the data stored in the object is performed by calling a function that belongs to the object. This function serves as an interface and calling it is termed *message passing*.

In addition to this concept of data hiding, the object oriented paradigm employs other ideas as well, one of which is *inheritance*. A programmer can base a new definition of an object on an already defined one. In such a case, the new object inherits all the definitions of the existing object and extend those definitions or add new ones.

The following is a simplified example that demonstrates the inheritance mechanism used in object-oriented programming. A *class* is the blueprint of an object defined in a programming language. Below we define three classes. (The methods in the class definitions are skipped for the sake of clarity):

```
class Item
{
string Name;
float Price;
string Location;
...
};

class Book : Item
{
string Author;
string Publisher;
...
};

class MusicCD : Item
{
string Artist;
string Distributor;
...
};
```

In this example, the Book class and the MusicCD class are *derived* or *inherited* from the Item class and through this inheritance, these inheriting classes inherently have what is defined in the Item class. In addition to the three inherited data fields Name, Price and Location, the Book class adds two more data fields, namely Author and Publisher.

All these features help to represent real world problems more easily and generate re-usable programs, enhancing the maintainability of the huge codes developed by tens or hundreds of programmers. These are commercial assets of the object oriented programming paradigm.

1.2.5 *The Concurrent Programming Paradigm*

Concurrent programming is a paradigm which intends to solve a problem by concurrently engaging more than one CPU. Each CPU will solve a part of the problem and then the partial solutions from each CPU are combined to yield the final solution. When assigned a task to carry out, each CPU will be on its own, acting independently. The focus of this paradigm is to manage the correct flow of the control, as well as the data, to and from these independently running pieces of programs.

In the future, due to the physical constrains on the manufacturing of CPUs, the speeding up of a single CPU will become less and less probable. To fulfill the increasing need for more computational power, the only way out might be to employ more and more CPUs working on the same problem. This will lead to a shift in favor of the concurrent programming paradigm.

1.2.6 *The Event-Driven Programming Paradigm*

From this paradigm's perspective, the programming world consists of events and actions tied to these events. When an event occurs, the action tied to that event is automatically triggered. This action may carry out some computational tasks as well as give rise to some new events. The programmer's job is to make a design of this chain reaction clockwork and implement the actions as pieces of the program (usually as functions).

- To serve all types of events (that can occur),
- not to get into deadlocks,
- handling events that occur while an action is being carried out

are kind of problems a programmer that does event driven programming has to deal with.

This paradigm has extensive applications in Graphical User Interface[4] (GUI) oriented application development, since GUIs have excessive amount of diverse user input (*i.e.*, events).

---

[4]A Graphical User Interface is the set of windows and all the stuff included in the windows that take care of the exchange of information between the user and the program. For example, when you open a browser, a window pops up; that window is the GUI for the browser.

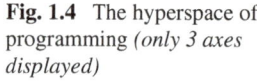

Fig. 1.4 The hyperspace of programming *(only 3 axes displayed)*

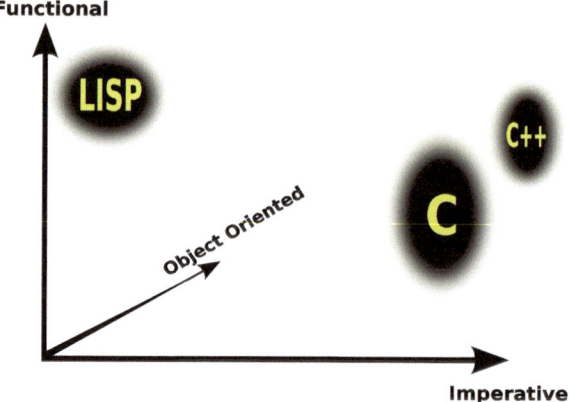

1.3 The Zoo of Programming Languages

Now we have presented some of the programming language paradigms together with more that we have not mentioned, there are about 10 programming paradigms. So, how come that there are over 700 programming languages? Are they simple re-implementations with some small syntactic differences? No, that would be too harsh a judgment.

The answer lies in the fact that most of these paradigms are not contradictory to each other. Actually, they are orthogonal. For a moment let us visit to a hyperspace of programming. Yes, its difficult to imagine but try to visualize it. The axes of this hyperspace are the paradigms (if there were only three paradigms, it would be simpler to visualize but still you can do it). A space spanned by a set of axes each of which is a programming paradigm. Then, we can view any programming language as a cloud in this space. As much as a language supports a paradigm, its cloud is located far away from the origin along that paradigm axis (see Fig. 1.4).

So, for example, the popular language C will be a cloud, quite advanced along the imperative axis (as shown in Fig. 1.4), lesser advanced along the functional axis, but not represented at all along the object oriented and logical axes. C++ would additionally be advanced in the object oriented axis direction (still nothing on the logical direction), as depicted in Fig. 1.4.

Why are we visualizing clouds and not points? This is because (a) these are fuzzy concepts, so it is not correct to quantify them with a single scalar: it is not reasonable to say that C is 81% functional (and not 80% nor 82%). (b) There is an additional factor that originates from the user, namely the programmer's personal style. One person may put more emphasis on the use of functions whereas another will be more concerned about the computational (machine code) overhead produced by function calls and tries to be more imperative. Therefore, personal tastes of the programmers moves around in the cloud.

You may ask whether there is a programming language that serves all paradigms?; *i.e.*, is there a 'cloud' that has high values on all axes in this programming hyperspace. This question is quite similar to the question "why is there no creature that can walk like an ostrich, run like a tiger, crawl like a snake, jump like kangaroo, swim like a human, remain underwater like a fish and fly like an albatross?".

Very similar to the problems in the design of such a super creature, the realization of a super programming language would present extreme difficulties due to conflicting requirements. Even if it were possible to construct such a language, it would be far from being versatile, fast, portable and so on. The reality is that languages that serve at most two or three paradigms are feasible and can be realized by programming language developers.

The development of programming languages is interesting in this sense. Figure 1.5 displays a historical overview of how this taxonomy developed.[5]

1.3.1 How to Choose a Programming Language for an Implementation

All paradigms, all programming languages and even all CPUs are equivalent. This is called the Turing Equivalence. We will return to the subject of the Turing Machine later in Sect. 3.3.1. For the moment, we are only introducing the term *Turing equivalence* which states that two computers P and Q are Turing equivalent if P can simulate Q and Q can simulate P. The proof is simple: A Von Neumann computer can simulate a Turing machine (a very simple, hypothetical, machine that has a mathematical definition) and a Turing machine can simulate any real world computer (this is a product of the Church–Turing thesis). The Church–Turing thesis is a conjecture which cannot be formally proven, but has near-universal acceptance. It reads as:

Everything computable is computable by a Turing machine.

So what? Are we in the darkness of the meaninglessness, again? All CPUs are equivalent! All paradigms are equivalent! All programming languages are equivalent! What does it mean if we can do with one what we can do with the other?

For clarification, think about this example: A man with a shovel and a bulldozer are equivalent too, if the task is displacing a certain amount of soil. For the common sense the key point lies in what we call 'efficiency' or 'easiness'. Turing equivalence does not say anything about these concepts. It is merely an equivalence about 'doability'.

Therefore, it is meaningful, indeed, to choose a language based on the consideration of efficiency and easiness. We make decisions based on these considerations in all other aspects of our life, all the time.

There are different factors in choosing among the programming language paradigms:

The domain and technical nature of the world problem: Consider   three   different computing tasks:

---

[5]From: Chen *et al.* (2005). Updated by the authors.

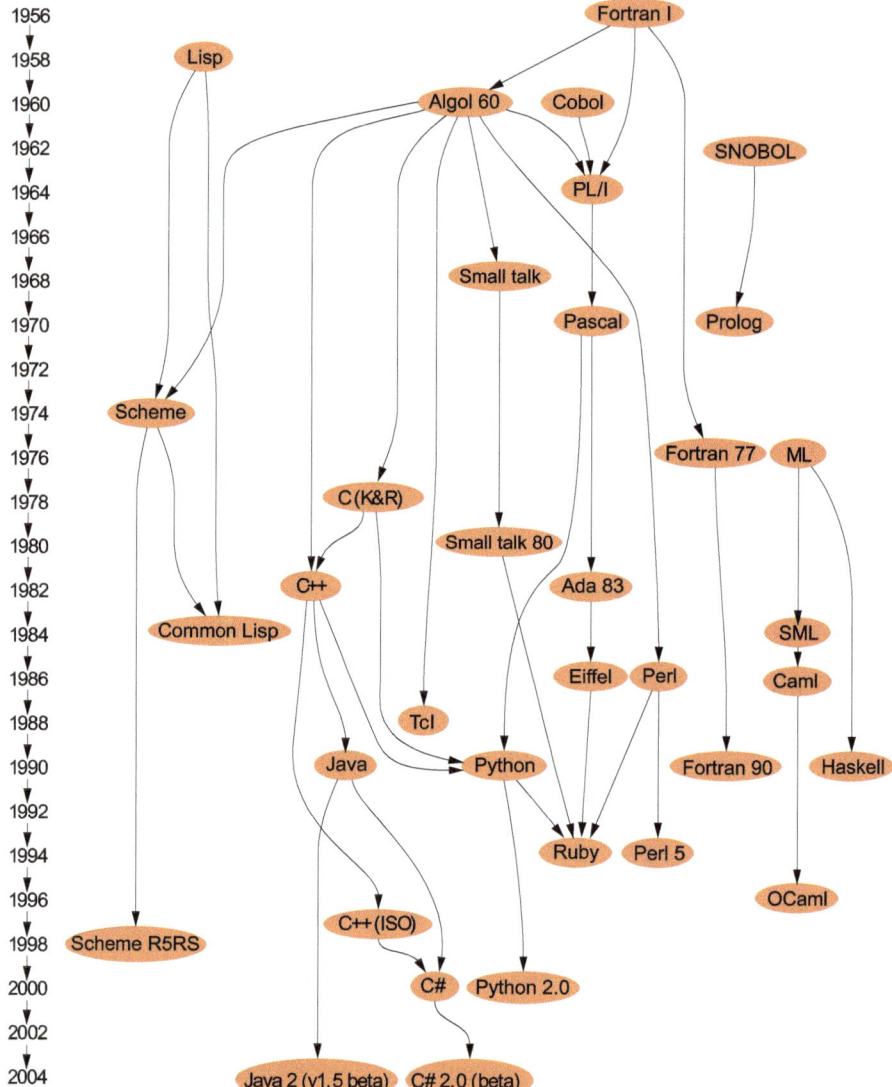

Fig. 1.5 A brief taxonomic history (1956–2005) of high level programming language (From: Chen *et al.* (2005). Updated by the authors)

(a) Finding the pixels of an image with RGB value of [202,130,180] with a tolerance of 5.4% in intensity.

(b) A proof system for planar geometry problems.

(c) A computer game platform to be used as a whole or in parts and may be extended or even rewritten by programmers at various levels.

(d) Payroll printing.

Any wise programmer will pick a fast imperative language (like C) for (a), a declarative language (like Prolog) for (b), an object oriented language (like C++) for (c) and Cobol for (d).

What would be the foolish way to go? That is fun to answer! Cobol for (a), (b) and (c).

Why is this so, because C is the fastest high-level language and the defined image processing task (a) is highly imperative; Prolog is the most profound and well-structured logic-declarative language especially suited for AI applications, in which domain the 'proof system' (b) belongs; Game programming is speed hungry and the re-usability issue of the task (c) is best fulfilled by an object oriented language, which leads a programmer to C++; Finally, payroll printing (d) can actually be done in any language but the archaic language Cobol is designed only to serve the domain of business, finance, and administrative systems for companies and governments.

Personal taste and experience: Among those 700 programming languages, certainly some are alike; or, some are alike as far as the task is concerned (*i.e.*, the difference is (ir)relevant for that specific task); or, for instance, the programmer has a rationale to favor a specific paradigm or language. As an example, think of a case where a programmer prefers the Lisp language (a profound representative of the functional paradigm) over Prolog (the best known declarative paradigm representative) because s/he has a library of programs at hand to carry out rule-based AI programming in Lisp (which s/he may have accumulated over his/her extensive years of AI programming experience).

Microsoft, used C, C++ and assembler in its Windows operating system. Apple, in its Mac OS X operating system used C, C++ and Objective C. The nonproprietary operating system Linux used C and assembler. For other programmers, taking also the other constraints into account, it is a matter of taste to choose among C++, Delphi or Objective-C.

Circumstance-imposed constraints: It is an interesting empirical fact that there is always a shortage of time when it comes to writing a program. However, sometimes, the project constraints are so tight that you know from the start that you have to go for a suboptimal solution; *i.e.*, a solution with compromises. You pick a scripting language (Perl, Php, Python, Ruby) for fast prototyping, knowing that it will be slow compared to an implementation in C. You select for Java being aware that it will be less efficient compared to C++, but knowing there is a huge pile of reusable code available in Java. As it is with life, choices made in the world of programming have their pros and cons.

Writing an experimental program to prove a concept developed in connection with your Ph.D. thesis and putting the concept into a commercial product are also different. The first code is presumably understandable only 'by you' and 'for you' whereas the second will be 'by a team of programmers in a software company' and 'for thousands of end users'. In the second case, you have to seriously consider the ease-of-use, maintainability, re-usability and portability (compatibility with another operating system), *etc.*, and, all these will impact on your choice of programming language.

Current trend: One way or another, current trends influence our choice of programming language for various reasons such as:

- Trendy languages usually come with gizmos for contemporary issues.
- There is a large professional interest, which, in turn, means dynamic answers
  in forums, documents, *etc.*
- The availability of a rich environment for learning (lectures, books, videos).
- Great collections of program libraries (even mostly free).
- It is easy to find a substitute programmer if someone drops out of the team.
- Customers are impressed to hear that their project will be realized using
  a trendy language since the disadvantages of older languages are more
  widespread.

There are many attempts to measure and inform the professional community
about the latest trend. Job advertisements mentioning a certain programming
language, lines of code written by the open software community, the teaching
books sold and search engine clicks are all counted and statistically evaluated
for this purpose.

In Fig. 1.6 the popularity change over the last 8 years from the TIOBE PCI is displayed. The TIOBE PCI (programming community index)[6] is a widely known
and acknowledged indicator for the popularity of programming languages. As
denoted on the TIOBE web page, the index is updated once a month; the ratings are based on the number of skilled engineers world-wide, courses and third
party vendors; the popular search engines Google, MSN, Yahoo!, Wikipedia and
YouTube are used to calculate the ratings.

1.4 How Programing Languages Are Implemented

Up to this point, you should have a fair idea of what a high level programming
language is.

When it comes to implementation, now we will discuss two ways to proceed
(later, we will also introduce an intermediate path). One approach is to set up a
machinery, a program, which takes as an input a program P in a high level language
and processes it, then produces a machine code equivalent of it. Then, whenever
we want the program to function, we make the Von Neumann machine execute the
translated machine code. This is the *compilative approach*. An alternative way is
to devise a machinery that, instead of producing the machine code, actually carries
out what the program P describes; immediately, statement by statement. This is the
interpretive approach.

---

[6]http://www.tiobe.com/index.php/content/paperinfo/tpci/.

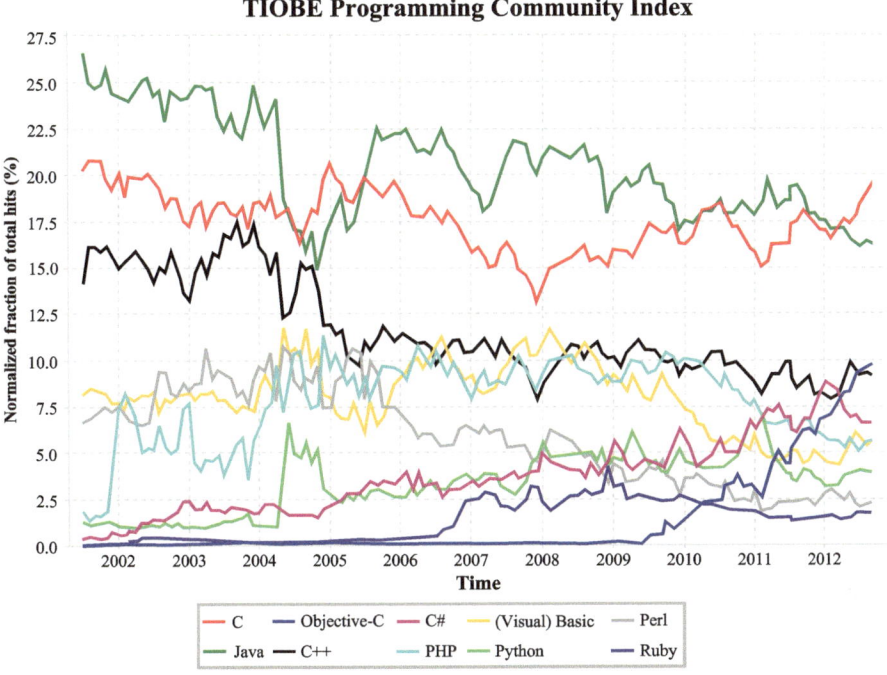

Fig. 1.6 Popularity change over years for highly used programming languages (Source: www.tiobe.com)

Fig. 1.7 Compilation to object code

1.4.1 Compilative Approach

In this approach, the high level language program is written by the programmer using a text editor in a text file which is then submitted to a program that does the translation. Such a translator program is called a *compiler*. The output of the compilation is a file that contains the machine code translation of the high level language program and some other information (Fig. 1.7). This content is called the *object code*. Why is the output of the compilation process not exactly the machine

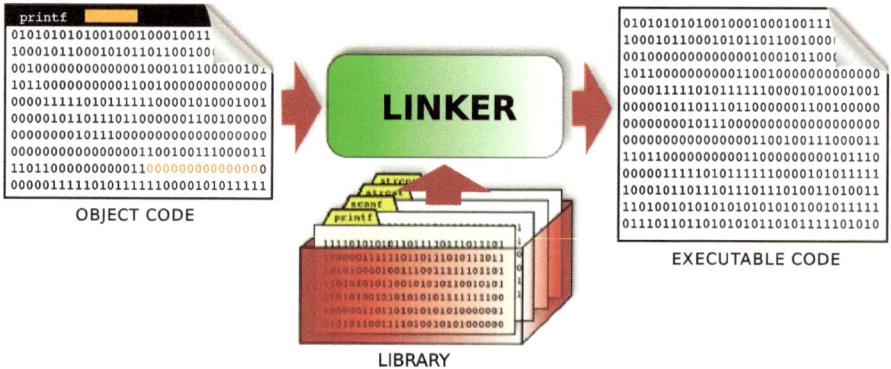

Fig. 1.8   Linking produces the executable code

code that will be run? Because it is quite likely that the programmer has made use of some code that he has not defined. For example, a *print directive*, or an arctangent calculation. Such codes are provided by the compiler manufacturer as a separate entity (not embedded into the compiler program), usually as a huge file, full of machine code pieces, which is called a *library*. The calls to these code pieces are left as holes in the machine code. The object code starts with a table followed with the machine code with holes in it. The table provides information about which hole is going to be filled with which code's reference.

After the first stage of compilation, a program called the *linker*, analyzes both the object code and the library. It creates a combined file where the compiled code is followed by the copies of the external code pieces that come from the library and were used by the programmer. Looking at the table of the object code and the library, the linker finds the matching names (for the code pieces) and substitutes into the holes the corresponding references (addresses). The result is a stand-alone machine code ready for execution. Actually this picture (Fig. 1.8) is a little simplified. In reality, it is also possible to use codes which are coming from other object files. Such combinations of object codes are possible because an object also carries a table about the names of the codes (functions and variables) it implements/defines. So, the linker is capable of analyzing more than one object code plus the library and fill the holes accordingly.

After the linking is carried out, the user, whenever s/he wants to, loads the machine code into the memory and starts executing it. There is a program called *loader* which is responsible for loading and starting machine codes (Fig. 1.9).

The compilative approach produces fast and executable machine codes, but it is not so suitable for an incremental development of a program. Compilation and linking, even in these days, take some time. Therefore, making small tweaks in the program or locating/correcting errors cannot be done interactively.

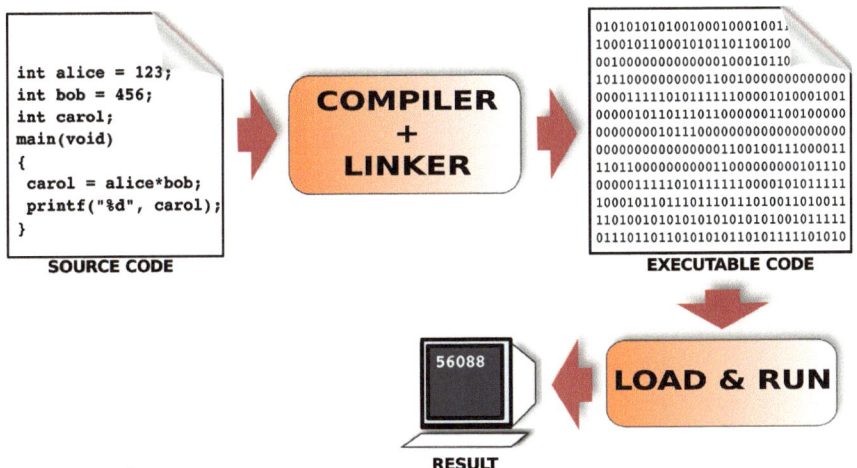

```
int alice = 123;
int bob = 456;
int carol;
main(void)
{
  carol = alice*bob;
  printf("%d", carol);
}
```

SOURCE CODE

COMPILER
+
LINKER

```
01010101010010010001001
10001011000101011011001001000
001000000000000100010110
101100000000011001000000000000000
000011111010111111100001010001001
000001011011101100000011001000000
000000000101110000000000000000000
000000000000000011001001110000011
110110000000000110000000000101110
000001111101011111100001010111111
100010110111011110111010011010011
110100101010101010101010010011111
011101101101010101101011111101010
```

EXECUTABLE CODE

56088

RESULT

LOAD & RUN

Fig. 1.9 Compilative approach: The whole program is first translated into an executable code (with the help of a compiler and a linker), loaded into the memory at a future time, run, then the result of the whole program is returned to the programmer

1.4.2 Interpretive Approach

In the interpretive approach, no target machine code is generated. Instead of having a stand-alone, executable and full translation of a program, written in a high-level language, we have a program that understands and obeys the commands given in the high level language. We talk to a program called an *interpreter* and issue those commands. For example, when we give an order to square a number and then take the sinus of it, our order is carried out immediately and the result is returned to us. Certainly, it is possible to fill a file with a sequence of orders (statements), and submit that file to be processed by the interpreter. Those statements will be carried out one by one, in real time.

Figure 1.10 displays a hypothetical conversation between a programmer and an interpreter, doing the same computation of the C language program shown in Fig. 1.9.

To be able to fulfill the high level commands, the interpreter has to have a kind of an internal ball park where variables can be created, function definitions be stored, function calls and expression evaluations be carried out. In addition to this, it has to have a front-end that receives those commands (statements), and maps them to the internal actions in the ball park. There is lots of work to do, in real time, first to decode (*i.e.*, interpret) the statement, and then to carry out the corresponding actions and keep the ball park tidy. Hence, an interpreter is slow; about 20 times slower than a compiler-generated machine code execution. But, on the other hand, an interpreter provides 100% interactivity while developing a program, enhancing rapid program, or algorithm development.

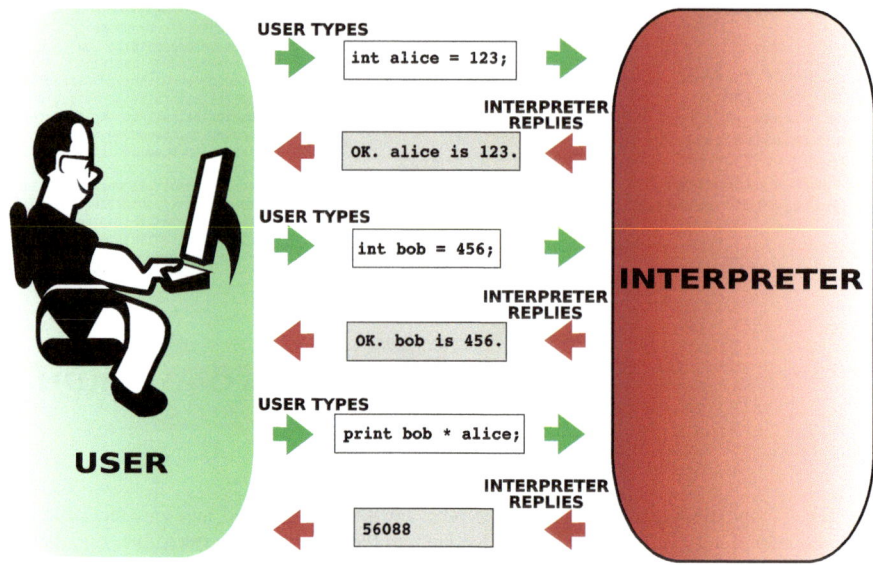

Fig. 1.10 Interpretive approach: Each high-level statement from the programmer is executed and the result is immediately returned to the programmer

1.4.3 Mixed Approaches

The interpretive approach is more user-friendly and elegant, but it has the huge drawback of being slow, sometimes to the point of unbearable! This is due, in part, to reinterpreting what might have been already interpreted; looping structures or functions for example. To overcome this problem, it is possible to compile, on the fly, such an expression into machine code. Then, when it is time to reuse it, instead of reinterpreting it, the interpreter simply executes the freshly compiled machine code (of that piece of code). If there is no repetition, this process would actually add to the processing time, but, in practice, most programs contain repetition to a great extent. This technique is called as *on-the-fly compilation*.

Compiling to machine code has its drawbacks too. There is certainly no standardization on the processors nor on the machine code. All manufactures are proud of having their own low-level languages for their CPU's. Though, they are all Von Neumann machines, they differ in the internal hardware components such as in number and the types/purposes of registers, the circuitry to undertake math calculations and other instructions. Therefore, a machine code compiled for a CPU brand A, will not run on a CPU brand B. One way to solve this problem is to write an *emulator* on the computer with CPU B, for the machine code of CPU A; *i.e.*, a kind of machine code interpreter. This approach has some realizations. Of course, the interpretation has a time cost which is a factor around three for CPUs of equal speed. However, there exists another solution: to set a low-level language which is not biased towards any CPU; *i.e.*, a kind of a machine language where the machine does not exist as a hardware, in other words, as a CPU. Then, for every brand of CPU, an interpreter will be written, that takes the code expressed in this low-level language in, and carries out the instructions. The idea is to keep this interpretation at a very simple level. This pseudo machine code is generically called as *p-code*. A good example is the popular language *java*. The interpreter that accepts java code is called *jvm*, an abbreviation for the *java virtual machine*. You can find the jvm for almost every platform, from powerful contemporary CPUs to the mobile phone CPUs.

1.5 How a Program Gets "Written"

The task of writing a program ranges from creating a couple of hundred lines up to a couple of million lines. As the number of lines of code increases, writing programs starts to become a team job; a team which sometime grows up to hundreds of programmers. A finalized program, possibly bundled with some data and documentation is named as *software*.

The realization of a software project is a discipline by itself, which is called *Software Engineering software engineering*, in which there are several methods, denotational mechanisms and dedicated tools (mostly software tools). In fact, it is not much different from any other field of engineering.

How such large software projects are managed is out of the scope of this book we refer the interested to textbooks on software engineering.

1.5.1 Modular & Functional Break-Down

Even a relatively small project of about a couple of thousand lines of code will have a functional break-down; *i.e.*, a division into a set of sub-components that are functionally distinct from each other. The first level of such a break-down corresponds to modules; for example consider a software for a library of books and periodicals. The modules for this library software might be the following:

- *The user interface module*: The piece of code that is responsible for communicating with the user sitting in front of the computer and using the developed or software. This module usually has screens containing informative text, parts of which are active (*e.g.*, clickable with the mouse), menus and text-fields to be filled in by the user.
- *The database module*: The piece of code that is responsible for storing and retrieving information. In this case, it is about library material (*i.e.*, books and periodicals) and the users of the library (their id, name, material they have checked out, *etc.*).
- *The control module*: The piece of code that is responsible for all the 'librarian'-style actions such as, asking for the library id, checking out books, warning about overdue items and generating lists of various items. While carrying out these actions, most probably, this module will heavily communicate with (*i.e.*, make use of) the 'database module' as well as the 'user interface module'.

Writing a program starts with such a break-down.

If the number of these modules is considerable, then this will affect the choice of the implementation language. Almost all practical programming languages provide features to decompose large programs into smaller components. Even when a language does not provide specific handles for this, the implementation often offers some *ad hoc* features which are used by software developers to put together the separately developed parts to form a more complex system.

Some programming languages provide additional features better to serve the modular implementation. This is done by explicit declarations of what is imported and exported in software terms from a certain code-module. Among these strongly modular languages, are Ada, Modula-2 and Python. The popular languages C, C++ and Java also provide constructs that makes it easier for the software developer to impose modularity.

1.5.2 Testing

While a program is being developed, a constant and continuous effort has to be made to ensure that the program conforms with the specifications (*i.e.*, user requirements), and meets the expectations. The former of these efforts is called *verification* and the latter *validation*. In other words, *verification* is asking the question

Is the program built right?

While *validation* is asking

Is it the right program?

There are two fundamental approaches to respond to these questions. The first is *to experiment with the behavior* of the software product, which is merely *dynamic testing*. The other is *static testing* which means analyzing the product (not only the code that makes up the program material but also its documentation *etc.*) and then to decide whether it will operate correctly by examining the logical consequences of its design. We will not go into the details about static testing, as this is subject to theoretical research. Companies, therefore take 'testing' (apart from the careful inspection of specifications and code by their in-house programming experts) to mean dynamic testing. Actually, both approaches are complementary and should be used together. It is also important to understand that, by testing, one cannot prove the complete absence of errors. In other words, simply because the test suite of trial examples for a system did not detect any errors, it cannot be concluded that the system does not contain any error. So, the verification is just a relative verification, 'modulo' your tests.

Usually, software projects are so large, in scale, that it is unrealistic to test them as a single unit. The way such systems are realized is in terms of smaller units, *i.e.*, modules, which in turn are built out of procedures, functions, *etc.*

Structure-wise, there are two testing approaches that are used in testing: *top-down* and *bottom-up* testing. Behavior-wise there are again two types of testing approaches: *black-box* and *white-box* testing.

Top-Down Testing

In the top-down approach, testing starts at a subsystem level. Even though some modules may not have actually been implemented before testing starts, they can be substituted by *stubs*. A stub is a program module which has exactly the same module interface as the intended final module, but is much simpler (in a sense hollow) in implementation; *i.e.*, it 'fakes' the subsystem by producing a simulated action or output. This is achieved by random data generation, or returning its input as the output, or directly consulting the tester for a result. Eventually, all stubs are replaced by their actual code. Clearly, this technique does not need to wait until all the modules are completed, and indeed it should to be started as soon as possible. It should be used in parallel with the development, so that as soon as a part of the software is coded, it is possible to start testing it.

Bottom-Up Testing

Bottom-up testing proceeds by starting from the smallest components. These components are tested individually, and then the module that integrates them is tested. As mentioned above, modules make up the subsystems; so, when all the modules have been tested, the subsystems are tested. Bottom-up testing has the disadvantage that until the very last line of code is written, the system is not ready for demonstration.

It is reasonable to suggest that a mixture of top-down and bottom-up testing should be used. In this mixed approach, the implementation may start with a single module, in which all kinds of bottom-up tests are performed and then this is mounted in a top-down test frame. This scheme is continued until all the modules are coded.

Black-Box Testing

In *black-box testing*, which is also known as *opaque-box* or *closed-box testing*, the item being tested is defined only by its input and output behavior. The actual test cases, *i.e.* examples, are designed from this point of view.

The advantage of black-box testing is that the tester does not have to understand (or even access) the source code to test it, the tester will only check whether the outputs match the desired outputs for the given inputs. The disadvantage of black-box testing is that the tester cannot look at the code and get hints from it, or locate the portion of the program where it is more likely to have a 'bug' and hence cannot design a 'test case' to catch likely errors.

The alternative to black-box testing is called *white-box testing* or *glass-box testing*.

White-Box Testing

In white-box testing, which is also known as *glass-box* or *clear-box testing*, the tester can look into the code to determine the tests to be implemented. Thus, the advantages are the disadvantages of the black-box testing, as stated above. However, this method has also its disadvantages in that by employing a tester with the 'inside knowledge' of the source code, we have the risk that the tester will also overlook the pitfall that the programmer overlooked once (for exactly the same reasons as the programmer had overlooked it).

The tester certainly cannot test all the possible inputs and outputs. Therefore, there must be a judgment, on some fair basis, that some of the input data are 'alike'. For instance, the input of 35 for a parameter that represents 'age' is not much different from the age input of 36. Hence, a tester may only try an input parameter of 35 here. The input classification of this kind, in which the set of all input data is partitioned into equivalence classes, is called *equivalence partitioning*. These equivalence classes are determined by using the available documentation, specification and perhaps more important the experience and the intuition of the tester to predict which classes of input value are likely to produce errors.

1.5.3 Errors

To Err is Human, To Forgive Divine

So states the English proverb; however, unfortunately, as it is with all the engineering disciplines, to err may have vital consequences in software development. A wrong calculation can cause planes to crash, buildings or bridges collapse. A programmer's minor error, finding its way into the control module of a life-support machine, can easily cost lives.

Errors are named as *bugs* in the software development jargon. The following excerpt from Wikipedia concerning 'Software bug' provides some insight to this funny term.

Problems with radar electronics during World War II were referred to as bugs (or glitches) and there is additional evidence that the usage dates back much earlier. Baffle Ball, the first mechanical pinball game, was advertised as being "free of bugs" in 1931.

The invention of the term is often erroneously attributed to Grace Hopper, who publicized the cause of a malfunction in an early electromechanical computer. A typical version of the story is given by this quote:

> In 1946, when Hopper was released from active duty, she joined the Harvard Faculty at the Computation Laboratory where she continued her work on the Mark II and Mark III. Operators traced an error in the Mark II to a moth trapped in a relay, coining the term bug. This bug was carefully removed and taped to the log book. Stemming from the first bug, today we call errors or glitch's [sic] in a program a bug.

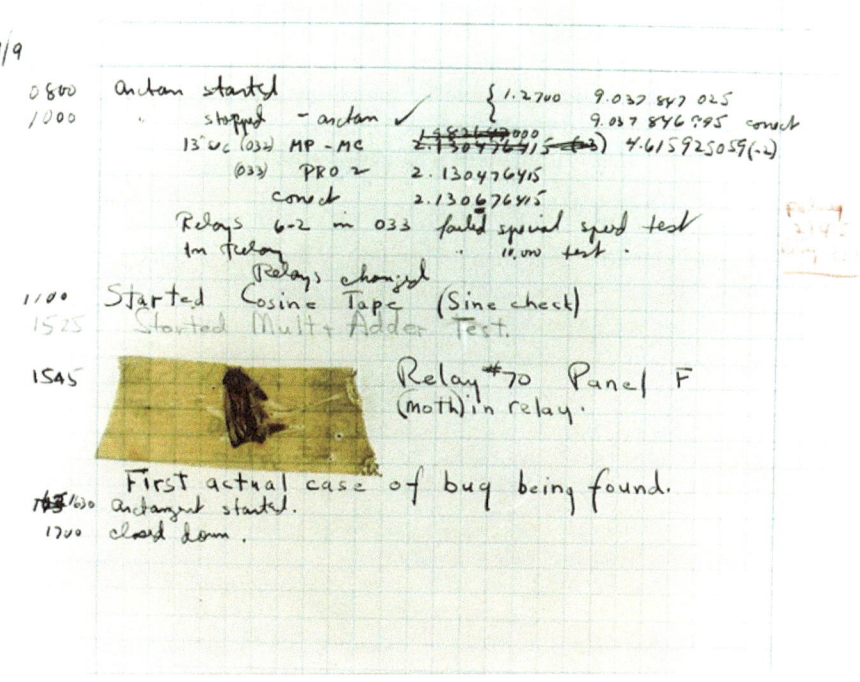

Fig. 1.11 Photo of what is possibly the first real bug found in a computer. (Photo courtesy of U.S. Naval Historical Center Online Library Photograph—NH 96566-KN)

Hopper was not actually the one who found the insect, as she readily acknowledged. The date in the log book was 9 September 1947, although sometimes erroneously reported as 1945. The operators who did find it, including William "Bill" Burke, later of the Naval Weapons Laboratory, Dahlgren, Virginia, were familiar with the engineering term and, amused, kept the insect with the notation "First actual case of bug being found." Hopper loved to recount the story. This log book is on display in the Smithsonian National Museum of American History, complete with moth attached. (See Fig. 1.11.)

Generally speaking, there are four types of programming errors (bugs).

- *Syntax errors (also known as* compile-time errors*):* The programmer does not obey the syntax rules of the programming language. For example, instead of entering:

      area = 3.1415 * R * R

  the programmer types:

      area = 3.1415 x R x R

  and since '*' is the infix operator for multiplication for this programming language not 'x' the programmer has made a syntax error. Syntax errors are the easiest errors to resolve. The compiler or the interpreter will issue the error, mostly indicating where exactly it occurred, with even in some cases, pointers on how to correct it.

- *Run-time errors*: Some errors cannot be caught at the moment the program is written. For example, assume that we are defining a function that will compute the square root of the discriminant of a quadratic equation:

$$SqrtDelta(a, b, c) = \sqrt{b^2 - 4ac}$$

All high-level imperative languages will allow a function to be defined for this computation. The following is an attempt to implement and test it in Python:

```
>>> def SqrtDelta(a,b,c):
>>>         return sqrt(b*b - 4*a*c)
>>>
>>> print SqrtDelta(1,3,1)
2.2360679774997898
>>> print SqrtDelta(1,1,1)
ValueError: math domain error
```

The last line causes a run-time error: the inputs given by the user lead to taking the square-root of a negative number, which is not allowed in the floating number domain.

Similarly, an attempt to divide a number by zero or accessing a memory portion that is not reserved for or forbidden to the running program will also cause a run-time error.

- *Logic errors*: Whenever you look at an outcome of a program and say:

    It wasn't supposed to do that!

you have a logic error. So, a logic error is when your program runs in an unexpected way.

Here is an example. Assume we want to compute the first root of a quadratic equation. So, we want to do the following

$$root_1 = \frac{-b + \sqrt{b^2 - 4ac}}{2a}$$

and you code this equation in Python as:

```
>>> root1 = (- b + sqrt(b*b - 4*a*c)) / 2*a
```

(Now, without reading further, can you spot the bug?)

The mistake is that the a in 2*a is not actually in the denominator. It is multiplying the whole fraction. The correct way would be to enclose the denominator terms into parenthesis: *i.e.*, (2*a).

Such a mistake will surface as 'unexpected results', which are not so easy to spot compared with a compile-time error.

- *Design errors* are like logic errors. The difference is that, in logic errors, your intention is correct but the way you convert it into a program contains a mistake, but, in design errors, your intention was incorrect.

  To have a concrete example, assume that you are given a cubic equation in the form of the following equation:

$$x^3 + ax^2 + bx + c = 0$$

and you are cooking up the solution to find the first root by the method which works only for a quadratic equation:

$$root_1 = \frac{-b + \sqrt{b^2 - 4ac}}{2a}$$

This is a design error.

1.5.4 Debugging

Removing a bug from a program is called *debugging*. The majority of the effort in a debugging phase will go into the debugging of logic errors. There are various debugging techniques, some of them are given below:

Use compiler features: Most contemporary compilers attempt to do semantic checks (*e.g.*, for the use of uninitialized variable or the forgotten return value in a function definition) and issue warnings. Configure your compiler so that it gives warnings about the semantics of what you are compiling. This is usually done by some comment line flags.

RTFM: The polite meaning is Read-the-*Fine*-Manual (for a different meaning of the term you can do a web search). Obscurities may occur especially when you are using library functions and the only cure is RTFM.

`print` *insertion*: This is the oldest debugging technique. Knowing the flow of the program, you insert printing statements at key positions. This way you can check either for the flow of the program (*i.e.*, whether the program flow reached that spot) or for the values of certain variables (that you suspect).

Intelligently inserted print statements is a very powerful tool in nailing down bugs.

Defensive programming: Insert statements that make sure that the variable values remain in their domains. Here are two self-explanatory examples:

```
if not -1<s<12 : print "s is out of range"
if n%2 == 1 : print "n expected to be even but found odd"
```

Use a debugger: A *debugger* is a computer program that is used to execute another program (your buggy program) in a controlled manner, sometimes step-by-step or instruction-by-instruction. As the debugger steps through your program, you can inspect the content of the variables in your program. In a decent debugger, you can put breakpoints (*i.e.*, stops) in the program so that, when the flow of execution comes to a breakpoint, the execution halts and you can, for example, investigate or alter the content of the variables.

Explain to a bystander: The bystander is a human innocent, ready-to-help-type programmer. As you try to explain your code to him/her, very often you will discover by yourself the idiocy you made.

1.5.5 Good Programming Practice

The following rules of programming style are from the book "The Elements of Programming Style" by Kernighan and Plauger (published by McGraw Hill, 1978; with kind permission of the authors):

 1. "Write clearly—don't be too clever."
 2. "Say what you mean, simply and directly."
 3. "Use library functions whenever feasible."
 4. "Avoid too many temporary variables."
 5. "Write clearly—don't sacrifice clarity for 'efficiency'."
 6. "Let the machine do the dirty work."
 7. "Replace repetitive expressions by calls to common functions."
 8. "Parenthesize to avoid ambiguity."
 9. "Choose variable names that won't be confused."
10. "Avoid unnecessary branches."
11. "If a logical expression is hard to understand, try transforming it."
12. "Choose a data representation that makes the program simple."
13. "Write first in easy-to-understand pseudo language; then translate into whatever language you have to use."
14. "Modularize. Use procedures and functions."
15. "Avoid gotos completely if you can keep the program readable."
16. "Don't patch bad code—rewrite it."
17. "Write and test a big program in small pieces."
18. "Use recursive procedures for recursively-defined data structures."
19. "Test input for plausibility and validity."
20. "Make sure input doesn't violate the limits of the program."
21. "Terminate input by end-of-file marker, not by count."
22. "Identify bad input; recover if possible."
23. "Make input easy to prepare and output self-explanatory."
24. "Use uniform input formats."
25. "Make input easy to proofread."
26. "Use self-identifying input. Allow defaults. Echo both on output."
27. "Make sure all variable are initialized before use."
28. "Don't stop at one bug."
29. "Use debugging compilers."

Fig. 1.12 Logo of Python

30. "Watch out for one-by-one errors."
31. "Take care to branch the right way on equality."
32. "Be careful if a loop exits to the same place from the middle and the bottom."
33. "Make sure your code does 'nothing' gracefully."
34. "Test programs at their boundary values."
35. "Check some answers by hand."
36. "10.0 times 0.1 is hardly ever 1.0."
37. "7/8 is zero while 7.0/8.0 is not zero."
38. "Don't compare floating point numbers solely for equality."
39. "Make it right before you make it faster."
40. "Make it fail-safe before you make it faster."
41. "Make it clear before you make it faster."
42. "Don't sacrifice clarity for small gains in 'efficiency'."
43. "Let your compiler do the simple optimizations."
44. "Don't strain to re-use code; reorganize instead."
45. "Make sure special cases are truly special."
46. "Keep it simple to make it faster."
47. "Don't diddle code to make it faster—find a better algorithm."
48. "Instrument your programs. Measure before making 'efficiency' changes."
49. "Make sure comments and code agree."
50. "Don't just echo the code with comments—make every comment count."
51. "Don't comment bad code—rewrite it."
52. "Use variable names that mean something."
53. "Use statement labels that mean something."
54. "Format a program to help the reader understand it."
55. "Document your data layouts."
56. "Don't over-comment."

In this book, we will be using *Python* as the programming language that will serve as the example or, a testbed for the concepts we introduce. The parts of the book in Python have a different background color (*i.e.*, green), and after covering a topic, it will be exemplified and discussed in Python.

1.6 Meet Python

Welcome to the world of Python (see Fig. 1.12 for its logo), a very popular programming language these days for its easy and clear syntax (*i.e.*, code readability), its standard library with wide range of tools and its support for multiple programming paradigms (*i.e.*, imperative, functional and object-oriented) and many other advantages it provides. Python was in its design phases at the end of 1980s and the first release appeared in 1991. With the release of the second version in 2000, it started attracting the interest of a wider population.

Python is an interpreted language; *i.e.*, as you have learned in Sect. 1.4, the computer can 'understand', or 'interpret' your code and compute the result of your code without producing an object file, or an executable file.

In this book, we will assume that you are using python in a Unix-like environment; however, the topics that we will cover, the codes that we are going to analyze and the illustrations that we will present are applicable in other platforms, though with minor modifications in rare cases.

In a Unix-like environment, you start talking to Python with the command `python` (if your operating system complains to you about not being able to find the command `python`, check your installation or your $PATH environment variable):

```
skalkan@divan:~$ python
Python 2.5.2 (r252:60911, Jan 24 2010, 17:44:40)
[GCC 4.3.2] on linux2
Type "help", "copyright", "credits" or "license" for more information.
>>>
```

Now, the Python interpreter is ready to interact with us, which is denoted by the >>> characters (These characters are called the *prompt* string of the interpreter and can be changed by the programmer). The first line after the `python` command tells us about the version (along with the information on the specific release number and the date) of the Python interpreter that we are using. The second line gives information about the compiler that was used to compile the Python interpreter: Do not be surprised; it is quite common that a C compiler like GCC is used to compile the interpreters for different programing languages. The third line gives the user pointers for more information and help about the interpreter. The fourth line tells the user that the interpreter is ready for interaction. To exit the interpreter, you can type CTRL-D (obtained by pressing first the CTRL key on your keyboard then while keeping it pressed also press the D key) or `exit()`.

The version of the interpreter is quite important since there are some major incompatibilities between versions. There are two major versions: (1) 2.x (namely, 2.5, 2.6 or 2.7) and (2) 3.x. Unfortunately, for some reasons that are not clear even to us, these two major versions are not compatible with each other. Since the 2.5, 2.6 and 2.7 versions of Python have a wider range of tools, facilities and applications available, we have adopted the 2.5 version of the interpreter throughout the book.

1.7 Our First Interaction with Python

Now we can start talking to the interpreter; we, as polite programmers, might say `Hello` first:

```
>>> Hello
Traceback (most recent call last):
  File "<stdin>", line 1, in <module>
NameError: name 'Hello' is not defined
>>>
```

and the interpreter complains, since it assumes that the word `Hello` is a name for something that had to be defined first (as we will see later). If we want the interpreter to take our words literally, we should enclose them between quotes, like `"Hello, please be more polite now"`:

```
>>> "Hello, please be more polite now"
'Hello, please be more polite now'
>>>
```

and the interpreter politely displays (*i.e.*, prints back) the *string* that we have written. What the interpreter has done is very simple: it has evaluated what we have typed (which was the `"Hello, please be more polite now"` *string* in this case) and prints back the result; since what we have written was a simple string, the result of the interpreter's evaluation was that same string itself.

Since it is getting boring playing around with the strings, we can try something else: We can test the mathematical capabilities of the Python interpreter:

```
>>> 3+4
7
>>>
```

This time, we have asked the interpreter to evaluate a different expression $3+4$, involving two numbers (*i.e.*, integers) and the interpreter happily answers our obvious question with the result 7.

1.8 Keywords

The important concepts that we would like our readers to understand in this chapter are indicated by the following keywords:

Program	Programming
Von Neumann Architecture	CPU
Memory	Imperative Programming Paradigm
Functional Programming Paradigm	Object-Oriented Programming Paradigm
Logical Declarative Programming Paradigm	Concurrent Programming Paradigm

1.9 Further Reading

For more information on the topics discussed in this chapter, you can check out the sources below:

- *Computer Architectures:*
  - *Von Neumann Architecture:*
    http://en.wikipedia.org/wiki/Von_Neumann_architecture
  - *Harvard Architecture:*
    http://en.wikipedia.org/wiki/Harvard_architecture
  - *Harvard vs. Von Neumann Architecture:*
    http://www.pic24micro.com/harvard_vs_von_neumann.html
  - *Quantum Computer:*
    http://en.wikipedia.org/wiki/Quantum_computer
  - *Chemical Computer:*
    http://en.wikipedia.org/wiki/Chemical_computer
  - *Non-Uniform Memory Access Computer:*
    http://en.wikipedia.org/wiki/Non-Uniform_Memory_Access
- *Programming Paradigms:*
  - *Introduction:*
    http://en.wikipedia.org/wiki/Programming_paradigm
  - *For a detailed discussion and taxonomy of the paradigms:*
    P. Van Roy, *Programming Paradigm for Dummies: What Every Programmer Should Know*, New Computational Paradigms for Computer Music, G. Assayag and A. Gerzso (eds.), IRCAM/Delatour France, 2009
    http://www.info.ucl.ac.be/~pvr/VanRoyChapter.pdf
  - *Comparison between Paradigms:*
    http://en.wikipedia.org/wiki/Comparison_of_programming_paradigms
- *Turing Machine:*
  http://en.wikipedia.org/wiki/Turing_Machine
- *Church–Turing Thesis:*
  http://en.wikipedia.org/wiki/Church-Turing_thesis
- *Programming Languages:*
  - *For a list of programming languages:*
    http://en.wikipedia.org/wiki/Comparison_of_programming_languages
  - *For a comparison of programming languages:*
    http://en.wikipedia.org/wiki/Comparison_of_programming_languages

– *For more details:*
Daniel P. Friedman, Mitchell Wand, Christopher Thomas Haynes: Essentials of Programming Languages, The MIT Press 2001.
- *Testing:*
http://en.wikipedia.org/wiki/Software_testing
- *Python:*
  – *For a history of Python:*
  http://en.wikipedia.org/wiki/Python_%28programming_language%29
  – *To set up your Python installation:*
  http://docs.python.org/using/index.html
  – *For a comparison between Python 2.x and 3.x:*
  http://wiki.python.org/moin/Python2orPython3

1.10 Exercises

1. Propose the most suitable programming paradigm for each of the following problems:
   (a) A computational environment where mathematical theorems or rules are proven.
   (b) A management system for a university where transfer of all the administrative documents between the departments as well as information about the students, the courses and the staff are managed.
   (c) A software to be run on a car that assists the driver.
   (d) The monitoring system of the airway control tower at a busy airport.
2. Propose whether a compilative or an interpretive programming language would be more suitable for each of the following problems:
   (a) A computational environment where mathematical theorems or rules are proven.
   (b) A management system for a university where transfer of all the administrative documents between the departments as well as information about the students, the courses and the staff are managed.
   (c) A software to be run on a car that assists the driver.
   (d) The monitoring system of the airway control tower at a busy airport.
3. Why do you think it is (currently) not possible to write programs using plain English, or any other language spoken by humans? When do you think we can write computer programs in our daily languages? (Hint: Have a look at the *Turing Test* and the *Chinese Room Argument*.)
4. Linux is an open-source operating system that is developed by hundreds, even thousands of programmers world-wide. If you were part of a team (composed of thousands of open-source programmers located world-wide) to develop an operating system (like Linux) from scratch,
   (a) give one reason to choose imperative programming paradigm.
   (b) give one reason to choose object-oriented paradigm.

5. The nervous system in humans is one type of a computing machine where the machine is composed of unit cells, called neurons; each neuron can work in parallel and perform its own computation; and, neurons can communicate with each other (*i.e.*, transfer information) using electrical currents. The nervous system is composed of the connections between neurons (of different types) and therefore, might be called the *Connectionist Machine*.
   (a) What are the differences between the Connectionist and the Von Neumann architectures?
   (b) State, with reasons if possible, for which programming paradigm(s) the Connectionist Architecture is more suitable.

Reference

Chen Y, Dios R, Mili A, Wu L, Wang K (2005) An empirical study of programming language trends. IEEE Softw 22(3):72–79

Chapter 2
Data: The First Ingredient of a Program

The Von Neumann architecture has some implications even on high-level programming languages. Below is an overview of these aspects:

- The Von Neumann architecture makes a clear distinction between the processing unit, namely the CPU, and the memory.
- The content of the memory is highly mixed containing:

  The orders to the CPU about all the actions: Register ⟷ memory transfer operations; arithmetic, comparison and bitwise operations on the registers; operations effecting the execution flow.
  Adjunct information needed to carry out some instructions: Addresses for the transfer operations, constants involved in arithmetic or bitwise operations.
  Raw information to be processed: Integer or floating point values, or sequences of them; address information of such raw data.

  All these types of information live in the memory. However, still, there is a distinction between them. Anything that is stored in the memory falls into one of these categories, and an error-free machine code, when executed, will consider this distinction: Actions will be treated as actions, adjunct information as adjunct information and raw information as raw information.
- Access to the memory is strictly address-wise. If you do not know the address of what you are looking for, you cannot locate it unless you compare every memory content with what you are looking for. In other words: Content-wise addressing is not possible.
- All information subject to processing by the Von Neumann architecture must be transformed to a binary representation.

  Among these implications of the Von Neumann architecture, the main implication is the distinction between 'actions' and the 'information' because this distinction affects the way we approach any World problem. Here, the term *World problem* refers to a problem of any subject domain, where a computerized solution is sought. Below are a few examples:

- Find all the wheat growing areas in a satellite image.

G. Üçoluk, S. Kalkan, *Introduction to Programming Concepts with Case Studies in Python*, DOI 10.1007/978-3-7091-1343-1_2, © Springer-Verlag Wien 2012

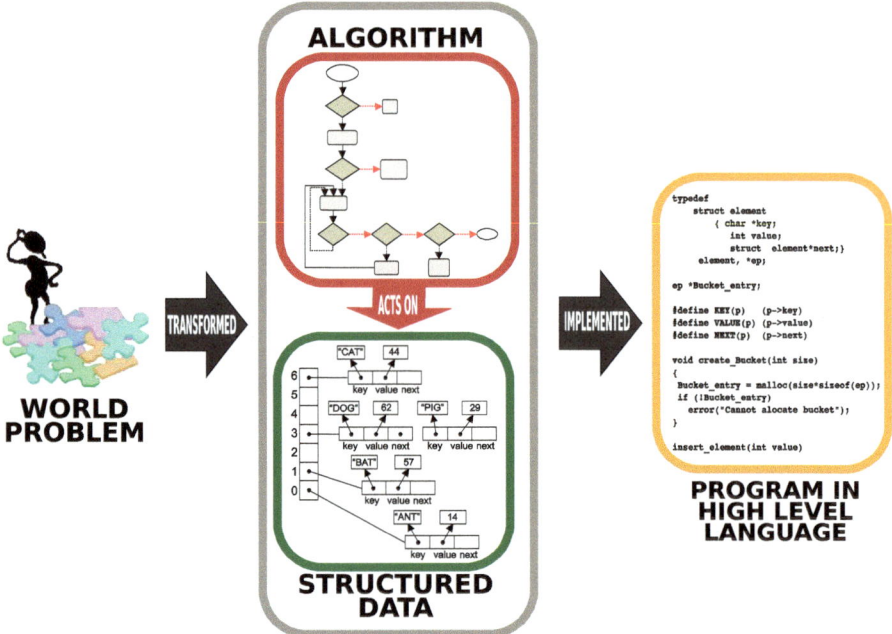

Fig. 2.1 Most of the time, a world problem is solved by a set of algorithms that act on structured data

- Given students' homework, lab and examination grades, calculate their letter grades.
- Change the amplitude of a sound clip for various frequencies.
- Predict China's population for the year 2040, based on the changes in the population growth rate up to date.
- Compute the launch date and the trajectory for a space probe so that it will pass by the outermost planets in the closest proximity.
- Compute the internal layout of a CPU so that the total wiring distance is minimized.
- Find the cheapest flight itinerary from A to B, given departure and return dates.
- Simulate a war between two land forces, given (i) the attack and the defense plans, (ii) the inventories and (iii) other attributes of both forces.

In such World problems, the first task of the programmer is to identify the information to be processed to solve the problem. This information is called *data*. Then, the programmer has to find an action schema that will act upon this data, carry out those actions according to the plan, and produce a solution to the problem. This well-defined action schema is called an *algorithm*. This separation of data and algorithm is visualized in Fig. 2.1. There can be more than one algorithm that can solve a problem and this is usually the case in practice. Actually, in Chap. 5, we will talk about the means for comparing the quality of two algorithms that solve the same problem.

2.1 What Is Data?

Practically, anything in the computer representation of a solution (for a World problem), which is not an instruction to the CPU, *i.e.*, not an action, can be called data.

Some data are directly understandable (processable) by the CPU. However, unfortunately, there are only two such data: *integers* and *floating points*. Furthermore, these data types are not full-fledged: Both integers and floating points are limited in size, which is determined by the processing capability of the CPU; *i.e.*, the range of the integer and the floating point numbers that can be represented is limited, and the limit is around 4–8 bytes at the time this book was written.

There are many more data types which are not recognized as directly processable entities by the CPU. To mention a few, we can quote fractions of numbers, real numbers of arbitrary precision, complex numbers, matrices, characters, strings of characters, distributions (statistical values), symbolic algebraic values.

Nonetheless, it is possible to write programs that implement these types of data. In fact, some of the high-level languages implement these types as part of the language: For example, high-level languages like Lisp, Prolog, Python and ML provide integers of arbitrary sizes; FORTRAN, an archaic language still in use, has support for complex numbers; BASIC supports numerical matrices; Mathematica, Matlab, Reduce and Maple provide, in addition to all of the above, symbolic algebraic quantities; and, almost all high-level languages have characters and strings.

Certainly, there are other less-demanded data types which are not provided by high-level languages but languages exist that facilitate defining new data types based on the existing ones. Therefore, it is possible, for example, to define a `color` data type with three integer attributes, `Red`, `Green` and `Blue`.

2.2 What Is Structured Data?

If the data is just a single entity then, in a low-level language, the programmer himself/herself can directly store it somewhere, a place known to him/her, in the memory. In fact, in a high-level language, there are language features that can do this automatically for the programmer. Soon, we will be looking into this subject.

What if we have more than 'one' of any type of data (*e.g.*, millions of integers)? One option is to store them in the memory consecutively, one after the other. Thus, if we want to fetch the 452389th item, we can easily compute the memory position as:

$$\langle \text{Address of the first byte of the first item} \rangle$$
$$+$$
$$(452389 - 1) \times \langle \text{Count of bytes occupied by a single item} \rangle$$

That was easy. We call this structured data an *array*. It is a very efficient organization of the data because after we have calculated the address of the 452389th item, accessing it is just a memory fetch. This benefit is due to the Von Neumann architecture: If you know the address, the content is always provided to you in a constant and short time.

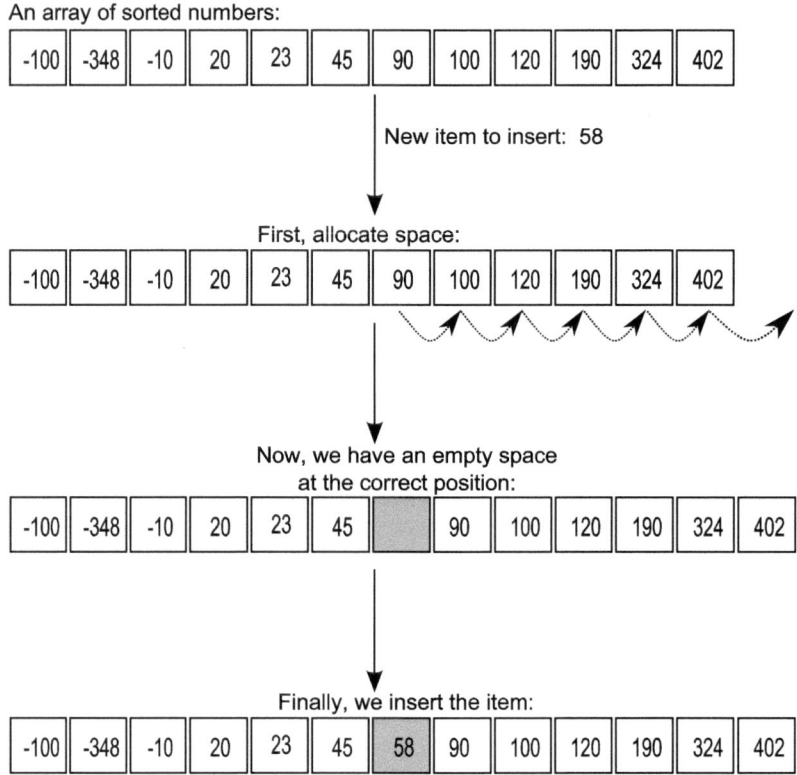

Fig. 2.2 An array becomes computationally inefficient when a new item needs to be inserted in the middle

However, what if your algorithm requires inserting some data at an arbitrary position of the array? As shown in Fig. 2.2, you would have to move all the items that are after the insertion point, and make new space for the new item. This could be the case for example if the array holds a collection of sorted numbers in order and you want to keep it sorted after the insertion. Unfortunately, the memory does not have a facility for shifting a range of its content down or up. Nonetheless, this can be performed by the CPU by shifting each item one by one. This is an extremely time consuming task especially for a large collections of data and therefore, not practicable.

Hence, we need other techniques for storing collections of data that make it easy and efficient to insert new items. The solution is to keep the data in "island"'s in the memory, in a structured manner, with each island holding an information item and the addresses of the neighboring islands. In this way, data can be organized into a collection of islands, where a certain item is located by knowing how to "jump" from one island to another and by comparing the item that we are looking for with the data on the islands. This technique is extensively used in programming.

Fig. 2.3 An address
reference is denoted by an
arrow

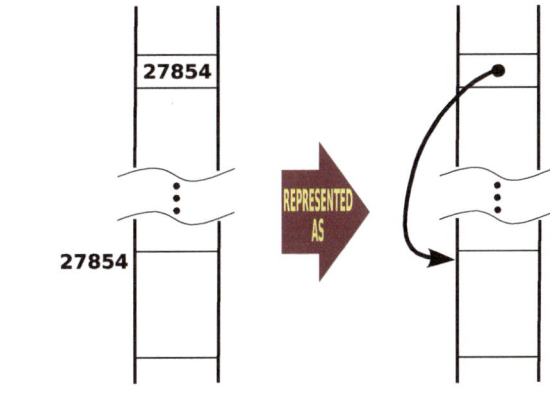

Fig. 2.4 A linked data
structure *(Colors are data,
arrows are links)*

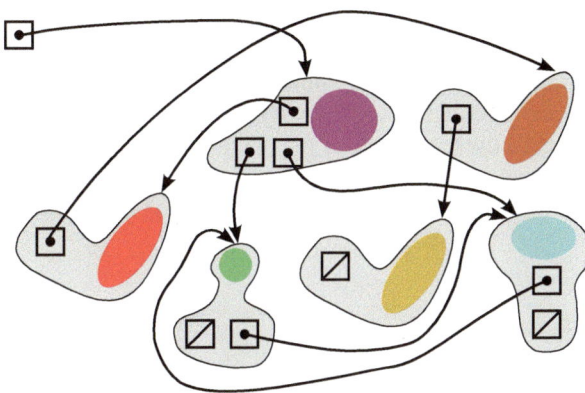

Whenever, as a part of an item of data, an address is kept which is the address of another data, the address holding position is called the *pointer* (or alternatively, the *link*) to that data. Denotationally, this is represented by drawing an arrow from the address holding position to that address, as shown in Fig. 2.3.

Therefore, keeping in mind that all the data islands are stored in the memory, Fig. 2.4 provides a pictorial example of a linked data structure:

Assume that we have N-many such islands, each island keeping some information which is required for our algorithm. Having more than one link per data island and organizing the links intelligently, we can locate (search and find) any information in $\log N$ many hops (How? Think about it). Moreover, removing an island or inserting another is achieved by just modifying a couple of arrows.

Therefore, by storing and organizing the data in a particular way, we can gain efficiency in various aspects. We will see that it is possible to reduce the time spent on locating some data searched for as well as inserting or deleting a data from a vast pool of data. This is an area of Computer Science called *Data Structures*.

Some high-level languages provide mechanisms to define those islands with "linkage fields"; Prolog, Lisp and ML, for example, provide syntactic features for automatically building and modifying such linked data structures. The 'list' construct in these languages is a good example of such embedded features.

2.3 Basic Data Types

From now on, we will use the adjective 'basic' to refer to the content of a high-level language. In this sense, 'basic' means a construct which is relatively easily implemented at the low level, *i.e.*, the machine code, and provided by a high-level language as built-in.

There are two categories of basic data:

- Numerical *(integers, floating points)*
- Symbolic (or non-numerical) *(character, boolean)*

All CPUs have support for numerical data whereas some may not support floating points. CPUs can add, subtract, multiply or divide numerical. A CPU-supported numerical data has a fixed size for representation (if the CPU uses 4 bits to represent integers, the magnitude of the maximum integer that can be represented on this CPU is around 15^1), and this fixed size will vary from CPU to CPU. At the time of writing this book, this limit is mostly 32 bits or 64 bits.

2.3.1 Integers

Integer is the data type used in almost all discrete mathematical applications, like enumeration, counting, combinatorics, number theoretics, geometry and many more.

The most common way to representing integers is *Two's Complement* using which we can represent integers in the range of $[-2^{n-1}, 2^{n-1} - 1]$ given n bits. In Two's Complement notation, a positive number has the leading bit as 0 whereas a negative number's leading bit in Two's Complement notation is 1. To convert a (positive or negative) decimal number x into its Two's Complement representation:

1. Convert $|x|$ into base-2, call it $b_{n-2} \ldots b_1 b_0$.
2. If $x > 0$, $0 b_{n-2} \ldots b_0$ is the Two's Complement representation.
3. If $x < 0$,
   (a) flip each bit—*i.e.*, $c_i = 1 - b_i$ for $i = 0, \ldots, n - 2$.
   (b) add 1 to $c_{n-2} \ldots c_0$; *i.e.*, $d_{n-2} \ldots d_0 = c_{n-2} \ldots c_0 + 1$.
   (c) $1 d_{n-2} \ldots d_0$ is the Two's Complement representation.

An important advantage of Two's Complement representation is that addition, subtraction and multiplication do not need to check the signs of the numbers. Another

---

[1]The exact value depends on how the CPU represents negative numbers.

important advantage is the fact that $+0$ and -0 have the same representations, unlike other notations.

The CPU arithmetic works rather fast (faster compared to floating points) in the integer domain. Furthermore, some obscure precision losses, which exist in representing floating point numbers, is not present for integers. Therefore, integers are favored over floating points when it is possible to choose between the two. It is frequently the case that even problems that are defined in a domain of reals (like computer graphics) is carried over to the integer domain, because of the gain in speed.

Some high-level languages do provide arbitrary precision integers, also known as *bignums* (short for big numbers), as a part of the language. In some cases, the usage is seamless and the programmer does not have to worry about choosing among the representations. Lisp, Prolog, ML, Python are such programming languages. In languages like C, Pascal and C++, facilities for bignums are available; therefore, the functionality is provided but not seamless (*i.e.*, the user has to make a choice about the representation type). As explained in the preceding section, bignums are not directly supported by the CPU; therefore, the provider has to represent them with a data structure and has to implement the algorithms himself to perform the arithmetic operations on them. Usually, bignums are represented as arrays of integers, each element of which is a digit in base-n, where n is close to the square root of the biggest integer that can be handled by the CPU's arithmetic (Why? Think about it).

It is possible that a high-level language offers more than one fixed-size integer type. Usually, their sizes are 16, 32, 64 or 128 bits. Sometimes, CPUs have support for two or three of them (having also different operations for different types of integers; for example, there are two different instructions to add integers of size 32 and 64, respectively).

2.3.2 Floating Points

Floating point is the data type used to represent non-integer real numbers. The internal representation is organized such that the number is converted into a binary fractional part and a multiplicative exponent part (*i.e.*, $F \times 2^E$, where F is the fraction, E the exponent). After this conversion, the fractional part is truncated to a fixed length in bits, and stored along with the exponent.

You might remember from your Mathematics courses that irrational numbers do not have fractional parts that can be truncated, neither do most of the rationals. In "... the fractional part is truncated...", "truncated" means "approximated". To observe this, feel free to take the square root of (let's say) 2.0, and then square the result, in any high-level language. You will never get back the answer, 2.0.

Let us have a closer look at the internal representation of floating points to understand what is going on and where the precision gets lost. Below is the IEEE 754 binary floating point standard, converting a real number into the internal representation (see also Fig. 2.5):

Fig. 2.5 IEEE standard for 32-bit floating point representation

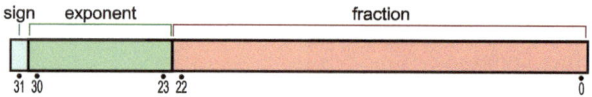

1. The whole part (the value to the left of the point) and the fractional part of a real number are expressed in binary.
2. The fraction 'point' is moved to the left (or right) so that the whole part becomes exactly 1. To compensate for the move and not to alter the value of the real number, a multiplicative power of 2 is introduced. It is possible, of course, that this power is negative.
3. The binary number 1 right before the point is skipped over, and the 23 digits (following the fraction point) in the fraction part are stored as the *mantissa*.
4. 127 is added to the power of the multiplicative factor and stored as the exponent.
5. If the original real number is negative, the sign bit is set to 1, otherwise to 0.
6. The values '0', $\pm\infty$, and 'NaN' *(Not-a-Number)* are represented by some exceptional combinations of mantissa and exponent values.

Therefore, mathematically, a real number is approximated to:

$$\left(1 + \sum_{n=1}^{23} \text{bit}_{[23-n]} \times 2^{-n}\right) \times 2^{\text{exponent}-127}$$

Where exactly is the loss? The answer is as follows: if the summation were extended to infinity, then any real number could be represented precisely. However, we do not have infinite number of bits; we have only 23 of them. Therefore, the truncation after the first 23 elements in the summation causes the loss. For example, the binary representation for a simple real number 4.1 has the whole part equal to 100, and yet, the fraction part has infinitely many binary numbers: *i.e.,* 00011001100110011 0011 .... Hence, using only 23 bits for real numbers such as 4.1 introduces a precision loss.

Is this a big problem? Yes, indeed it is. Here are some examples of everyday problems that occur in scientific computing:

• Let us say we have 32 bits for representing floating points. Therefore, you have *only* 2^{32} real numbers that can be correctly represented. However, we know from Mathematics that even in the range [0, 1], there are infinitely many real numbers (actually, it is worse than that: to be precise, there are 'uncountably many'). In other words, uncountably many real numbers are approximated to one real number that is representable by the computer. We call this precision loss *roundoff* error.

What makes it even worse is that we easily make wrong estimates on roundoff errors. In fact, there is no correlation between the representability in the decimal notation and representability in the binary notation. For example, to us, 0.9 might seem less prone to roundoff errors compared to 0.9375. Actually, it is just the other way around: 0.9375 is one of the rare real numbers that is represented without any loss, and 0.9, despite its innocent look, suffers from the roundoff error (take your pencil and paper and do the math! When you get tired of it, you can go and watch the movie "Office Space" (1999), where you can learn how to make millions out of roundoff errors).

• Many numerical computations are based on multiplicative factors which are differences of two big numbers (by big numbers, we mean numbers whose whole parts $\gg 0$). The whole parts are represented in the mantissa, and as a result, the fractional parts lose precision. Therefore, for example, $(1.0023 - 1.0567)$ yields a different result from $(1000.0023 - 1000.0567)$, although, mathematically, the results should be the same (Try it!).

• The irrational number π is extensively used in scientific and engineering computations. To get a close-to-correct internal floating point representation for π, we have to type 3.1415926535897931. The sinus of π, *i.e.*, $\sin(\pi)$, should yield zero, but it does not: the result of $\sin(\pi)$ on a computer is $1.2246467991473532 \times 10^{-16}$, which is definitely a small number but not zero. Therefore, a comparison of $\sin(\pi)$ against 0.0 would fail.

• You might remember that, in your Mathematics courses, you were told that addition is associative. Therefore, $(a + b) + c$ would yield the same result as $a + (b + c)$. This is not the case with floating number computations. The losses in the intermediate computations will differ, and you will have a different result for different ways numbers are added. As an example:

set $a = 1234.567$, $b = 45.67834$ and $c = 0.0004$:

$(a + b) + c$ results in 1280.2457399999998,

$a + (b + c)$ results in 1280.2457400000001.

• Precision does not mean accuracy. Assume that you are working with the (IEEE 754 standard) 32-bit float representation introduced above. You want to compute an area and you take π as 3.141. You add, multiply, divide and what you get are numbers that are precise in 7 decimal digits. However, your accuracy is not more than 4 digits in any computation that involves π, since the π value (3.141) you have taken is accurate only up to 4 digits: All those higher digits are nonsense as far as accuracy is concerned.

What is the bottom line then? Here are some rules of thumb about using floating points:

• If you can transform the problem to a problem in the integer domain, do so: As much as you can, refrain from using floating points.

• Use the most precise type of floating point in your choice of high-level language. C, for example, has `float`, `double` and `long double`, which, these days, correspond to 32, 64 and 128 bit representations, respectively.

• Use less precision floating points only when you are short of memory.

• It is very likely that you will have catastrophic roundoff errors when you subtract two floating points close in value.

• If you have two addends that are magnitude-wise incomparable, you are likely to lose the contribution of the smaller one. That will yield unexpected results when you repeat the addition in a computational loop where the looping is so much that the accumulation of the smaller addends is expected to become significant. It will not.

- The contrary happens too: Slight inaccuracies might accumulate in loops to significant magnitudes and yield non-sense values.
- You better use well-known, decent floating point libraries instead of coding floating point algorithms yourself.

2.3.3 Numerical Values in Python

Just to remind you our first interaction with Python from Chap. 1, let us have a look at a simple computation involving some numbers:

```
>>> 3+4
7
```

In this interaction, the numbers 3 and 4 are integers, and Python has a certain *name*, *i.e.*, a *type*, for all integers: int. If you ask Python what int is, it will tell you that it is a type:

```
>>> int
<type 'int'>
```

We could also ask the type of a constant number, or a combination of them:

```
>>> type(3)
<type 'int'>
>>> type(3+4)
<type 'int'>
```

The int type in Python has fixed-size representation, which depends on the CPU. If you need to work with integers that exceed the fixed-size limit of your CPU, you can use the long data type in Python. If you want your constant numbers to be represented as long integers, you need to enter the L letter after them:

```
>>> type(3L)
<type 'long'>
>>> type(3L+4L)
<type 'long'>
>>>
```

int type in Python has fixed-size representation (based on the CPU) whereas long type is only limited by the size of available memory.

For floating point numbers, Python has another type:

```
>>> type(3.4)
<type 'float'>
>>>
```

and similar to `int` numbers, we can do simple calculations with the `float` data:

```
>>> 3.4+4.3
7.7
>>> 3.4 / 4.3
0.79069767441860461
```

– Useful Operations on Numerical Values in Python

Let us have a look at some useful simple operations with numerical values in Python (in Chap. 3, we will look at more operations and how they are interpreted by the CPU):

- *Absolute value of a number*: The `abs(Number)` function can be used for the absolute value of a number.
- *Hexadecimal or octal representation of an integer*: The `hex()` and `oct()` functions can be used for this purpose.
- *Exponent of a number*: Typing `pow(Number1, Number2)` or Number $**$ Number2 in Python results in *Number1^{Number2}*.
- *Rounding a floating point number*: The `round(Float)` function rounds the given floating point number to the closest integer.
- *Conversion between numbers*: You can use the `int(Number)`, `float(Number)` and `long(Number)` as constructors to convert a given number to `int`, `float` and `long` respectively:

```
>>> long(3.6)
3L
>>> float(3L)
3.0
>>> int(3.4)
3
```

Note from the examples that converting a `float` number to an integer number results in losing the fraction part (without rounding it).

2.3.4 Characters

As stated earlier in this book, we attempt to generate computer solutions for some of our world problems. These problems are not always about numbers, they can also be about words or sentences of a natural language. The written language is made up of fundamental units called *graphemes*. Alphabetic letters, Chinese/Japanese/Korean characters, punctuation marks, numeric digits are all graphemes, and there is a demand to have these represented on the computer. In addition to graphemes, certain basic actions of the computer-external world interactions need also to be represented on the computer: "make a beep sound", "eject the half printed paper from the printer", "end a line that is being printed and start a new one", "exit", "up", "down", "left", "right" are all such interaction actions. We call them *unprintables*. Since the semantics of graphemes is very different from numbers and numerical values, they are not at the center of CPU design. The CPUs nowadays do not have any built-in feature for graphemes.

Whenever there is no built-in representation provided by the CPU architecture, then programmers are free to make their own choice. In the case of representing graphemes, we have several options which all involve constructing a mapping from the set of graphemes and unprintables to binary representations. In more practical terms, being a computer manufacturer, you make a table of two columns: one column is for the graphemes and unprintables and the other is for the binary representations that you choose for the graphemes. You manufacture your interaction devices, the so-called input/output devices, to represent graphemes and interpret the binary representations of graphemes according to this table. A grapheme is represented in the memory in binary. For the CPU, the representation does not have any meaning—it is just a set of binary numbers. At most, without interpreting it, the CPU can aid to copy such binary data from one memory position to another or just compare whether two such binary representations are identical.

Throughout the history of computers, there has been many such tables that link graphemes with binary representations. Almost all large computer manufacturers had their own tables. Later, local authorities responsible for standardization began to standardize those tables. Table 2.1 shows the ASCII (American Standard Code for Information Interchange) table, which was defined by the American Standards Association, in 1963.

As you may have observed, the ASCII table uses 7 bits. The first 32 entries are the unprintables. For decades, the USA was the dominant computer manufacturer and this table affected the way programs were written for years. Even today, the ASCII table is still extensively used world wide, although it is solely organized to reflect a subset of the local needs of the USA. The ASCII table includes the dollar sign ($), however, apparently, it falls short to satisfy the needs of foreign trade; the symbols for sterling (£) and yen (¥) are absent. Furthermore, none of the diacritics which are widely used in European languages are included in the ASCII table; *e.g.*, the table does not have Ö, Ü, Ç, Å or È letters. The punctuation characters suffer, too. It is difficult to understand why the tilde is there but the section sign is not.

For these reasons, many countries had to extend the ASCII table and add their additional characters using the 8th bit set. In such extensions, the letter Ç has a numerical value that is not between the numerical values of letter C and D, making alphabetical sorting a problem. A solution to this problem is having another table

Table 2.1   The ASCII (American Standard Code for Information Interchange) table

NUL	00000000	SYN	00010110	,	00101100	B	01000010	X	01011000	n	01101110
SOH	00000001	ETB	00010111	-	00101101	C	01000011	Y	01011001	o	01101111
STX	00000010	CAN	00011000	.	00101110	D	01000100	Z	01011010	p	01110000
ETX	00000011	EM	00011001	/	00101111	E	01000101	[	01011011	q	01110001
EOT	00000100	SUB	00011010	0	00110000	F	01000110	\	01011100	r	01110010
ENQ	00000101	ESC	00011011	1	00110001	G	01000111	]	01011101	s	01110011
ACK	00000110	FS	00011100	2	00110010	H	01001000	^	01011110	t	01110100
BEL	00000111	GS	00011101	3	00110011	I	01001001	_	01011111	u	01110101
BS	00001000	RS	00011110	4	00110100	J	01001010	`	01100000	v	01110110
HT	00001001	US	00011111	5	00110101	K	01001011	a	01100001	w	01110111
LF	00001010	SPC	00100000	6	00110110	L	01001100	b	01100010	x	01111000
VT	00001011	!	00100001	7	00110111	M	01001101	c	01100011	y	01111001
FF	00001100	"	00100010	8	00111000	N	01001110	d	01100100	z	01111010
CR	00001101	#	00100011	9	00111001	O	01001111	e	01100101	{	01111011
SO	00001110	$	00100100	:	00111010	P	01010000	f	01100110	|	01111100
SI	00001111	%	00100101	;	00111011	Q	01010001	g	01100111	}	01111101
DLE	00010000	&	00100110	<	00111100	R	01010010	h	01101000	~	01111110
DC1	00010001	'	00100111	=	00111101	S	01010011	i	01101001	DEL	01111111
DC2	00010010	(	00101000	>	00111110	T	01010100	j	01101010		
DC3	00010011	)	00101001	?	00111111	U	01010101	k	01101011		
DC4	00010100	*	00101010	@	01000000	V	01010110	l	01101100		
NAK	00010101	+	00101011	A	01000001	W	01010111	m	01101101		

for the ordering of these letters. However, this makes working with such extension tables inherently slower. It is an undeniable fact that since many of such existing mappings are limited in size and scope, incompatible with multilingual environments, and cause programmers no end of trouble.

Years later, in the late 80's, a nonprofit organization, the Unicode Consortium, was formed with a goal to provide a replacement for the existing character tables that is also (backward) compatible with them. Their proposed encoding (representation) scheme is called the *Unicode Transformation Format (UTF)*. This encoding scheme has variable length and can contain 1-to-4 8-bit-wide components (in the case of UTF-8), or 1-to-2 16-bit-wide components (in the case of UTF-16). Gaining wide popularity, UTF is now becoming part of many recent high level language implementations such as Java, Perl, Python, TCL, Ada95 and C#.

Characters in Python

Python has a data type for a collection of characters (called 'string') and does not have a separate data type for individual character. However, taking a character as a subset of the string class (*i.e.*, a character is a string of length one), you can write programs making use of characters. We will come back to characters in Python when we introduce strings.

Although characters are not explicitly represented with a type in Python, we have the following functions that allows us to work with characters:

- The function `chr(ascii)` returns the one-character string corresponding to the ASCII value `ascii`.
- The `ord(CharString)` is the reverse of `chr(ascii)` in that it returns the ASCII value of the one character string `CharString`.

2.3.5 Boolean

Boolean is the type of data that represents the answer to questions like $3.4 > 5.6$ or $6/2 \stackrel{?}{=} 3$. CPUs has built-in support for asking such questions and acting accordingly to the answers. Therefore, the concept of *True* and *False* must be understood by CPUs. CPUs recognize 0 as the representation of *False* (*falsity*). Mostly, any value other than 0 stands for *True* (*truthness*). If the CPUs process any boolean calculation, the result will be either 0 or 1; 1 representing the *True* truth value that CPUs generate.

High-level languages have a similar mapping. Generally, they implement two keywords (like `TRUE`, `FALSE` or `T`, `F`) to represent the two boolean values.

When the interpreter or the compiler sees these keywords, it translates them into internal representations of values 0 or 1. High-level languages make additional checks to ensure that those values are created

- either by the programmer entering the keyword, or
- as a result of a comparison operation.

Although they will be represented as 1s and 0s internally, on the surface (*i.e.*, in the high-level language) these keywords will not be treated as integers.[2]

Boolean Values in Python

You can check yourself whether or not Python has a separate data type for boolean values by asking it a simple comparison:

```
>>> 3 > 4
False
>>> type(3 > 4)
<type 'bool'>
```

Therefore, Python has a separate data type for boolean values and that data type is called `bool`. The `bool` data type can take only two values: `True` and `False`.

We can use the `not` keyword for negating a boolean value. For example, `not True`, and `not 4 > 3` are `False`.

Since everything is internally represented as binary numbers, we can check for the mapping of the `True` and `False` values to the integers:

```
>>> int(False)
0
>>> int(True)
1
```

which tells us that `False` is internally represented as 0 (zero), and `True` as 1 (one).

In Python, like many high-level languages, numerical values (other than 0 and 1) have a mapping to boolean values as well:

```
>>> not 0
True
>>> not 1
False
>>> not 2.5
False
```

---

[2]Except in C and its descendants. C does not provide a distinct boolean type and assumes that the integers 1 and 0 play the True/False role.

From this interaction, we understand that Python interprets any numerical other than 0 as `True`. Moreover, any non-empty instance of a container data type, which we will see in the remainder of this chapter, is interpreted as `True`; and otherwise, any data is `False`. For example:

```
>>> not ""
True
>>> not "This is some text"
False
>>> not ()
True
>>> not (1, 2, 3)
False
```

2.4 Basic Organization of Data: Containers

In Sect. 2.2, we introduced the necessity of storing collection of data in the memory and retrieving it later. Furthermore, we argued that storing the data in an intelligently organized way can provide efficiency and flexibility.

In computer science, a data structure with the sole purpose of storing elements is called a *container*. If a high-level language implements a container type, we expect the following functionalities from it:

- Construct a container from a set of elements and store them.
- Destruct a container and free the associated memory.
- Access the stored elements for use.

In addition to those aspects, if we have the right to set/delete/change the individual elements, then the container is said to be *mutable*. Otherwise, it is *immutable*.

As far as the internal representation is concerned, the simplest way to implement a container is to store the elements in adjacent memory locations. If the elements are homogeneous, *i.e.*, of the same type, then we call this an *array* representation. If they are heterogeneous, *i.e.*, of different types, this is a *tuple* representation.

In the following subsections, we will introduce three basic containers:

- Strings (mutable or immutable)
- Tuples (immutable)
- List (mutable)

2.4.1 Strings

Strings are the containers to store a sequence of characters. The need for strings is various; world problems intensively contain textual information and Computer

Science itself relies heavily on strings. For example, the implementations of programming languages themselves, compilers as well as interpreters, is partly a string processing task.

The internal representation of strings is based on storing the binary representations of characters that make up the string, scanned from left to right, in adjacent memory cells in the increasing address order. The count of characters in a string is not fixed: *i.e.*, we can have a string instance with three characters or a thousand characters. The count of characters that make up the string is named as the *length* of the string. Zero-length strings, *i.e. empty strings*, are also allowed.

Since there is a flexibility in the length of a string, there is a problem of determining where the string ends in the memory. There are two solutions for this representational problem:

1. Store at a fixed position (usually just before the string starts), the length of the string as an integer.
2. Store at the end of the string a binary code which cannot be a part of any string. In other words, put an ending marker which is not a character that could take a place in a string.

Both of these approaches do exist in high-level language implementations. For example, Pascal takes the first approach, whereas C takes the second. Both approaches have their pros and cons. The first approach limits the length of a string to be at most the biggest integer that can be stored in that fixed position which is a disadvantage. On the other hand, in this approach directly reaching the end of string is extremely easy. You just add the length of the string to the starting address of the string and you get the address of the last character in the string, that is an immense advantage. The second approach has the advantage that there is no limitation on the length of a string, however, the disadvantage is that to reach to the end of the string, you have to undertake a sequential search through all the characters in the string for the binary code of the ending-mark.

Strings are usually immutable. Inserting new characters and/or deleting characters is not possible. Altering of individual characters is technically doable but many high-level languages depreciate it. However, high-level languages provide syntactic features to form new strings by copying or concatenating (*i.e.*, appending) two or more strings. You must keep in mind that such processes are not carried out *in place* and are costly. In other words, when you concatenate a string S_1 with another string S_2 to form a new string S_3, first, the lengths of both S_1 and S_2 are obtained; then, a fresh memory space that will hold $length(S_1) + length(S_2)$ many characters is allocated. All bytes that make up S_1 are copied to that fresh memory location, then, when the end of S_1 is reached, the copying process continues with the characters of S_2. Therefore, a simple concatenation costs a memory allocation plus copying each of the characters in the strings to some new location. If the end of a string is marked by a terminator then, in addition, the length calculation requires access to each member of both S_1 and S_2.

Strings in Python

Python provides the `str` data type for strings:

```
>>> "Hello?"
'Hello?'
>>> type("Hello?")
<type 'str'>
```

The simplest thing we can do with strings is to get their lengths, for which we can use the `len(string)` function:

```
>>> len("Hello?")
6
```

– Accessing Elements of a String

Using brackets with an index number, *i.e.*, `[index]`, after a string, we can access the character of the string residing at the given index number. For example, `"Hello?"[0]` returns the character `'H'`, and `"Hello?"[4]` the character `'o'`. Note that indexing the elements of a string starts at zero and not at one. This means that to access the last element of the string, we would need to provide `len(string)-1` as the index.

Luckily, we don't need to use `len(string)-1` to access the last element of a string since Python provides a very useful tool for that: *negative indexing*. In other words, if the index number is negative, the indexing starts from the end of the string; *i.e.*, `"Hello?"[-1]` gives us `'?'` and `"Hello?"[-2]` the character `'o'`. Note that negative indexing starts with one (as the last element in the list) and in general, an index of `-i` refers to the character of the string at position `len(string) - i` in *positive indexing*.

Python provides additional tools to access a subset of a string using *ranged indexing*; *i.e.*, `[start:end:step]`, where `start` is the starting index, `end` is the ending index, and `step` specifies that every `step`th element of the string until the index `end` will be returned. For example:

```
>>> "Hello?"[0:4:2]
'Hl'
>>> "Hello?"[2:4]
'll'
>>> "Hello?"[2::2]
'lo'
>>> "Hello?"[::2]
'Hlo'
```

As seen in these examples, we can skip any of the `start`, `end` and `step` values in `[start:end:step]` (*i.e.*, we can just write `[start::step]`, [start::], [::step] *etc.*), and in these cases, Python will assume that the following default values are given: start: 0, end: the end of the string and step: 1. However, if a negative step value is specified, then the start corresponds to the last element, and end corresponds to the first element. In other words:

```
>>> "ABC"[::-1]
'CBA'
```

> If the subfields of [start:end:step] are omitted, Python assumes default values for them (see the text for some examples).

In Python, strings, lists and tuples have similar representations and therefore, as we will see later, they have similar means for accessing their elements.

– Constructing Strings

We can get a string in either of the following ways:

- Enclosing a set of characters between quotation marks, like "Hello?", in the code.
- Using the str() function as the constructor and supplying data of other types. For example, str(4.5) constructs a string representation of its floating point argument 4.5 and returns '4.5'.
- Using the raw_input() function as follows to get a string from the user:

```
>>> a = raw_input("--> ")
--> Do as I say
>>> a
'Do as I say'
>>> type(a)
<type 'str'>
```

– Useful Operations on Strings

- *The length of a string*: As we shown above, we can use the len(string) function to find the number of elements of a string: For example, len("Hello?") returns 6 since there are six characters in the string.
- *Searching for a substring in a string*: To do this, we can use the string.index() function, for example: "Hello?".index("o?") returns 4 since the substring 'o?' starts at index four.

- *Counting the occurrence of a given substring in a string*: Can be achieved by using the `string.count()` function, for example: `"Hello?".count('lo')` returns 1 since there is only one occurrence of the substring `'lo'`.
- *Concatenating two strings*: Python provides the plus sign + to concatenate two strings: `"Hell"` + `"o"`? yields `"Hello?"`.
- *Making the string lowercase or uppercase*: We can use the `string.upper()` and the `string.lower()` functions respectively to make a string uppercase or lowercase. For example, for a string `"Hello?"`, the call to `"Hello?".upper()` result in `'HELLO?'` whereas the `"Hello?".lower()` would give us `'hello?'`.
- *Checking the characters in a string*: The function calls `string.isalpha()`, `string.isdigit()` and `string.isspace()` respectively check whether all the characters in a string are alphabetical, digital or whitespace (*i.e.*, space, newline and tab characters).
- *Splitting a string into substrings*: Often, we will need to split a string into two or more substrings based on a given separator. We can use the `string.split([string])` function for that (`[string]` denotes that the `string` argument is optional. Test it on your Python interpreter and see what happens when you don't supply a string argument to the `split()` function). For example, `"Hello?".split("e")` gives us a list of two substrings: `['H','llo?']`.
- *Checking for membership*: We can use the `in` and `not in` operators to check whether a substring occurs in a string: `substring in string`, `substring not in string`.
- *Minimum and maximum characters*: The functions `min(string)` and `max(string)` return the characters in the string that have respectively the minimum and the maximum ASCII values. For example, for the string `"Hello?"`, `min("Hello?")` and `max("Hello?")` respectively give us `'?'` and `'o'` since with ASCII values 63 and 111, `'?'` and `'o'` respectively have the minimum and the maximum ASCII values in the string.
- *Repeating a string*: We can multiply a string with a number, *i.e.*, `string*number`, and the result will be the concatenation of `number` many copies of the `string`. For example, `"Dan"*3` is `'DanDanDan'`.

2.4.2 Tuples

The term *tuple* is borrowed from *set theory*, a subfield of mathematics. A tuple is an ordered list of elements. Different from tuple in Mathematics, in Computer Science a tuple can have elements of heterogeneous types. A very similar wording will be given in the following subsection for the definition of *lists*. Having almost the same definition for lists and tuples could be somewhat confusing but this can be resolved by understanding their difference in use and their function in life. Tuples are used to represent a *static form* of aggregation. There is a known prescription and you, the programmer, will bring together the components that make up that prescribed aggregate.

For example, in a computer simulation of a physical event, you will extensively be dealing with coordinates, *i.e.*, a 3-tuple of floating point numbers. You will send 'coordinates' to functions, and form variables of them. However, they will neither become a 2-tuple nor a 4-tuple; like the 3-musketeers, the grouping is unique. Similarly, assume you want to represent an 'employee record' which may consist of six fields of information:

ID, FIRSTNAME, LASTNAME, SALARY, ADDRESS, STARTDATE

As you can see, the types of the fields are not at all homogeneous. ID is an integer; FIRSTNAME, LASTNAME and the ADDRESS are three strings, whereas SALARY is a floating point, and STARTDATE is likely to be a 3-tuple. Since after setting the structure of the aggregate information once (in the example that is what makes up an employee record), it is illogical to change it in the subparts of the program, thus, you make it a tuple.

We will see that lists, too, serve the purpose of grouping information but they are dynamic; *i.e.*, the information in a list can be altered, new elements can be added and removed, *etc*.

As far as high-level language implementations are concerned, the immutability constraint is sometimes turned into an advantage when it comes to compilation. Compared to lists, tuples lead to fast and simple machine code. However, apart from this, the only use of tuples in favor of lists is to prevent programming errors.

Tuples in Python

Python provides the `tuple` data type for tuples. You can provide any number of elements of any type between parentheses `()` to create a tuple in Python:

```
>>> (1, 2, 3, 4, "a")
(1, 2, 3, 4,'a')
>>> type((1, 2, 3, 4, "a"))
<type 'tuple'>
```

– Accessing the Elements of a Tuple

Tuples have exactly the same indexing functionalities as strings to access the elements; *i.e.*, you can use the following that was introduced for strings:

- Positive Indexing: *e.g.*, (1, 2, 3, 4, "a") [2] returns 3.
- Negative Indexing: *e.g.*, (1, 2, 3, 4, "a") [-1] yields 'a'.
- Ranged Indexing, *i.e.*, [start:end:step]: *e.g.*, (1, 2, 3, 4, "a") [0:4:2] leads to (1, 3).

 Strings, Tuples and Lists in Python have the same indexing mechanisms.

– Constructing Tuples

There are several ways to constructing tuples:

- Writing a set of elements within parentheses: *i.e.*, (1, 2, 3).
- Using the tuple() function as a constructor and supplying a string or a list as argument: tuple("Hello?") gives us the tuple ('H', 'e', 'l', 'l', 'o', '?'), and supplying the [1, 2, 3] to tuple() function results in the (1, 2, 3) tuple (Note the difference between the brackets and the parentheses).
- Using the input() function as follows to get a tuple from the user:

```
>>> a = input("Give me a tuple:")
Give me a tuple:(1, 2, 3)
>>> a
(1, 2, 3)
>>> type(a)
<type 'tuple'>
```

– Useful Operations on Tuples

Like strings, tuples have the following operations:

- *The number of elements of a tuple*: We can use the len(tuple) function to find the number of elements in a tuple: For example, len((1,2,3,4,'a')) returns 5.
- *Searching for an element in a string*: One can use the index() function location = my_tuple.index(element) as follows, for example: (1,2,3,4,'a').index(4) returns 3. Note, that unlike stings, you cannot use the index() function to find a subtuple within a tuple.
- *Counting the occurrence of a given element in a tuple*: One can use the count() function location = my_tuple.count(element) as follows, for example: (1,2,3,3,'a').count(3) returns 2. Note,

that unlike strings, cannot use the count() function for counting the occurrence of a subtuple within a tuple.

- *Concatenating two tuples*: Python provides the plus sign + to concatenate two tuples: (1, 2) + (3, 4) yields (1, 2, 3, 4).

2.4.3 Lists

Similar to tuples, lists store a sequence of ordered information. From the programmers point of view, the only difference between tuples and lists is that lists are mutable and tuples are not. You can extend a list by inserting new elements and shrink it by removing elements. However, this ability has deep implementational impacts. Once a tuple is created every member's position in the memory is fixed but this is not the case for a list. In lists, both the size and content can be dynamically adjusted. This brings the problem of structuring the data (the elements of the list) so that these changes to the size and content can be easily and efficiently performed. There exists various implementation alternatives for lists, which fall into two categories:

(a) Dynamic array solutions.
(b) Linked data structures solutions.

In type (a) implementations, reaching any member takes a constant number of steps (*i.e.*, reaching the first, the middle, the end of the list, or any other member in the list requires the same number of steps) which is better than type (b). However, in type (b), the insertion or deletion of elements takes a constant time which is not so for type (a). High-level languages are divided on this subject; for example, Lisp and Prolog implement lists as linked structures whereas the Python implementation is based on dynamic arrays.

The list as a container concept is quite often confused with the linked list data structure. Linked list data structures can serve as implementations of the list abstract data type (the container). As stated, there can be other types of implementations of lists.

Lists are heterogeneous, *i.e.*, the members of a list do not have to be of the same type. Mostly, lists themselves can be members of other lists, which is extremely powerful and useful for some problems. When you have this power at hand, all structures that are not self-referential[3] become representable by means of lists. Some languages, like Lisp, allow even self reference in lists. Therefore, complex structures like graphs become efficiently representable.

---

[3]Structures are self-referential if they are (recursively) defined in terms of themselves. We will come back to self-referential structures in Chap. 4.

Lists in Python

Tuples are immutable, *i.e.*, unchangeable, sets of data. For mutable sets of data, Python provides the `list` data type:

```
>>> [1, 2, 3, 4, "a"]
[1, 2, 3, 4,'a']
>>> type([1, 2, 3, 4, "a"])
<type 'list'>
```

Note that, unlike tuples, a `list` in Python uses brackets.

– Accessing the Elements of a List

Lists have exactly the same indexing functionalities as strings and tuplesto access the elements; *i.e.*, you can use the following that we already introduced for strings and tuples:

- Positive Indexing: `[1, 2, 3, 4, "a"][2]` returns 3.
- Negative Indexing: `[1, 2, 3, 4, "a"][-1]` returns `'a'`.
- Ranged Indexing, *i.e.*, `[start:end:step]`: `[1, 2, 3, 4, "a"][0:4:2]` leads to `[1, 3]`.

– Constructing Lists

There are several ways of constructing Lists:

- Writing a set of elements within brackets: *i.e.*, `[1, 2, 3]`.
- Using the `list()` function as a constructor and supplying a string or a tuple as argument: `tuple("Hello?")` gives us the list `['H', 'e', 'l', 'l', 'o', '?']`.
- Using the `range()` function: `range([start,] stop[, step])`
- Using the `input()` function as given below, to get a list from the user:

```
>>> a = input("Give me a list:")
Give me a list:[1, 2, "a"]
>>> a
[1, 2, 'a']
>>> type(a)
<type 'list'>
```

– Modifying a List

You can substitute an element at a given index with a new one: *i.e.*, `List[index] = expression`. Alternatively, Python allows changing a subset of the list with new values:

```
>>> L = [3, 4, 5, 6, 7, '8', 9, '10']
>>> L[::2]
[3, 5, 7, 9]
>>> L[::2] = [4, 6, 8, 10]
>>> L[::2]
[4, 6, 8, 10]
>>> L[]
[4, 4, 6, 6, 8, '8', 10, '10']
```

Note that, in the above example, we have given the name L to the list in the first line. We call L *a variable*, and later in this chapter we will discuss in detail giving names to data (*i.e.*, variables).

Python provides the `L.append(item)` function to add one item to the end of the list L:

```
>>> L =  [4, 4, 6, 6, 8, '8', 10, '10']
>>> L.append("a")
>>> L
[4, 4, 6, 6, 8, '8', 10, '10', 'a']
```

Alternatively, you can add more than one item to a list using the `L.extend(seq)` function:

```
>>> L.extend(["a", "b"])
>>> L
[4, 4, 6, 6, 8, '8', 10, '10', 'a', 'a', 'b']
```

If you want to add a new element in the middle of a list, you can use the `L.insert(index, item)` function:

```
>>> L=[1, 2, 3]
>>> L
[1, 2, 3]
>>> L.insert(1, 0)
>>> L
[1, 0, 2, 3]
```

To remove elements from a list, you can use either of the following:

- `del` *statement*: `del L[start:end]`

  ```
  >>> L
  [1, 0, 2, 3]
  ```

```
>>> del L[1]
>>> L
[1, 2, 3]
```

- L.remove() *function*: L.remove(value)

```
>>> L
[2, 1, 3]
>>> L.remove(1)
>>> L
[2, 3]
```

- L.pop() *function*: L.pop([index])

```
>>> L=[1,2,3]
>>> L.pop()
3
>>> L
[1, 2]
>>> L.pop(0)
1
>>> L
[2]
```

 List modification is meaningful only for named lists; *i.e.*, if you run (for example) the append() function like [1, 2, 3].append(4), you will not observe an effect, although the list [1, 2, 3] might have been changed.

– Useful Operations on Lists

- *Reversing a list*: L.reverse() function
  A list can be reversed using the reverse() function.

```
>>> L = [1, 2, 3]
>>> L.reverse()
>>> L
[3, 2, 1]
>>> L[::-1]
[1, 2, 3]
>>> L
[3, 2, 1]
```

In this example, we also see the difference between the `reverse()` function and the `[::-1]` indexing (which gives the elements of a list in reverse order): `[::-1]` does not change the list whereas the `reverse()` function does (*i.e.*, it is *in-place*)!

- *Searching a list*: `index = L.index(item)` function
  The `index()` function returns the index of the `item` in the list L. If `item` is not a member of L, an error is returned.
- *Counting the occurrence of an element in a list*: `n = L.count(item)` function
  The `count()` function counts the number of occurrence of the `item` in the list L.
- *Range of a list*: `value = min(L)` and `value = max(L)` functions
  We can easily find the minimum- and maximum-valued items in a list using the `min()` and `max()` functions. For example, `min([-100, 20, 10, 30])` is `-100`.
- *Sorting a list*: `L.sort()` or `L2 = sorted(L)` functions
  There are two options for sorting the elements of a list: `L.sort()` or `L2 = sorted(L)`. They differ in that `sort()` modifies the list (*i.e.*, it is *in-place*) whereas `sorted()` does not.

2.5 Accessing Data or Containers by Names: Variables

We are mostly used to the word 'variable' from our Mathematics classes. Interestingly, the meaning in programming is quite different from the mathematical one. In Mathematics, 'variable' stands for a value which is unknown or undetermined. In programming though, it refers to a value that is at hand and hence, is very well-known. Literary speaking, a variable, in programming, is a storage which can hold a data element of the high-level language and in the program, is referred to by a symbolic name, given by the programmer.

2.5.1 Naming

The symbolic name is the handle that the programmer uses for reaching the variable. What this name can consist of differs from language to language. Mostly, it is an identifier which starts with a letter from the alphabet and continues either with a letter or a digit. Examples of possible names are `x`, `y`, `x1`, `xmax`, `xmin2max`, `a1a`, `temperature`. Whether there is a distinction between upper case and lower case letters, and the inclusion of some of the punctuation characters in the alphabet (*e.g.* '_', '-', '$', ':') is dependent on the language. Moreover, some languages limit the length of the identifiers whereas others do not.

2.5.2 Scope and Extent

The way variables are created differ among high-level languages. Some need a dec-
laration of the variable before it is used whereas some do not. Some high-level languages allow the creation and annihilation of a variable for subparts of a program
where some do this automatically. The subparts of a program can exist in various
forms. Although not restricted to this, they are mostly in the form of subroutines, a
part of the program which is designed to carry out a specific task and is, to a great
extent, independent of other parts of the code. Subroutines are functional units that
receive data (through variables that are named as parameters) process it and as a
result, produce action(s) and/or data.

In addition to the parameters, many high level languages also allow the definition
of local variables in subroutines. The situation can become quite complex when
a high-level language (like Pascal) allows subroutine definitions inside subroutine
definitions. This is done with an intention of limiting the subroutine's existence and
usability to a locality.

All this creation and annihilation of variables, the nest-ability, both definition-
wise and usage-wise, in subparts of a program result in the emergence of two important properties of variables:

- Scope
- Extent (or lifetime)

Scope is about where the language allows or disallows accessing a variable by re-
ferring to its name; *i.e.*, scope determines the program parts in which a variable
is usable. Disallowing mostly occurs when a subpart (*e.g.* a subroutine) defines a
variable with the exact same name of a variable that already exists in the global
environment (the part of the program which is exterior to that subpart but is not
another (sibling) subpart). The variable of the global environment is there, lives
happily but is not visible from the subpart that has defined a variable with the
same name.

Extent or so called *lifetime* is the time span, from the creation to the annihilation of
the variable, during the flow of the program execution.

2.5.3 Typing

Depending on the high-level language, variables may or may not be defined with a
restriction on the type of data they will hold. The difference stems from the language
being;

- statically typed, or
- dynamically typed.

In the *statically-typed* case, the language processor (the compiler or interpreter)
knows exactly for what kind of data the variable has been established. It is going to

hold a single type of data, and this is declared by a statement in the program (prior to using the variable). Therefore, whenever a reference in the program is made to that variable, the interpreter or compiler knows exactly what type of content is stored in the corresponding memory location. This is the case in C, Pascal and Java.

If it is a *dynamically-typed* language, the content of the variable can vary as far as types are concerned. For example, the same variable can first store an integer then, in accordance with the programmer's demand, it can store a floating point. In this case, every piece of data in the memory is tagged (preceded) with a byte that specifies the type of the data. Lisp, Perl and Python are such languages.

Statically-typed languages are relatively faster, since at run time (*i.e.*, when the program is running) there is no need to perform a check on the type of the data and make a decision about how to proceed with an action (*e.g.* to decide whether a multiplication instruction is that of a floating point or an integer type).[4]

2.5.4 What Can We Do with Variables?

The answer is simple: you can do whatever you wanted to do with the 'data' stored in the variable. You can replace the data, or use the data. Certain uses (syntaxes) of a variable (name) have the semantic (meaning) of "I want to replace the content of the variable with some new value (data)". All other uses of the variable (name) have the semantics of "I want to have the data (or sometimes a copy of it) inserted at this position". An assignment instruction example, common to many high-level imperative languages, would read:

```
average = (x + y) / 2.0
```

Here, `average`, `x` and `y` are three distinct variables. The use of `average` is syntactically different from the use of `x` and `y`. Being on the left of the assignment operator,[5] the equal sign, the data stored in the variable `average` is going to be replaced with a new value. This new value is the result of the calculation on the right side of the assignment operator and that calculation also makes use of two variables: `x` and `y`. Since they appear on the right-hand side of the assignment operator this time, the semantic is different, meaning *"use in the calculation the values stored in those two variables"*. In the course of the evaluation, those two values will be added then the sum will be divided by two.

---

[4]Processors have different sets of instructions for floating point and integer arithmetic.

[5]The assignment operator exists in all imperative languages. '=', ':=' are the most common notations used for assignment. '<-', '«', '=:', ':' are also used, but less frequently.

2.5.5 Variables in Python

As discussed above, programming languages almost always provide a means for naming the locations of the stored information, and these names are called *variables*. In Python, to create a variable is as easy as writing a name and assigning a value to that name:

```
>>> a = 4
>>> b = 3
>>> c = a + b
>>> a
4
>>> b
3
>>> c
7
```

One of the goodies of Python is visible in the previous example: we used the variables a, b and c without first defining them, or declaring what they are; Python can evaluate the right side of the equal sign and discover the type of the value. If the variable has already been created, the existing variable is used and the value stored in the variable is over-written. If the variable has not already been created, a new one is created with the type of the expression on the right-hand side of the assignment operator (*i.e.*, =).

The left-hand side of the assignment operator has to be a valid variable name; for example, you cannot type a+2 = 4, (we will come back to what can be put on the left hand side of an assignment operator in Chap. 3).

– Variable Naming in Python

Like in other programming languages, in Python only certain combinations of characters can be used as variable names:

- Variable names are case sensitive, therefore the names a and A are two different variables.
- Variable names can contain letters from the English alphabet, numbers and an underscore _.
- Variable names can only start with a letter or an underscore. So, 10a, $a, and var$ are all invalid whereas _a and a_20, for example, are valid names in Python.

Since the following keywords are already used by Python, you cannot use them as variable names:

```
and        del        from      not        while
as         elif       global    or         with
assert     else       if        pass       yield
break      except     import    print
class      exec       in        raise
continue   finally    is        return
def        for        lambda    try
```

– Scope and Extent of a Variable in Python

The scope and the extent of a variable in Python depends on where it is defined. Since we will cover more complex Python constructs later in the book, we will return to the topic of scope and the extent of variables in the following chapters.

– Typing of Variables in Python

As discussed above, variables can be either statically or dynamically typed. In Python, variables are dynamically-typed. The following example displays this property:

```
>>> a = 3
>>> type(a)
<type 'int'>
>>> a = 3.4
>>> type(a)
<type 'float'>
```

That means, in Python, (i) you do not need to specify the type of the variable and (ii) you can change the type of the variable by assigning new data of a different type.

– Using Variables in Python

You can use variables in Python as you would use data: you can assign a tuple, a string or a list to a variable and manipulate it in any way that you would manipulate the data, for example:

```
>>> a = (1, 2, 3, 'a')
>>> type(a)
<type 'tuple'>
>>> a[1]
2
>>> a[-1]
'a'
```

– Variables, Values and Aliasing in Python

Each data (or object) in Python is assigned a unique identifier (basically, an integer) which can be accessed by the id() function. Having unique identifiers, Python manages memory space such that multiple occurrences of the same data are stored only once whenever possible. For example:

```
>>> a = 1
>>> b = 1
>>> id(1)
135720760
>>> id(a)
135720760
>>> id(b)
135720760
```

Here, we see that the data '1' and the variables a and b all hold the same content; *i.e.*, the data '1' is represented once and all these three cases make use of only one stored '1'.

However, it is safe to change the content of one variable without affecting the content of the other (following the previous interaction):

```
>>> a = 2
>>> b
1
>>> id(a)
135720748
>>> id(b)
135720760
```

In the following example for lists (which are mutable containers), however, the variables are *linked* to the same memory location and changing one variable means changing the other one, due to mutability:

```
>>> a = ['a', 'b']
>>> b = a
>>> id(a)
3083374316L
>>> id(b)
3083374316L
>>> b[0] = 0
>>> a
[0, 'b']
```

In this example, although we did not explicitly access the list pointed to by the variable a, we could change it since variable b became an *alias* to the variable a in the assignment b = a.

 In Python, mutable data types (we have only seen lists up to now) are affected by aliasing. Although this can be a beneficial property at times, it is often dangerous to assign variables of mutable content to each other such as, a = b.

2.6 Keywords

The important concepts that we would like our readers to understand in this chapter are indicated by the following keywords:

Structured Data	Tuples
Basic Data	Variables
Integers	Static Typing
Floating Points	Dynamic Typing
Characters	Mutable Types
Boolean Values	Immutable Types
Strings	Aliasing
Lists	Scope&Extent of Variables

2.7 Further Reading

For more information on the topics discussed in this chapter, you can check out the sources below:

- *Two's Complement*:
  http://en.wikipedia.org/wiki/Two%27s_complement
- *IEEE 754 Floating Point Standard*:
  http://en.wikipedia.org/wiki/IEEE_754-2008
- *ASCII*:
  http://en.wikipedia.org/wiki/ASCII
- *UTF—UCS Transformation Format*:
  http://en.wikipedia.org/wiki/UTF-8
- *Mutable and Immutable Objects*:
  http://en.wikipedia.org/wiki/Mutable_object
- *For naming conventions and the reserved keywords in Python*:
  http://docs.python.org/reference/lexical_analysis.html#identifiers
- *Aliasing*:
  http://en.wikipedia.org/wiki/Aliasing_%28computing%29

2.8 Exercises

1. Find the Two's Complement representation of the following numbers: 4, −5, 1, −0, 11. How many bits do you require for all these numbers?
2. Find the IEEE 754 32-bit representation of the following floating points: 3.3, 3.37, 3.375.
3. You can use either a comma , or a plus sign + to combine different values or variables in a print statement. Experiment with the Python interpreter to see the difference.
4. Write a Python code that inputs two numbers from the user and then displays their arithmetic, geometric and harmonic means. Do you see any relation between the arithmetic mean, geometric mean and the harmonic mean? (Hint: For a set of numbers $x_0, \ldots, x_N$, arithmetic, geometric and harmonic means are respectively defined as: $1/N \sum_{x_i} x_i$, $1/N \prod_{x_i} x_i$ and $N / \sum_{x_i} 1/x_i$.)
5. Write a Python code that inputs the coefficients of two lines $y = a_1 x + b_1$ and $y = a_2 x + b_2$ from the user and finds their intersection. (1st Hint: You can assume that the lines are not parallel. 2nd Hint: The x coordinate of the intersection can be found by equaling $a_1 x + b_1$ to $a_2 x + b_2$. Putting that x coordinate in the equation of one of the lines leads us to the y coordinate of the intersection.)
6. Write a Python code that inputs the coordinates of the corners of a triangle (*i.e.*, $(x_0, y_0), (x_1, y_1), (x_2, y_2)$) and compute the area of the triangle.
7. What happens when you call the append() function on a list with another list as the argument? (For example: For a list L = [1, 2, 3], what is the output of L.append([4, 5])?)
8. What happens when you call the extend() function on a list with another list as the argument? For example: For a list L = [1, 2, 3], what is the output of L.extend([4, 5])?
9. Write a piece of Python code that takes the first half of a list, reverses it and appends it to the end of the second half. For example: For a list L = [1, 2, 10, 20], the result of your Python code should be [10, 20, 1, 2].
10. Write a piece of Python code that checks whether a word is palindrome. A palindrome is a word or phrase or number which reads the same forward and backwards. Examples are; *radar, racecar, wasitaratisaw*. (Hint: You can make use of the == operator to check the equality of two sequences.)
11. Write the following in Python and study their outputs: help(help), help(type), help(int), help(long), help(float), help(bool), help(str), help(list).
12. From the help page of the list type, find out how to calculate the number of bytes that a list occupies.
13. What happens when you try to index a string with a number greater than the length of the string? Do you get the same result for tuples and lists?
14. What happens when you try to change the elements of a tuple? For example: for a tuple T = (1, 2, 3), what is the result of T[0] = 3 ?
15. Do the sort() and the sorted() functions sort in increasing or decreasing order? How can you change the sorting order? (Hint: Use the help page of the list data type or the sorted() function.)

16. Type `import sys` and `help(sys)` into your Python interpreter and look for how you can access the following:
    (a) The maximum `int`, `float` and `long` that can be represented by your Python interpreter on your machine.
    (b) The version of the Python interpreter.
    (c) The name of the platform that the interpreter is running on.

Chapter 3
Actions: The Second Ingredient of a Program

In the previous chapter, we have introduced data an essential but static component of programming. It is static in the sense that data has no ability to act: Data cannot change itself, create new data, or even display itself. It is the actions of a high-level language that will provide all these. Actions are what will be performed in terms of CPU instructions at the machine code level.

3.1 Purpose and Scope of Actions

A program, as stated previously, is a solution to a world problem. World problems form a broad spectrum including: mathematical computations involved in mortgage calculations, weather forecasting, processing sensory data of a person's cardiac activity or remote sensing of a fired hostile missile. Providing a (computerized) solution requires many actions to be taken in a program. Providing a (computerized) solution requires many actions to be taken in a program. These actions can be classified into two categories:

- *Creating and/or modifying data*: This is actually what computation is all about. Given some data, based on rules that govern the specific computational domain, these types of actions infer new data. That is what we do when we multiply two numbers, solve a quadratic equation, calculate the fuel for a spacecraft to travel from Earth to the Moon, or find the net profit a bank has made over all its fiscal transactions. This type of computation is one, or a combination of two or more, of the following:
  - Evaluating a mathematical expression.
  - Looking up or modifying some structured data (*e.g.*, a container, a tree, a graph, *etc.*),
  - Storing the results of computations.
  - Making a decision about how to proceed with the computation,
  - Altering the flow of the computation.

G. Üçoluk, S. Kalkan, *Introduction to Programming Concepts with Case Studies in Python*, DOI 10.1007/978-3-7091-1343-1_3, © Springer-Verlag Wien 2012

High-level programming languages provide the facilities to undertake these actions:

- The evaluation of an expression is similar to what we are used to doing in our math classes, but there are some restrictions. For example, there is no concept of unknowns or variables as in mathematical terms, and writing down an equation never has the implicit meaning of 'solving the equation for an unknown'. The information that appears in an expression is either a constant or a value stored in the memory (*i.e.*, a 'variable' in programming terms). Therefore, all calculations are merely arithmetical.

- High-level languages have built-in facilities for constructing and navigating structured data. In the previous chapter, some basic structures, such as containers, were introduced. A decent high-level language will provide programming handles (like pointers, functions for dynamic memory allocation) even if it does not offer direct syntax for actions on certain kinds of structured data.

- Storing any result obtained in computations into the memory is provided in all high-level languages through variables. This type of action is called *assignment*.

- Asking questions (and deciding which action to take based on the answer) is an action by itself. However, the questions will be answered either in the affirmative or negative; *i.e.*, the answer is either yes or no.
  - if $x*y < 3.1415$ then $\langle$*do some action*$\rangle$
  - if `"ali" in class_111_list` then $\langle$*do some action*$\rangle$
  - if `tall("ali")` then $\langle$*do some action*$\rangle$

The so-called "truth value" on which the decision action is based is crisp and two-valued. As we will see later, this is due to the very nature of *Deterministic Turing Machine* (DTM), the theoretical machine which all processors and programming languages are equivalent to.

The first two of the examples given above are simple; *i.e.*, they can be answered with a clear 'yes' or 'no'. But, what about the third one? Let `"ali"` be of height 1.75. Should he be considered "tall"? Being 'tall' is a fuzzy concept. Unfortunately, having a fuzzy answer and, based on the answer, a choice among a spectrum of possible actions is inherently not possible. These types of fuzzy actions have to be 'simulated' in this crisp world. That is achievable, but it requires quite an amount of programming effort.

Another related concept is determinism. In other words, under the same circumstances, any decision action always produces the same outcome. It is actually possible to implement probabilistic actions in today's computers. Making use of an external (*i.e.*, external to the Von Neumann architecture) random (or pseudo-random) phenomenon, it is possible to import the probability concept into the world of programming. One of the most common external phenomena used is the tick-count of a real-time clock in micro seconds. This, of course, requires certain electronic circuitry to be built into the computer and hooked up to the Von Neumann architecture.

Below you will find more information on how this is done.

- *Interaction with the external environment*: A Von Neumann machine, by itself, does not say much about the interaction of the machine with the outer world. Today's computers communicate with external devices, the so-called *peripherals*, by a complicated mechanism, the details of which are beyond the scope of this textbook and belong in a *Computer Organization* textbook, However, here is a brief introduction to the way in which computers communicate with other devices: There are basically two types of methods.
  - Memory-mapped I/O,
  - Port-mapped I/O.

In 'memory-mapped I/O', the electronic circuitry that forms the connection to a peripheral device writes to and reads from a segment of the memory, which is a part of the Von Neumann architecture. An electronic mechanism prevents simultaneous access to the memory bus (which is required since multiple peripherals and circuits would want to access the memory simultaneously).

  - The peripherals gain access to that memory segment, then write or read some data.
  - The CPU gains access to that memory segment, then writes or reads some data.
  - In addition, most of the time, it is possible that the peripheral, by means of the interrupt mechanism, makes the CPU suspend whatever it is doing and execute a piece of machine code stored in the memory. This piece of code, called *the interrupt service routine*, will presumably perform some quick action related to the peripheral's data. After having executed the interrupt service routine, the CPU will resume its previous task (that was suspended).

The 'port-mapped I/O' is similar to the 'memory-mapped I/O'. The difference is that in the port-mapped I/O, a wire running from the CPU to the memory device carries the signal which tells that the address on the address bus is not an address of the physical memory. So, the actual physical memory does not respond and stays silent. The address bus and that wire are also listened to by the peripherals' electronics. If it is not a memory access but a port I/O (the wire carries that information) and if the address is in the concern of a peripheral, the electronics connecting that peripheral are activated. Then, it is the peripheral that provides data to, or consumes data from, the data bus. The functionality of interrupts in port-mapped I/O is exactly the same as the interrupts in the memory-mapped I/O.

There are two reasons for a program to interact with the environment:

1. To react to a change in the external environment.
2. To produce an effect on the external environment.

Examples of the first reason are; Getting the typed input from the keyboard, updating the coordinates of the mouse icon due to the movement of the mouse, receiving a data package that arrived over the Ethernet, an image sent by the camera connected to the PC or a signal sent by the X-ray device wired to your PC.

Examples for the second reasons are; Displaying a text or an image on the screen, storing some data on the hard disk or a USB stick, printing a document on the printer, launching a missile, sending a request to Google over the Internet via a modem connection are examples.

3.1.1 Input-Output Operations in Python

In this section, we will describe the Input/Output actions in Python.

Getting Input from the User in Python

You can make use of either of the following to get input from the user:

raw_input function: `raw_input([prompt string]): string`
  The `raw_input` function reads the characters from the keyboard until an EOF (End of File) is provided (EOF is CTRL-D on Unix and CTRL-Z&Return on Windows). If the optional prompt string argument is provided, the `raw_input` function displays the argument string as the prompt to the user before reading the input. The entered text can be used for example, as follows:

```
>>> a = raw_input("--> ")
--> Do as I say
>>> a
'Do as I say'
>>> type(a)
<type 'str'>
```

input function: `input([prompt string]): value`
  The `input` function is similar to the `raw_input` function with the difference that the entered text is evaluated in Python and the resulting value is returned. As specified in the help page of the `raw_input` function (you can reach the help page of the `raw_input` function by typing `help(raw_input)` at the interpreter), the `raw_input` function is equivalent to `eval(raw_input([prompt]))`, where the `eval()` function evaluates, or interprets, the input string as a Python expression and raises an error if the entered text is not valid in Python.
  Since the entered text is evaluated as a Python expression, caution against malicious input should be taken in the usage of the input function.

The following example demonstrates the difference between the `input` and `raw_input` functions:

```
>>> input("Give me something: ")
Give me something: 3+4
7
>>> raw_input("Give me another text: ")
Give me another text: 3+4
'3+4'
```

Displaying Data to the User in Python

Python provides the print statement to display data to the user: print expr1, expr2, expr3, ..., exprN. print accepts at least one expression, evaluates the expressions and displays the value to the user.

```
>>> a=1
>>> b=20
>>> c="Test"
>>> print "These are what I want to display:", c, a, b
These are what I want to display: Test 1 20
```

We have provided Python with four expressions of different types, and it could display them back to us. If we try something harder with fewer expressions (three in the first case and two in the second case):

```
>>> print "These are what I want to display:" + c, a, b
These are what I want to display:Test 1 20
>>> print "These are what I want to display:" + c, a + b
These are what I want to display:Test 21
```

Python can evaluate the expressions that we have provided and displays the results of the expressions. In the following case, we give the print statement only one expression. Since the input expression includes the addition of a string with integers, Python complains:

```
>>> print "These are what I want to display:" + c + a + b
Traceback (most recent call last):
  File "<stdin>", line 1, in <module>
TypeError: cannot concatenate 'str' and 'int' objects
```

– Formatted Output in Python

Python provides two different ways to format a string for printing it to the user:

1. *C style string formatting*: In this style, the programmer can call the print function as follows: print "I am %f meters tall" % 1.86,

which would print `'I am 1.860000 meters tall'`. In this style, `%f` is the *data identifier* and at the end of the string, after the `%` sign, the data (*i.e.*, `1.860000`) is provided.

The following data identifiers can be used (see the pointers in the "Further Reading" section for a complete list and more-detailed description):

Identifier	Description
d, i	Integer
f, F	Floating point
e, E	Floating point in exponent form
s	Using the `str()` function
r	Using the `repr()` function
%	The % character itself

Multiple data can be formatted in a single string as in the examples below:

```
>>> print "I am %f tall, %d years old and \
        have %s eyes" % (1.86, 20, "brown")
I am 1.860000 tall, 20 years old and have brown eyes
```

Note the extra zeros at the end of `1.860000`. You can use `%s` if you don't want to see extra zeros:

```
>>> print "I am %s tall, %d years old and \
        have %s eyes" % (1.86, 20, "brown")
I am 1.86 tall, 20 years old and have brown eyes
```

2. *New style string formatting*: In the new style formatting, the delimiters (*i.e.*, `%f`, `%d`, *etc.*) of the C style are replaced by the curly braces (`{}`). For example: `print "I am {0} meters tall".format(1.86)`, which would print `'I am 1.86 meters tall'`.

The number within the curly braces specifies which data supplied as the argument to `format()` corresponds to the identifier. If we have more than one data, then:

```
>>> print "I am {0} tall, {1} years old and \
        have {2} eyes".format(1.86, 20, "brown")
I am 1.86 tall, 20 years old and have brown eyes
```

The numbers 0, 1 and 2 can be replaced with names:

```
>>> print "I am {height} tall, {age} years old and \
        have {color} eyes".\
        format(height=1.86, age=20, color="brown")
I am 1.86 tall, 20 years old and have brown eyes
```

 If a sentence is too long, you can use the \
character then continue the sentence on the
next line.

Since we can give names to the data and the data identifiers, we can use a
data more than once, or even we can change the order:

```
>>> print "I am {height} tall, {age} years old.\
        I am {height} tall.".format(age=20, height=1.86)
I am 1.86 tall, 20 years old. I am 1.86 tall.
```

3.2 Action Types

In high-level programming languages, actions are performed in two forms:

- Expression evaluation,
- Statement execution.

The key distinction between these two forms is that expression evaluations return a
value whereas statement executions do not.

As far as statements are concerned, programming languages differ in the syntax they admit. This is the case even for some very basic actions common in all
high-level programming languages: C, Pascal, Fortran and Python all have different
syntax for the conditional (if) statement, though the semantics (meaning) is just
the same.

Stemming from mathematics, expressions are far more standardized. The difference, if any, is due to the way variables and function calls are denoted.

3.2.1 Expressions

Expressions are actually prescriptions of how to do a calculation. In a calculation,
values are combined under *operations* to yield new values. Anything that is subject to an operation is called an *operand*. Hence, an operand or operands enter an
operation which produces a value (Fig. 3.1).

Two of such operations single out due to their extensive usage: binary and unary
operations (Fig. 3.2).

Church–Rosser Property and the Side-Effect in Expressions

An expression can contain many operands and operations and now, we will take a
closer look at the evaluation scheme in order to understand how *big* and *complex*

Fig. 3.1 N-ary operation

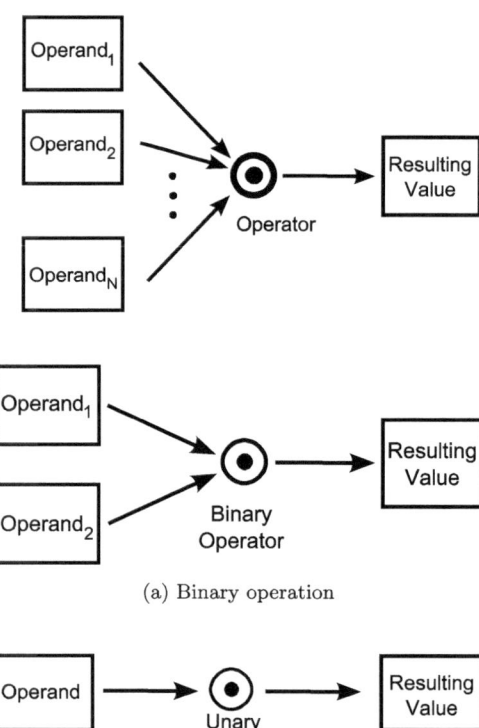

Fig. 3.2 Extensively used operations

(a) Binary operation

(b) Unary operation

expressions are interpreted by the computer. There is a reason for this: things are not exactly as we would expect them to be.

In mathematics, the evaluation of a mathematical expression is said to have the so-called *"Church–Rosser property"*, which is about reduction or rewriting systems. Such systems are defined as sets of reductions or rewriting rules on some objects. An object, by means of application of the rules, will finally be transformed into (*i.e.*, reduced to) a form to which no further rule can be applied anymore. In a reduction system, the sequence of rule applications might not be unique. For example, a reduction system on strings may have a single rule which says

- "If both ends of a string are consonants, remove any one."

Now, assume that we start with the string BRING. Figure 3.3 displays a tree of possible actions the rule set (which has actually a single rule) allows. Each path that leads to a leaf (underlined in red) is a valid reduction. As clearly visible in Fig. 3.3, various reductions can lead to different end-results. Starting with any object, if all the results obtained for that object are the same, this reduction system would be said to possess the Church–Rosser property.

In mathematics, expression evaluation has the Church–Rosser property, but, in programming, expression evaluation does *not* have the Church–Rosser property.

Fig. 3.3 Failure in possessing the Church–Rosser Property

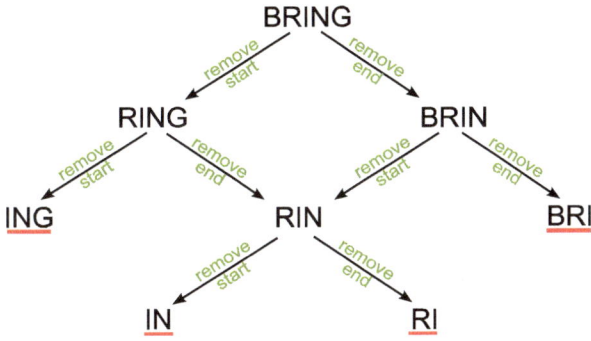

Therefore, a programmer has to know exactly the way an expression is evaluated.

Two factors, which are not present in mathematics, are the cause of failure for the Church–Rosser property of expression evaluation in programming:

1. *The limitations due to the fixed-size representation of numbers*: In the preceding chapter, the problems related to the fixed-size representation of numbers were introduced. The fixed-size representation makes calculations vulnerable to overflows and round-off errors. Calculating $A \times B / B$ may overflow even if both A and B are within the limits of the binary representation. If $A \times B$ overflows, then there is no chance that the division will save the situation. This observation is valid, of course, under the assumption that the multiplication is performed prior to the division. If it is the other way around, and the division is performed first, A will be multiplied by 1, which is certainly a safe calculation. Hence, the Church–Rosser property does not exist.

2. *Side-effects in the evaluation of some operations and function calls*: In order to properly understand this, it is necessary to describe what a side-effect is in computer science terminology.

   In computer science, a function or an operation is said to have a *side effect* if, besides producing a value, it either alters some existing global variables[1] (variables with a lifespan longer then the function call), or it has an observable interaction with the exterior world (such as printing a message on the screen or deleting a file on the hard disk).

For example, assume a function $f(n)$ sets a global variable x to n and then returns n^2. Further assume that x has an initial value of 0. Then, the result of a simple expression like $(f(2) + x)$ depends on the evaluation order of the operands of the addition: If the left operand is evaluated first, the result is obtained as $(4 + 2) = 6$, and if the right operand is evaluated first, the result is $(4 + 0) = 4$. Interestingly, in both cases after the evaluation, the global variable x contains 2. Hence, the possibility of having side-effects in programming disobeys the Church–Rosser property.

---

[1] A global variable is a variable that is accessible by all functions.

Numerous books that introduce certain programming languages leave issues related to the absence of Church–Rosser property in programming unexplained. A considerable number of books take the easy way out using an explanation similar to the one given below:

> In expression evaluation, inner-most parentheses are evaluated first; when no parentheses are left (or when we are inside a parenthesis), operators with highest precedence are sorted out first; if the precedence of the operators are equal, the left operation goes first.

This is not true, and not a single assertion is correct. Here are the facts about expression evaluation:

- Most languages do not define the order of evaluation. This is deliberate in order to leave the compiler writers a degree of freedom, which is particularly necessary for code optimization. Therefore, to be 100% certain, a programmer should refrain from all side effects and consider the worst case scenario for overflows. These are the areas which lead to the annihilation of the Church–Rosser property; so, if you can guarantee that there will be no side effects, then you can consider that the Church–Rosser property exists.
- Unless highly optimized, the most commonly used algorithm for expression evaluation (or the generation of the code that will do it) is a two-phase algorithm. The first phase is Dijkstra's *Shunting-yard algorithm* which translates an infix expression into postfix, and the second phase is the *postfix evaluation algorithm*.

Since it is the commonly used algorithm, to introduce it will clear off the untrue assertions that many books put on display just to beat the bush.

The Most Commonly Used Expression Evaluation Algorithm

Expression!Evaluation As stated above, this is a two phase algorithm:

Phase I: Translate the infix expression into postfix.
Phase II: Evaluate the postfix expression to obtain the resulting value.

Before going into the details of the phases, it is necessary to explain the term *postfix expression*, and why it is useful for this very purpose (*i.e.*, expression evaluation). *Expression!Evaluation*

We are used to expressions where the operator sits between the operands. If $\square$ and $\triangle$ are two operands and $\odot$ is the operator,

$$\square \odot \triangle$$

is the way we denote the operation. When any of the operands is a different operation, then the situation becomes complicated. Let us say $\circledast$ is another operator and

■ is an operand

Which operation is going to be performed first? In this case, there is a hidden code. Beside the semantics (meaning) of the operators, we need to think about the *precedence* of the operators; *i.e.*, the relative priorities of the operators. For example, multiplication has a higher precedence over addition, and exponentiation has the highest precedence. If two operators of equal precedence clash then we consult the *associativity*. We are taught in school that apart from exponentiation, all arithmetical operators are left associative. Last but not least, if you are dissatisfied with what the hidden code imposes, you can override it by using parentheses. Although this works, it is complicated. We don't have this feeling when we perform arithmetic with pen and pencil because that is a rewriting technique. We are absolutely free to jump to any part of the expression, sort it out and even undertake some rewritings in parallel. We use our experience and intelligence in doing this. Furthermore, mostly we have an overall grasp of the 'whole expression'. However, this is certainly not the way a computer can proceed.

The irregularity (having to jump from a subpart to another subpart of the expression) in the calculation is due to the existence of parentheses and precedences.

Two other denotations, namely the *prefix* and the *postfix* notations, are free of these troublemakers. As their name implies, the operands follow the operator in the prefix notation, and the operator follows the operands in the postfix notation:

$$\underbrace{\square \odot \triangle}_{\text{INFIX}} \qquad \underbrace{\odot \square \triangle}_{\text{PREFIX}} \qquad \underbrace{\square \triangle \odot}_{\text{POSTFIX}}$$

Let us take a look at an example. Consider the mathematical expression

$$A + \frac{B^{C^{D}} \times (E - (F - G - H))}{K}$$

The common arithmetical operators used in programming are as follows:

Arithmetics	Programming
Addition $(+)$	$+$
Subtraction $(-)$	$-$
Multiplication $(\times)$	$\star$
Division $(\div)$	$/$
Exponentiation	$\char`\^$ or $\star\star$

Therefore, the mathematical expression given above would be written in a programming language that admits infix expressions as:

A-B^C^D*(E-(F-G-H))/K

The prefix form would be:

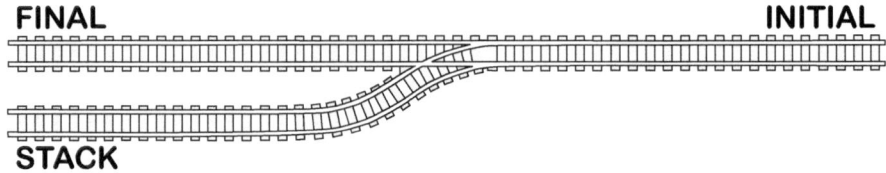

Fig. 3.4 Railroad shunting-yard

$$-A/*^{\wedge}B^{\wedge}CD-E--FGHK$$

And the postfix would be:

$$ABCD^{\wedge\wedge}EFG-H--*K/-$$

The postfix notation is algorithmically very easy to evaluate and convert to from the infix notation.

Phase 1: Dijkstra's Shunting-Yard Algorithm

The name comes from the resemblance to the task of putting railroad cars into a desired order according to their destination. The way to do this is to have a shunting-yard, as shown in Fig. 3.4. So, how does it function? Let us see it on an example. Assume that we have a train which is in the order of a red car, followed by a yellow car, then by a green car. We want to change the order to red, green and yellow.

Here is how it is done:

Making use of the shunting-yard, we are able to transform an infix expression into a postfix expression as follows (see Fig. 3.5):

- Place the infix expression at the INITIAL position on the shunting-yard.
- From left to right, consider, one by one, each item (operator, operand or parenthesis) of the expression as a railroad car to be moved.
- If the item is an operand, move it straightaway to the end of the sequence formed at the FINAL position.
- If the item is an operator, it will go to the STACK, but the following conditions must be fulfilled prior to this move:
  - The operator to be placed on the STACK must have exactly a lower precedence than the operator that will leave the STACK first. If the operator to be placed is right associative, then equality in precedence is also allowed.
  - If it is an opening parenthesis that would leave the STACK first, then the operator is allowed to the STACK.
  - If none of the conditions above holds and the STACK contains elements, move the operators out of the STACK straightaway to the FINAL position, until either an opening parenthesis becomes the first in the STACK or the STACK is emptied.

After these conditions are fulfilled, move the operator to the STACK.

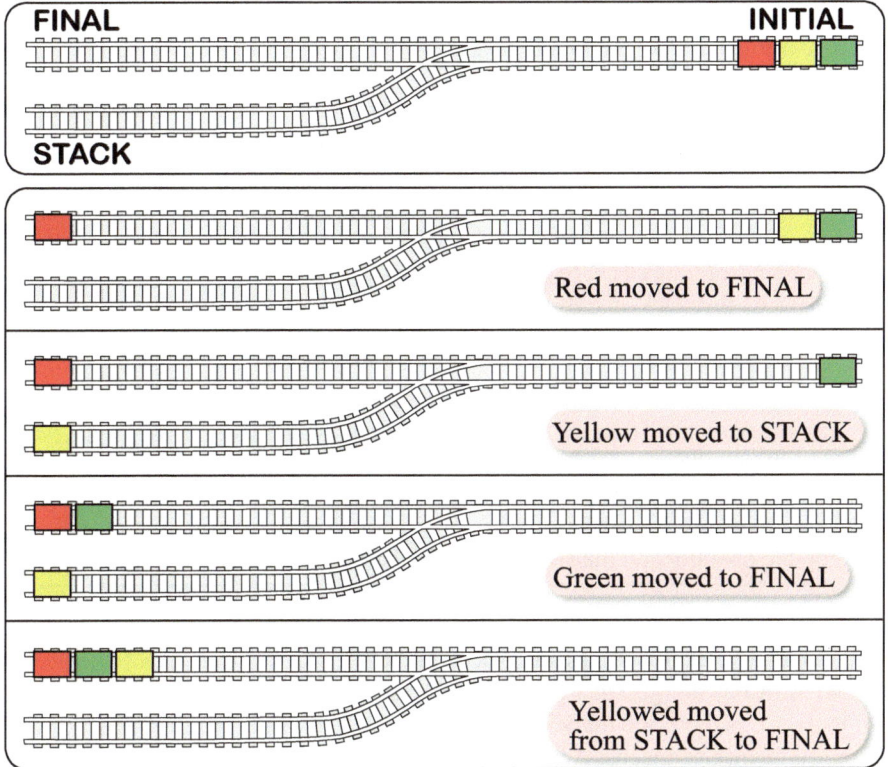

Fig. 3.5 How the shunting-yard functions

- If the item is an opening parenthesis, move it to the **STACK**.
- If the item is a closing parenthesis, discard it. But, also move elements from the **STACK** until either an opening parenthesis becomes the first in the **STACK** or the **STACK** is emptied. If it is an opening parenthesis, remove it from the **STACK** and discard it (do not move it to the FINAL position).
- If no more items exist to be considered, move all the items, if any, straightaway to the FINAL position.

Before showing an example of the algorithm in practice, we think it is the right time to introduce a more formal denotation of the algorithm. You will meet the following type of denotation very frequently.

To speak using computer science terminology, we need to know:

token is any one of {operand, operator, parenthesis} that makes up the expression.
top of the stack is the element which will come out first from the **STACK**.
pop is moving out the top of the stack.
push is placing a new element on the **STACK**. Due to the nature of the **STACK** this
    element becomes the 'top of the stack'.

Algorithm 3.1 Dijkstra's Shunting-yard algorithm

Get next token t from the input queue

if t is an operand **then**

    Add t to the output queue

if t is an operator **then**

    while There is an operator τ at the top of the stack, and either t is left-associative and its precedence is less than or equal to the precedence of τ, or t is right-associative and its precedence is less than the precedence of τ **do**

        Pop τ from the stack, to the output queue.

    Push t on the stack.

if t is a left parenthesis **then**

    Push t on the stack.

if t is a right parenthesis **then**

    Pop the operators from the stack, to the output queue until the top of the stack is a left parenthesis.

    Pop the left parenthesis.

if No more tokens to get **then**

    Pop the operators on the stack, if any, to the output queue.

---

input queue is the infix expression placed at the INITIAL position, as a sequence of tokens. Removal (get) is always from the left.

output queue is the place marked as FINAL where the postfix expression is formed as a sequence of tokens. Append (add) is always from the left.

Now we are ready for a more formal definition of the shunting-yard algorithm, shown in Algorithm 3.1.

It is time to have a complete walk-through of an example. We will consider the mathematical infix expression given above, and applying the shunting-yard algorithm, we will obtain the postfix form of the expression. Figure 3.6 displays the progress of the algorithm step-by-step for each token.

Phase 2: Postfix Evaluation

Similar to phase 1, this phase also employs a stack. However, this time it is not the operations but the values that are pushed and popped from the stack. It has a relatively easier algorithm as shown below (see also Algorithm 3.2):

- Process the postfix expression from left to right. Consider each token.
- If the token is an operand, then evaluate it. There are three possibilities:
  - The operand is a constant; push that value onto the stack.
  - The operand is a variable; fetch the value associated with it from the memory, and push that value onto the stack.
  - The operand is a function call; perform the function call, obtain the return value, push it onto the stack.

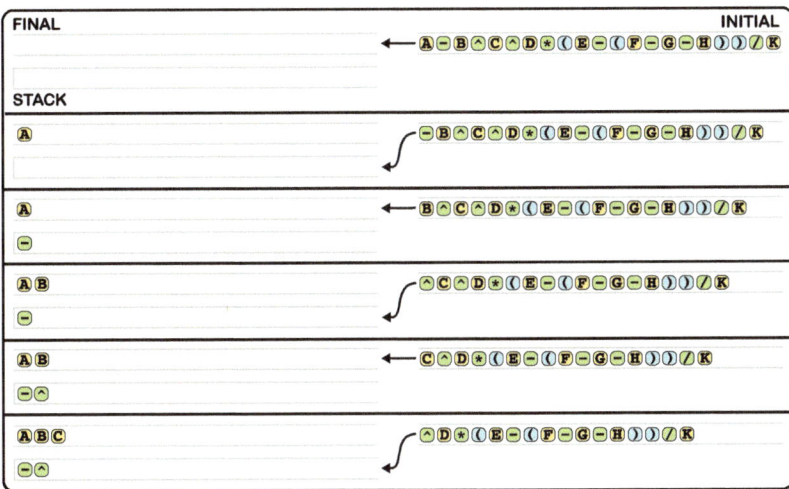

Fig. 3.6 A step-by-step illustration of how the infix to postfix conversion is carried out. The example continues in the next page

- If the token is an operator, then perform a pop operation twice. The first pop operation will provide the value of the right operand and the second the value of the left operand. Now, perform the operation between these two values and push the result onto the stack. *(If it is a compilation, then, at this position, the compiler will insert some machine code that will perform a pop operation from the stack into a register and then a second pop operation into another register. This piece of code is followed by a machine code instruction that performs the operation on the registers. The resulting value will be generated in a register, which thereafter is pushed onto the stack.)*
- When all tokens are exhausted, there will be only one single value on the stack and that is the resulting value for the whole expression.

A Corollary

Now, let us consider the first phase. All the operands are directly moved to the postfix expression. Since the token consumption is strictly left to right, the relative order of the operands will not change during the conversion from infix to postfix. In other words, if we erase all the operators from the infix expression and do the same for the postfix expression, what remains (*i.e.*, a sequence of operands) is the same. So, Phase-1 does not alter the operand ordering.

Now, let us consider the second phase. This phase is also a strict left to right one pass algorithm. When tokens are consumed from the postfix expression, *the operands are evaluated* and pushed onto the stack. So, it is obvious that any operand is evaluated before any operator to its right and after any operator to its left.

However, the order of the operands was not changed neither in phase-1 nor in phase-2. So, the operands will get evaluated strictly in the left to right order as they

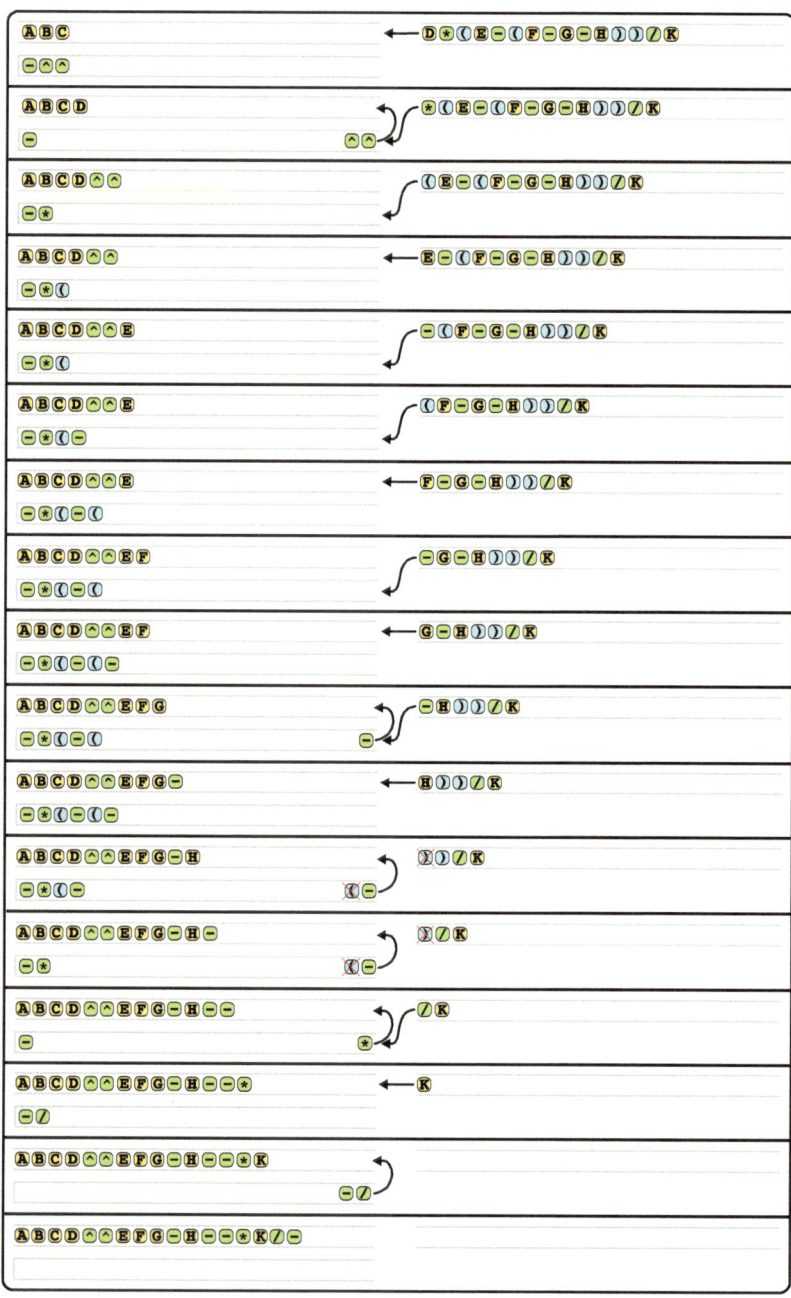

Fig. 3.6 (*Continued*)

Algorithm 3.2 Postfix evaluation algorithm

Get next token t from the postfix expression
if t is an operand **then**
  obtain its value and push onto the stack.
else
  pop from stack as $value_{right}$
  pop from stack as $value_{left}$
  being t an operator, calculate $value_{left}$ t $value_{right}$ and push the result onto the stack
if No more tokens to get **then**
  return pop from stack (That is the overall result)

---

appear in the infix expression. They will be evaluated but the values they are reduced to will enter the stack and wait for a while. This is a proof that the wide-spread 'parentheses are evaluated first' dogma is simply incorrect.

3.2.2 Expressions and Operators in Python

As mentioned above, operators (*i.e.*, actions) are important ingredients of a programming language. We have already seen simple operations (like addition, multiplication and division) in the previous chapter when the different data types of Python were introduced.

Python uses the *infix* notation for operators; *i.e.*, the operator is placed between the operands, as in x + 4.

In this section, we will cover the basic operators of Python in more detail.

– Arithmetic Operators in Python

The arithmetic operators in Python are common to both int and float data. Below is a list of the arithmetic operators for numerical values:

Operator	Operator Type	Description
+	Binary	Addition of two operands
–	Binary	Subtraction of two operands
–	Unary	Negated value of the operand
+	Unary	Positive value of the operand
*	Binary	Multiplication of two operands
/	Binary	Division of two operands
**	Binary	Exponentiation of two operands (Ex: $x**y = x^y$)

Once you start working with the operators and the numbers, you will soon realize that sometimes Python may not give you what you expected:

```
>>> 6/4
1
```

Python tells you that the division of 6 by 4 is 1, which is intriguing. The reason for this unexpected behavior is that if the arguments of the division operator / are both integers, it performs *integer division*, neglecting the remainder of the division. If you do not want the remainder to be neglected, you have to use float numbers:

```
>>> 6.0/4.0
1.5
```

In fact, we could have just typed 6.0/4 and obtained the same result since having only one float argument is sufficient for Python to perform floating point division.

Alternatively, we could explicitly call a function to convert a number to a float:

```
>>> float(6)/4
1.5
>>> 6.0 / 4
1.5
```

In general, if the types of the operands of an operator are not the same, Python converts the data type of the smaller capacity (for example, a bool is smaller than an int which is smaller than a float) to the type of the bigger capacity:

```
>>> True / 4
0
>>> True / 4.0
0.25
```

In the first case (True/4), True is converted to the type of the second operand (*i.e.*, int), and the division operator performs integer division (hence, the result is 0 due to 1/4). In the second case, the second operand is a float; the True value is converted to a float, and floating point division is performed (hence, the result is 1.0/4.0, which is 0.25).

– Precedence & Associativity of Arithmetic Operators

As in the expression a + b + c * d, when multiple operators are combined in a single expression, the evaluation of the expression relies on which operator is interpreted first (this is called *operator precedence*) and if the operators have equal precedence, how they are combined (which is called *operator associativity*). For example, the expression a + b + c * d is understood by Python as ((a + b) + (c * d)) and not as, for example, (a + ((b + c) * d)).

The precedences of the operators specify the order of operators of different precedence. For example, in a + b + c * d, multiplication (*) has a higher precedence than addition, and therefore d is multiplied by c and not b+c or a+b+c. Associativity, on the other hand, determines how the operators of the same precedence will be combined; *i.e.*, is the expression a+b+c equivalent to (a+b)+c or a+(b+c)? Note that although, in mathematics, these two expressions might be the same, in programming, they do not have to be the same. This was discussed in relation to floating point numbers in the previous chapter, and in this chapter related to the side effects. Since the addition operator is left-to-right associative, the expression a+b+c is interpreted as (a+b)+c.

Below is the precedence and associativity of arithmetic operators (from highest precedence, at the top, to the lowest at the bottom):

Operator	Type	Associativity	Description
**	Binary	Right-to-left	Exponentiation
+, −	Unary	Right-to-left	Positive, negative
*, /, //, %	Binary	Left-to-right	Multiplication, Division, Remainder, Modulo
+, −	Binary	Left-to-right	Addition, Subtraction

– Container Operators in Python

Containers, or sequences (*i.e.*, strings, tuples and lists) have very different semantics from numbers; therefore, the set of operators that can be applied on them is different. Although in some cases the symbols may be the same, the semantics is different:

• *Concatenation*: Python can concatenate two sequences with the + operator:

```
>>> "I" + " am a string"
'I am a string'
>>> [1, 2, 3] + [3, 4, 5]
[1, 2, 3, 3, 4, 5]
>>> (1, 2) + (3, 4)
(1, 2, 3, 4)
```

• *Repetition*: Python provides a handy operator * for repeating sequences:

```
>>> "Noo"*3
'NooNooNoo'
>>> [1, 2] * 3
[1, 2, 1, 2, 1, 2]
>>> (3, 4) * 2
(3, 4, 3, 4)
```

- *Membership*: Python has in and not in operators for checking the membership of an item:

```
>>> "o" in "Noo"
True
>>> 2 in [1, 2, 1, 2, 1, 2]
True
>>> 4 not in (3, 4)
False
```

- *Indexing*: The indexing mechanisms (that we have talked in the previous chapter) that use brackets ([]) are also operators.

Below is the updated list of the precedence and associativity of the operators in Python:

Operator	Type	Associativity	Description
[]	Binary	Left-to-right	*Indexing*
**	Binary	Right-to-left	Exponentiation
+, –	Unary	Right-to-left	Positive, negative
*, /, //, %	Binary	Left-to-right	Multiplication & *Repetition*, Division, Remainder, Modulo
+, –	Binary	Left-to-right	Addition, Subtraction, *Concatenation*
in, not in	Binary	Right-to-left	Membership

– Relational Operators in Python

You will often need to compare the values of two data types, and Python provides the following operators for comparing different data. In Python, relational operators are defined for every data type, whether it is basic (*e.g.*, int, float or bool) or a container (*e.g.*, tuple, str or list).

As in arithmetic operators, if the operands of a relational operator are not of the same data type, the *smaller* one is converted to the data type of the *larger* one. Whenever this conversion is not possible (such as in checking the equality between [1, 2, 3] and 3.0), the result of the relational operation is False (*i.e.*, the interpreter does not complain to you about the incompatibility of the operands!).

== (*Equality Operator*): The equality operator returns the `bool` value `True` if the operands are equal. Below is a description of what *equal* means for different data types:

- Two values of basic data types are equivalent if the values are exactly the same. For example, 3 equals `3.0`, `True` equals 1, *etc.*
- Two strings are equivalent if they represent exactly the same set of characters in the same order. For example, `"Book"` is not equivalent to `"Books"` or `"book"` (*i.e.*, equality on strings is case-sensitive!).
- Two tuples are equivalent if they have exactly the same elements in the same order.
- Similar to strings and tuples, two lists are equivalent if they have the same elements in the same order.

< (*Less-than Operator*): The less-than operator returns the `bool` value `True` if the value of the first operand comes earlier than the value of the second operand. The *comes-earlier* is determined based on the data type, and below is a description of what *comes-earlier* means for different data types:

- A value of basic data type comes earlier than another basic-data-type value if the first value is smaller than the second value. For example, 3 is less than (comes earlier than) `4.0`, `-4.45667` is less than `-1.25`, and `True` is less than 2, *etc.* (what is the result of `False < True`?).
- A string comes earlier than another string if the first is earlier than the second string in the lexicographical ordering based on the ASCII values of the characters (Reminder: you can check the ASCII value of a character using the `ord()` function). In other words, `"b" < "bac"`, `"b" < "xyz"` are `True`, whereas `"b" < "BACK"`, `"b" < "1"` and `"b" < "/"` are `False`.
- A tuple comes earlier than another tuple if the first differing elements of the tuples satisfy the less-than operator. If the first differing element does not exist in one of the tuples (because one of them is shorter), the shorter tuple is less-than the longer one. Example: `(1, 2) < (1, 2, 3)` returns `True`, so do `(2, 2) < (3, 3, 3)` and `(2, 2, 1, 2, 3, 4) < (4, 1, 2, 3)`, whereas `(2, 2) < (1, 2, 3)` would return `False`.
- The less-than operator behaves in exactly the same way for lists. In other words, `[2, 2] < [3, 3, 3]` is `True` whereas `[2, 2] < [1, 2, 3]` is `False`.

<= (*Less-than-or-Equal Operator*): The less-than-or-equal operator between two operands `op1` and `op2` returns `True` if either `op1 < op2` or `op1 == op2` returns `True`; otherwise, the result is `False`.

> (*Greater-than Operator*): The greater-than operator between two operands op1 and op2 returns True if both op1 < op2 and op1 == op2 returns False; otherwise, the result is False.

>= (*Greater-than-or-Equal Operator*): The greater-than operator between two operands op1 and op2 returns True if either op1 > op2 or op1 == op2 returns True; otherwise, the result is False.

!= (*Not-Equal Operator*): The Not-equal operator != yields True if the equal operator == yields False; otherwise, the result is False.

Note that in Python, relational operators can be chained. In other words, a RO b RO c (where RO is a relational operator) is interpreted as:

(a RO b) and (b RO c).

In most other programming languages, a RO b RO c is interpreted as:

(a RO b) RO c.

Below is the updated list of the precedence and associativity of the operators in Python:

Operator	Type	Associativity	Description
[]	Binary	Left-to-right	*Indexing*
**	Binary	Right-to-left	Exponentiation
+, -	Unary	Right-to-left	Positive, negative
*, /, //, %	Binary	Left-to-right	Multiplication & Repetition, Division, Remainder, Modulo
+, -	Binary	Left-to-right	Addition, Subtraction, Concatenation
in, not in, <, <=, >, >=, ==, !=	Binary	Right-to-left	Membership, *Comparison*

– Logical Operators in Python

For manipulating truth values, Python provides and, or and not operators:

and Operator: Boolean-Expr-1 and Boolean-Expr-2
The and of two boolean expressions is True if both arguments of the operator are True; otherwise, the result is False.

or Operator: Boolean-Expr-1 and Boolean-Expr-2
The or of two boolean expressions is True if either argument of the operator is True; otherwise, the result is False.

not Operator: `not Boolean-Expr`

The `not` of one boolean expression is `True` if the expressions evaluates to `False`; otherwise, the result is `False`. Note that `not` operator is unary; *i.e.*, it accepts one argument.

Summary of the Precedence and Associativity of Operators in Python

Below is the updated list of the precedence and associativity of the operators in Python:

Operator	Type	Associativity	Description
`[]`	Binary	Left-to-right	Indexing
`**`	Binary	Right-to-left	Exponentiation
`+, -`	Unary	Right-to-left	Positive, negative
`*, /, //, %`	Binary	Left-to-right	Multiplication & Repetition, Division, Remainder, Modulo
`+, -`	Binary	Left-to-right	Addition, Subtraction, Concatenation
`in, not in, <, <=, >, >=, ==, !=`	Binary	Right-to-left	Membership, Comparison
`not`	Unary	Right-to-left	Logical negation
`and`	Binary	Left-to-right	Logical AND
`or`	Binary	Left-to-right	Logical OR

3.2.3 Statements

The statement form of actions is a concept attached to imperative programming. In the imperative context it is a 'unit of order'. Though syntaxes of statements may vary from language to language, certain basic types of statements are common to almost all imperative languages.

There are two types of statements:

- Basic statements
- Compound statements

Compound statements are those that control the execution of other statements which are embodied into that statement. Any statement not of this nature is a basic statement. Statements dedicated to the input and output of values (**read**, **print** statements), unconditional branching (the **goto** statement) are among the examples of basic statements.

The simplest example of a compound statement is the conditional statement (commonly referred to as the if statement). A conditional statement has two subcomponents. Namely a boolean expression β and a statement σ.

if β **then** σ

When the conditional statement is executed, first the boolean expression β is evaluated; if the result is TRUE, then the statement σ is executed. A variant of the if statement has an additional statement subcomponent.

if β **then** σ_1 **else** σ_2

σ_2 is the statement which is going to be executed if the boolean expression evaluates to FALSE.

Other compound statements commonly found in imperative languages are the repetitive statements: The while statement and the for statement.

The while statement resembles the if statement. Similar to the if statement, the while statement also has a boolean expression β and a statement σ as subcomponents.

while β **do** σ

if the boolean expression β evaluates to TRUE then the statement σ is executed. After σ is executed the flow of execution jumps back to the start of the evaluation of the boolean β. This looping continues until β no longer evaluates to TRUE. Of course, it is expected that the execution of the β statement alters the ingredients of the σ which eventually causes an evaluation to FALSE. Otherwise the execution will enter a vicious circle, technically called an *infinite loop*.

The for statement is designed to have a variable 'v' takes values from a set and with each set value of the variable, has an execution of a statement σ. This set can be for example, a range of numbers, characters or a list. For instance:

for $v = 1$ **to** 5 **do print** $v, v * (v - 1)$

This will print the following output:

```
1 0
2 2
3 6
4 12
5 20
```

Compound statements can be nested as well. Here is an example:

for v **in** ["michael","john"]
    for u **in** ["marry","michelle","jill"]
        if $length(v) \overset{?}{=} length(u)$ **then**
            print $v,$ " is the perfect match for ", u

will print

```
john is the perfect match for jill
```

Another compound statement extensively used is *statement grouping*. It quite often occurs that a single action expressed as a statement is insufficient for the task. More than one action has to be carried out in the place where only a single statement was allowed. Statement grouping serves this purpose; it groups statements such that they appear as a single statement. Some languages use the BEGIN and END keywords to enclose the grouped statements, others use parentheses (mostly curly braces), and Python fulfills this need by indentation.

The way assignments are handled is a gray area. For some languages (such as Pascal, Fortran, Basic, Python), assignments (changing the value of a variable) are considered as statements. However, there exists languages for which assignment is an operation and has a value (the same value of the assigned value) along with a side effect (the side-effect of changing the value of a variable). If assignment is a statement, then of course, there is no value associated with it:

```
a := 3.1415*(b:=2.7182^2)+1;
```

is an illegal Pascal statement, since assignment is a statement and does not possess a value. But an expression in C as:

```
a = 3.1415*(b=2.7182^2)+1
```

is perfectly valid. This is closely related to whether the language allows expression evaluations on their own or not. Some languages allow the expression evaluations to be written down into a statement. In such a statement the action which is carried out is 'only evaluating an expression'. The resulting value of the evaluation is purged, simply discarded. At first sight, this might seem awkward. Why perform an expression evaluation then throw the result away? Such a need occurs when we want to evaluate an expression for its side-effect. 99.9% of this type of statements comprises of extremely simple evaluations such as a single function call, or an assignment (if assignment is considered as an operation in that particular high level language).

For example, the printf() function of the C language prints its argument on the standard output device (which is normally the screen):

```
printf("I love you my darling more than anything")
```

The evaluation of the function call above has a very profound side effect (that's the wishful thinking of the programmer), it displays the message on the screen. Also, it returns the count of characters that got printed on the screen. It returns a value, because printf() is a function and function calls are expressions and expressions always return a value. It is very likely that the programmer is merely interested in the side effect of printing the expression (and presumably the side effect of the side effect: impressing 'the darling') and does not care about how many characters were printed (42 actually). So, to make the function 'function', the programmer will turn the call into a statement (this is done in C by appending a semicolon after the expression).

```
printf("I love you my darling more than anything");
```

– Assignment Statement in Python

Using the equal sign (=), we can assign data to variables. The equal sign is called the assignment statement (not an operator!). Python provides shortcuts for assignments of the form a = a OP b and allows the programmer to write it equivalently as 'a OP= b'. OP can be any of the arithmetic operators that we introduced in previous sections (*i.e.*, +, −, *, %, //, /, **). We call assignments of the form 'a OP= b' as *combined assignment*. Note, however, that the variable 'a' must be an existing variable.

Below is an example:

```
>>> b += 4
Traceback (most recent call last):
  File "<stdin>", line 1, in <module>
NameError: name 'b' is not defined
>>> b = 5
>>> b **= 2
>>> b
25
```

Multiple assignment can be performed simultaneously like a = b = c = 10, in which case all the variables get the same values.

 Unlike most other high-level programming languages, in Python, = is a statement and not an operator, which means that an assignment statement in Python does not return value and cannot be used as part of an expression, like: a=3+(b=4), which is valid in, *e.g.*, C but not in Python.

Let us clarify these important points: (1) Actions of the form a += b += 10 or a += 10 * d+= 8 are not allowed in Python. (2) Neither are the following permitted in Python: a += 10 + d=10. (3) It is not possible to use actions such as a = 10 + d=10 although you can perform multiple assignments like a = b = c = 10.

3.3 Controlling Actions: Conditionals

Now, we will introduce the *Turing Machine*, which we have already referred to several times. This will give an insight into why some components of computation are designed in the way they are. In particular, you will see that conditionals are an inherent property of the Turing Machine.

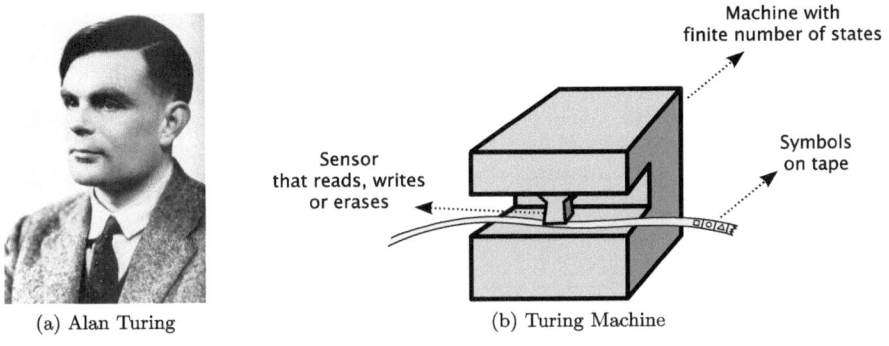

(a) Alan Turing   (b) Turing Machine

Fig. 3.7 Alan Turing and his machine

3.3.1 The Turing Machine

In 1937, Alan Turing, a mathematician (and not an electrical engineer), published
an article entitled:

On computable numbers, with an application to the Entscheidungsproblem[2]

and introduced a simple theoretical architecture that was able to undertake computation.

A Turing machine, as shown in Fig. 3.7, is a theoretical machine that manipulates
(reads, writes and erases) symbols on an infinite tape according to a rule table. At
each cycle, the Turing Machine reads the symbol under its head then prints a symbol
at the current tape position and the tape moves to the left or right (according to the
rule table).

Every Turing Machine has:

- a set of symbols that it can read and write on the tape (the set, by default, includes
  a special *blank* symbol),
- a set of states, one of which is marked as the initial state and some of which are
  marked as the final states.
- a transition function which maps all symbols for all possible non-final states to a
  3-tuple ⟨*symbol to print, new state, tape movement direction*⟩

State is some intrinsic variable of the Turing Machine; when the machine starts,
it is in the *initial* state. The machine stops when it reaches one of the *final* states.
The tape movement direction is one of {LEFT,RIGHT,DONTMOVE}. On the tape,
any place which had not been written on before contains a *blank* symbol. Turing
Machines may start with a blank or written tape. This does not form a degree of
freedom, since any machine with some written tape can be replaced with a machine
with one more state but a blank tape. This is so that the machine first starts in that

---

[2]"Entscheidungsproblem" means "decision problem" in German.

state and fills out the tape; then, it changes state and continues with what the machine with the written tape would do.

The members of the symbol set are certainly not restricted to being alphanumerical, but in many examples a subset of alphanumerics are used. Below is a widely known example, the three-state busy beaver Turing Machine.

The machine has three non-final states {**A**, **B**, **C**} and one final state **HALT**. **A** is the initial state. The symbol set is {0, 1} where 0 is the *blank* symbol.

State now	Read symbol	Write symbol	Move tape	Next state
A	0	1	RIGHT	**B**
A	1	1	LEFT	**C**
B	0	1	LEFT	**A**
B	1	1	RIGHT	**B**
C	0	1	LEFT	**B**
C	1	1	RIGHT	**HALT**

As an exercise, you are invited to get a pencil and paper to investigate what this machine actually does.

Before we end this introduction to the Turing Machine, one special Turing Machine is worth mentioning: The *Universal Turing Machine* (UTM). The UTM is a Turing Machine that can simulate any Turing machine (with its tape) that is provided to it on tape (with some encoding). Actually, the UTM is an abstraction of the Von Neumann architecture.

The Turing machine abstraction is used in proving various theorems about computing. We will not go into their details, but let us observe some of the properties of the Turing Machine. Due to the Church–Turing conjecture, any such observed properties will also be the properties of any processor, any programming language and any program that is written.

Discreteness: The machine has finite number of discrete states and symbols. The Universe though is a continuum. Many physical events are based on real numbers. The states in a Turing Machine are countable but real numbers are not. Therefore, there is simply not enough number of states to compute real numbers. The same is true even for functions on natural numbers. There are uncountably many such functions that are not computable by any Turing Machine (TM).

Determinism: You can run a TM a zillion times, it will carry out the same sequence of transitions a zillion times. We call this property determinism. It is possible to simulate nondeterminism on a TM if the nondeterminism is bounded (a subclass of nondeterminism). However, even this equivalence refers solely to what can be computed, and not how quickly. The payment is an extra non-polynomial time factor, but in real life, this 'time' factor is the main criteria that counts.

Conditional: The transition function can be viewed as a set of conditionals. Each row of the table then reads as:

if the machine is in state X and the symbol read is Y **then** ...

So, a conditional structure exists *per se* in the TM.

3.3.2 Conditionals

Conditionals exist in all high level languages. Mostly in the form given below:

if ⟨*boolean expression*⟩ **then** ⟨*action*⟩

It is the way to have an action take place depending on the outcome of a boolean expression evaluation. In the programming context, an 'if' has a different meaning to its causal meaning in natural language. Consider the statement below that you might read in a magazine

If you refrain from consuming fat, sugar and wheat products, you will have a longer life.

This conditional statement of English conveys us an information about 'probabilities'. The outcome is not 100% guaranteed: maybe in five years, you will be run over by a truck and die. What the sentence says is that the probability of living longer increases with the mentioned diet. Actually, it also contains a hidden assertion that:

Consuming fat, sugar and wheat products shortens your life.

In programming, the causal relation is not probabilistic and does not contain any hidden information. If the conditional is going to be carried out, first the boolean expression is evaluated; if the outcome is TRUE, the action, which was subject to the conditional, is carried out.

At the machine code level, the instruction that exists with a conditional meaning is called *conditional branching*. It is an instruction which alters the content of the instruction counter depending on the value of a register. A conditional action in a high-level language, for example;

if ⟨*boolean expression*⟩ **then** ⟨*action*⟩

will translate into

> compute the ⟨*boolean expression*⟩,
> leave the result in the relevant register r
> branch to α if $r \overset{?}{=} 0$
> carry out ⟨*action*⟩
> α :   ⟨*some actions that follow the* **if**⟩

In programming, it is quite often that there is an alternative action which will be carried out if the condition (the result of the boolean expression evaluation) fails. Theoretically, this could be achieved by a second conditional which tests for the negation of the boolean expression:

if ⟨*boolean expression*⟩ **then** ⟨*action$_{TRUE}$*⟩
if ¬⟨*boolean expression*⟩ **then** ⟨*action$_{FALSE}$*⟩

This is impractical, time consuming and open to problems if the ⟨*boolean expression*⟩ contains side effects. For this purpose, a variant of the if statement, namely the 'if-then-else' statement exists.

if ⟨*boolean expression*⟩ **then** ⟨*action$_{TRUE}$*⟩
else ⟨*action$_{FALSE}$*⟩

The evaluation of the ⟨*boolean expression*⟩ is carried out only once. If the outcome is TRUE, the ⟨*action$_{TRUE}$*⟩ statement is carried out; if the outcome is FALSE, the ⟨*action$_{FALSE}$*⟩ statement is carried out. An if-then-else statement will translate into

compute the ⟨*boolean expression*⟩,
leave the result in the relevant register r
branch to α if $r \stackrel{?}{=} 0$
carry out ⟨*action$_{TRUE}$*⟩
branch to β
α :   carry out ⟨*action$_{FALSE}$*⟩
β :   ⟨*some actions that follow the* **else**⟩

Some languages mark the end of the ⟨*action$_{FALSE}$*⟩ by an **endif** keyword.

Sometimes, the ⟨*action$_{FALSE}$*⟩ statement is treated as another if-then-else statement. This is called the *else-if ladder*. For these cases, some languages provide a keyword of **elseif**. This is especially useful in languages where the sub-actions (⟨*action$_{FALSE}$*⟩ or ⟨*action$_{TRUE}$*⟩) need to be indented to denote the level of nestedness. Python is such a language.

All functional languages and some imperative languages provide an expression version of conditional. In this case, one boolean expression and two other expressions (one for the TRUE case and one for the FALSE case), have to be provided. Since an expression has to evaluate to a value under all circumstances, a conditional expression that provides only a value for the success (*i.e.*, TRUE) case does not exist.

3.3.3 Conditional Execution in Python

In this section, we cover how we can change the flow of execution in Python.

– if Statements in Python

Python, like most other programming languages, provides the if statement:

```
1  if <condition−expression> :
2           <statements −1>
3  else :
4           <statements −2>
```

where the first line specifies the condition that must be met for executing the statements that start on the next line; *i.e.*, if the <condition-

expression> is True, the <statements> are executed one after the other; otherwise, the execution continues with the statements in the else: part.

The syntax is important here: The identifier if if statement is followed by the conditional expression which is then followed by a column ':'. The indentation (*i.e.*, the tab or space at the beginning of the lines) of the statements is important: The statements have to have *at least* one space or one tab character at the beginning of the lines. This is how Python understands the end of the statements that will be executed when the conditional expression is met. Similarly, the statements in the else part should be properly intended.

 You can indent your Python code using tabs or space. However, it is a good programming practice to use only one of them while indenting your code: *i.e.*, do not mix them!

else part of an if statement is optional and can be omitted. Below is a simple example: if statement

```
1  a = 3
2  b = 5
3  if  a < b  :
4              print "a  is  less  than  b"
5              c = a
6  if  c >= a:
7              print "c  is  greater −than−or−equal−to  a"
```

and if we write this into a file test.py and ask Python to interpret it using the command python test.py in a terminal window, we would obtain the following output:

```
skalkan@divan:~$ python test.py
a is less than b
c is greater-than-or-equal-to a
```

– – Multiple if Statements

In Python, any number of if statements can be combined as follows: if statement

```
1  if  <condition −expression −1>  :
2              <statements >
3  elif  <expression −2>  :
```

```
4              <statements>
5  .
6  .
7  .
8  elif <expression—M> :
9              <statements>
10 else:
11             <statements>
```

where the condition expressions are checked one by one until one of them is met, in which case the corresponding statements are executed (again, they have to be indented). If none of the expressions is `True`, then the statements in the `else` part are executed. If there is no `else` part, the execution continues with the rest of the code.

– – Nested if Statements

An `if` statement can be placed within another one as follows, for example (since `if` construct is a statement, we can place `if` statements anywhere in a code where we can put statements): `if statement`

```
1 if <condition—expression—1> :
2             <statements—1>
3             if <condition—expression—2>:
4                     <statements—2>
5             else:
6                     <statements—3>
7 else:
8             <statements—4>
```

`Indentation` The indentation is extremely important here:

- If `<condition-expression-1>` is `True`, `<statements-1>` are executed, and after executing `<statements-1>`,
  - if `<condition-expression-2>` is `True`, `<statements-2>` are executed.
  - If `<condition-expression-2>` is `False`, `<statements-3>` are run.
- If `<condition-expression-1>` is `False`, `<statements-4>` are executed.

– Conditional Expressions in Python

Python provides a shortcut for simple `if-else` statements:

```
<expression-1> if <condition-expression>
else <expression-2>
```

Below is a very simple example:

```
>>> a = 4
>>> b = 5
>>> a if a < b else b
4
```

3.4 Reusable Actions: Functions

A *Function* (or sometimes synonymously called as *subroutine, procedure* or *subprogram*) is a grouping of actions that performs a certain task under a given name. When that piece of code is activated (*called*), an order that refers to this name is issued. The form in which this order is issued differs from language to language. Mostly a syntax that resembles the use of mathematical functions is adopted. In modern languages this 'named' piece of code can receive parameters. These parameters are variables that carry information from what is known as the *call point*, to the function. The life span of these parameter variables is from the activation (call) of the function until the return (ending) of the function.

Functions in programming are quite different from mathematical functions:

- A mathematical function returns a value whereas a function in programming may or may not return a value.[3] This solely depends on the purpose of the function. If the function is designed to clear the screen and then display a heading on the top of the screen, there is no need to have a value returned. Of course the language will take the necessary precautions to prevent an accidental use of such a nonexistent value (for example, as a part of an expression).
- Normally, a mathematical function returns a value that only depend on its arguments.[4] Therefore, the result is always the same given that the arguments are the same. This is not necessarily the case for the functions in programming. Though programmers are advised not to do so, functions can make use of variables exterior to their definition and have a longer lifespan than the activation of the function.
- A mathematical function will never produce a side effect but a function of programming may do so.

---

[3] Archaically, not value returning functions were named as subroutines or procedures.

[4] Excluding stochastic functions.

What is the use of functions in programming? The answer is three-fold:

Reusability: If we did not have functions in programming, we would still survive. However, the coding cost would be enormous. Every action that is repeated at a different point of the program would have to be a duplicate code. For example, if our program would needed to "capitalize the first characters of all the words in a string" at 10 different points, then at those 10 different points in the program that piece of code would have to be duplicated. What a waste of programming effort and code space! With the ability to define functions, only at a single point a function, let's say with the name `Capitalize_String`, that does 'the capitalization of a string' will be defined, and at the required 10 different points in the program, that function will be called with different string arguments.

Structuredness: Here is a small example. In C, there is a ternary operator for conditional expressions. The usage is

> *boolean expression* ? *value*$_{TRUE}$: *value*$_{FALSE}$

Now, can you guess what the expression below evaluates to?

```
a<(b<c?b:c)?a:(b<c?b:c)
```

Now consider the following

```
max(a,max(b,c))
```

We have not provided you with the definition of the function `max()` but the name of the function is sufficient for you to complete your guess. The expression is for finding the maximum among the contents of the variables a, b and c. In the previous line (*i.e.*, `a<(b<c?b:c)?a:(b<c?b:c)`), everything was on the display but making the guess was not so easy, was it?

So, functions aid in structured programming, which certainly reduces code complexity. Everything becomes more readable and understandable. This is an important aspect when you professionally write code.

All the benefits of the functional paradigm: In Sect. 1.2.2, we introduced the functional programming paradigm. When this paradigm is followed, functions are restricted to receive data only through arguments and produce data only by their return values. Thus, side effects, except for the cases involving interaction with the external environment, are avoided. Hence, a function written conforming to the functional paradigm is like a mathematical function: The solution to a problem is merely manufactured by a functional composition. The programmer 'discovers' such a functional break down, codes the functions, compose them to act on the initial data, and the result is there. This type of a solution does not suffer from unexpected side effects or variable alterations; therefore, testing and debugging gets easier.

Another aspect strongly emphasized in the functional paradigm is *recursion*. Simply, recursion in functions means that a function that will solve a problem which is represented by some data Δ has a definition that makes use of a call to the function itself with a sized down Δ. In Chap. 4, this very powerful technique will be explained in detail. Recursion provides very elegant solutions to many 'scalable' problems.

As there is no such thing as a free lunch (called the 'No free lunch' theorem), there is a price to be paid. Each function call has a time-cost overhead. So, the more you force functional composition or recursion, the slower your program will be. Moreover, creating a clean functional breakdown or discovering the recursive relations that lead to the solution is sometimes more difficult than the quick-and-dirty programming of the imperative paradigm.

Even if we are not as restricted as 'functional programming', the use of functions in professional programming is essential. General algorithms which are coded as functions become very valuable because they can be reused again and again in new programs. Collections formed from such general purpose functions are called *libraries*. Over decades, libraries have been formed for almost all application areas. They exist nowadays in all good high-level programming language for networking, scientific computing, graphical user interfacing, computer graphics, gaming and for a multitude of other uses.

3.4.1 Alternative Ways to Pass Arguments to a Function

At first sight, this seems to be an semantically ill-structured topic. Something like "alternative ways of writing down "I love you". One would assume that what counts is the meaning of "I love you" and not how it was written on paper. This is not so. The way arguments are evaluated, and passed down to the function can produce drastically different side effects. The key is in the answer to the question 'what is actually passed down to the function?'

Let us consider the possibilities using a series of examples. Let us assume that, in a programming language, you define a function f as:

```
1: define f(x)
2:     x[0] ← "jennie"
3:     x ← ["suzy", "mary", "daisy"]
4:     return x
```

Just at the point of calling the function f, the code looks like:

```
...
11: s ← ["bob", "arthur"]
12: print f(s)
13: print s
...
```

Now what is your expectation for the two line output of this code?

(a) | ["suzy", "mary", "daisy"] |
     | ["bob", "arthur"] |

(b) | ["*suzy*", "*mary*", "*daisy*"] |
     |---|
     | ["*suzy*", "*mary*", "*daisy*"] |

(c) | ["*suzy*", "*mary*", "*daisy*"] |
     |---|
     | ["*jennie*", "*arthur*"] |

(a) is an example of call-by-value.

- When the function is called at line 12, a copy of the list container is made and assigned to the parameter variable x. Due to this step, the variable x is created; a brand new object ["*bob*", "*arthur*"], which is a copy of the content of s, is created and attached to x.
- Then, the first element of this copy is changed to "*jennie*" at line 2. So, the copy-list is modified to ["*jennie*", "*arthur*"].
- The next line (line 3) in the function creates another new object: the ["*suzy*", "*mary*", "*daisy*"] list. The former content of x (namely ["*jennie*", "*arthur*"]) is purged and the new object is attached to the variable x. After line 3 executes, the state of the memory looks like:

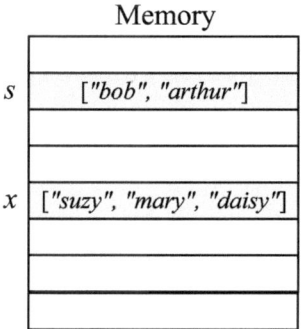

Memory

- The returned value is the new created object. The first **print** statement at line 12 prints this returned value.
- The second **print** statement at line 13 prints the untouched value of s.

If a call strategy is 'call by value', there is no possibility of altering the value at the calling point (the value attached to s in the example). All changes are made on the copy.

(b) is an example of call-by-reference.

- When the function is called at line 12, the variable x *refers* to s itself (that is why it's named as call-by-reference).
- The first element of x (also known as s) is changed to "*jennie*" at line 2.
- The next line (line 3) in the function creates a new object: the ["*suzy*", "*mary*", "*daisy*"] list. The former content of x (namely ["*jennie*", "*arthur*"]) is purged and the new object is assigned to the variable x. What has changed is actually the content of s because x is just a renaming for s. The state of the memory after line 3 is executed looks as follows:

Memory

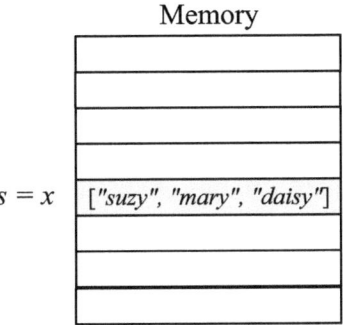

$s = x$ ["suzy", "mary", "daisy"]

- The returned value is the newly created object. The first **print** statement at line 12 prints this returned value.
- The second **print** statement at line 13 prints the value of s. Since the value of s was changed to ["*suzy*", "*mary*", "*daisy*"], the printing of s outputs this value.

So, in this strategy, computations and changes are done on the original (calling point) variables. The parameters are just renames.

(c) is an example of call-by-sharing.

- When the function is called at line 12, the variable x is created. This new variable point to the same object that s does. This is not a copy: There is a single ["*bob*", "*arthur*"] object in this case, which is assigned to both s and x. In this case, the variables actually hold the addresses of the object, not the object itself. Therefore, 'assigning the object to a variable' means 'storing the address of the object in the variable'. So, it is quite possible that two or more variables are set to contain the same address.

Memory

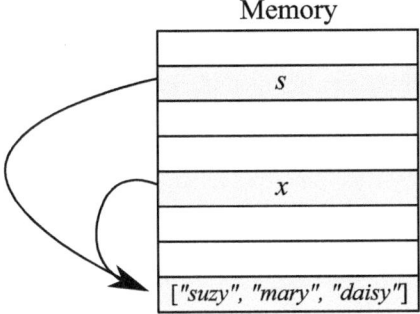

- The first element of x is changed to "*jennie*" at line 2. Since there is a single object, and the same object is also assigned to s, if we were to ask whether the value of s is changed at line 2 too, we would receive the answer 'yes'.
- The next line (line 3) in the function creates a new object: the ["*suzy*", "*mary*", "*daisy*"] list. The former assignment of x (which was the address of ["*jennie*", "*arthur*"] object) is removed (note: that object still remains assigned to s). Now, ["*suzy*", "*mary*", "*daisy*"] is assigned to x.

- The returned value at line 4 is the newly created object. The first **print** statement at line 12 prints this returned value.
- The second **print** statement at line 13 prints the value of *s* namely the [*"jennie"*, *"arthur"*] object.

In call-by-sharing, *x* and *s* are two variables sharing the same value at the moment of calling function *f*. Changes can be performed on the shared object by means of variable *x*. However, an assignment to *x* means breaking the sharing (*i.e.*, the address stored in both of them is no longer the same) and assigning a 'new' (address) value to *x*.

3.4.2 Functions in Python

Defining New Functions in Python

A new function can be defined in Python as follows:

```
1  def  function –name ( parameter –1,  ... ,  parameter –N ):
2              statement –1
3                .
4                .
5              statement –M
```

def is the keyword that specifies that a new function is being defined. The def keyword is followed by the name of the function. The naming conventions for functions are the same as the ones with variables (see Chap. 2). Following the name of the function, a list of parameters separated by comma is provided in parentheses; these parameters are the information that the function will *manipulate*. The list of parameters (*i.e.*, parameter-1, ..., parameter-N) is followed by a column ':'. The intended statements after the column define what the function does. It is important to emphasize the indentation: Like in if statements, the statements belonging to a function definition have to be indented properly.

Let us give an example definition for a function that reverses the digits in a number:

```
1  def  reverse_num ( Number ):
2      ''' reverse_num :  Reverse  the  digits  in  a  number '''
3      str_num  =  str ( Number )
4      print  "Reverse  of ",  Number,  "is ",  str_num [:: –1]
```

After this definition, we can use the function as follows:

```
>>> reverse_num(123)
Reverse of 123 is 321
>>> reverse_num(123.45)
Reverse of 123.45 is 54.321
>>> reverse_num("Car")
Reverse of Car is raC
```

– Returning Values in Functions in Python

A function can return a value using the `return <expression>` statement.
When the `return` statement is executed, the function finishes its execution
and returns the result of the `<expression>` to the calling function.
   Below is an example:

```
1  def  f(Number):
2      return  Number ** Number
3
4  def  g(Number):
5          a = 10
6          b = 20
7          print  f(a) * f(b)
```

Multiple values can be returned in a function by providing the values separated
by a comma: `return <exp-1>, <exp-2>, .., <exp-N>`. In such a
case, a tuple which consists of `<exp-1>, <exp-2>, .., <exp-N>` is
created and returned.

– Default Parameters in Python

It is possible to specify default values for the parameters of a function, which
will be used when no values are supplied for these parameters. For example,
we can re-define our `reverse_num` function to take `Number` as `123` if no
argument is supplied:

```
1  def  reverse_num(Number=123):
2      ''''''reverse_num: Reverse
3                  the  digits  in  a  number''''''
4      str_num = str(Number)
5      print "Reverse of", Number, "is", str_num[::-1]
```

In this example, the lines enclosed within ''''''' are documentation strings and are
printed when `help(reverse_num)` is called.

> There are two different ways to write comments in Python: (1) You can use # in which case the rest of the line is not interpreted. (2) You can enclose multiple lines: """" <lines of text> """". The comments that are written using the second option are basically documentation strings and available through the `help` page.

After this definition, we can call `reverse_num` as `reverse_num()` (which is equivalent to `reverse_num(123)`) or `reverse_num(<expr>)`.

In case of multiple parameters, the parameters following a default-valued parameter should be given default values as well, as in the following example:

```
1  def f(Str, Number=123, Bst="Some"):
2     print Str, Number, Bst
```

In this case, the following calls are possible: `f("A")`, `f("A", 20)` or `f("A", 20, "B")`.

– Changing Data Using Functions in Python

Consider the following simple example in Python:

```
1  def f(N):
2          N = N + 20
3
4  def g():
5          A = 10
6          print A
7          f(A)
8          print A
```

If you call function `g()`, you would get the following result:

```
>>> g()
10
10
```

The reason for this rather annoying result is that (as explained in Sect. 3.4) in Python, functions receive parameters by sharing (*call-by-sharing*). In Python, every variable is just a reference to data. In other words, when a function is called with parameters, the parameters are also just references to the existing data. Due to this concept of sharing data, (i) when we assign a new value to a variable, the original data that is pointed to by the other variable is not changed! For this reason, variable A in the above Python code still points to the same data; *i.e.*, number 10. (ii) Although the new values that are assigned to the parameters of a function are lost, the changes to the parts of the data that is shared by the parameters are kept (in Python, partial changes to data are possible only for mutable data types, as we have seen in Chap. 2). For demonstrating item (ii), we provide a simple example using another data type; namely, a `list`, which is a mutable type in Python, is used:

```
1  def  f(List):
2            List[0]  =  'A'
3
4  def  g():
5            L  =  [1,  2,  3]
6            print  L
7            f(L)
8            print  L
```

If we call function `g()`, we get a different result:

```
>>> g()
[1, 2, 3]
['A', 2, 3]
```

 Python uses call-by-sharing for passing arguments to functions (see Sect. 3.4.1).

So, the conclusion is that if you have to change non-mutable data types, you should use the `return` statement to get the changes made in a function. If the type of the data to be changed is mutable, you can change the elements of your data. However, as seen in the following example, if your changes are not limited to the elements of the list, you will lose the changes:

```
1  def  f(List):
2            List  =  List[::-1]
3
4  def  g():
5            L  =  [1,  2,  3]
6            print  L
```

```
7                 f(L)
8                 print L
```

```
>>> g()
[1, 2, 3]
[1, 2, 3]
```

– Global Variables in Python

One way to share data between functions is to use *global* variables. Below is an example:

```
1 N = 10
2 def f():
3             global N
4             def g(Number):
5                     C = 20
6                         return N * Number
7             N = g(N)
```

To be able to access the variable N in function f(), we used the global keyword followed by the name of the variable. If we had not specified N as global, function f() would have just created a *local* variable with the name N and the changes made to N would not have effected the global variable N.

– Nested Functions in Python

In Python, functions can be defined within other functions. For example:

```
1 def f(N):
2             Number = N
3             def g():
4                     C = 20
5                         return N * Number
6             print "Number", N, "and its square:", g()
```

There are several important points here:

- Function g() can access all the local variables as well as the parameters of function f().
- Function f() cannot access the local variables of function g().
- Function g() cannot be used before it is defined. For example, the second line could not have been Number = 10 * g(10).

- The indentation is extremely important to understand which statement belongs to which function. For example, the last line is part of function f() since they are at the same indentation.

3.5 Functional Programming Tools in Python

We mentioned previously that Python is a multi-paradigm programming language, supporting Functional, Imperative and Object-Oriented programming. In this section, we will briefly introduce the functional aspects of Python:

3.5.1 List Comprehension in Python

Simple operations can be performed easily on all the elements of a list with the syntax: [<expr> for <var> in <list>], where <expr> is an expression involving variable <var>, and for each element in <list> as a value for variable <var>, the expression <expr> is evaluated.

For example:

[3*x for x in [1, 2, 3, 4, 5]] yields [3, 6, 9, 12, 15].

3.5.2 Filtering, Mapping and Reduction

Any function (whether user-defined or not) can be applied to a list. We have three ways for applying functions to a list:

1. *Filtering*: filter(function, list)
   In filtering, a function that returns a bool value is applied to a list, and the items of the list for which the function returns True are returned. Below is an illustrative example:

```
1 def Positive(N):
2         if N > 0: return True
3         return False
```

The function Positive() can be used in filtering as follows: filter(Positive, [-10, 20, -2, 5, 6, 8, -3]) which results in [20, 5, 6, 8].

2. *Mapping*: map(function, list)
   In mapping, a function that returns any value is applied to a list, and for each item of the list, the function is called. The results of the function are combined in a list and returned. Here is an illustration:

```
1 def Mod4(N):
2         return N % 4
```

which can be used as follows: `map(Mod4, range(1, 10))` yielding
`[1, 2, 3, 0, 1, 2, 3, 0, 1]`.

3. *Reduction*: `reduce(function, list)`

   In reduction, a *binary* function is used to compute a single value from a list:

```
1 def greater(A, B):
2         return A if A > B else B
```

which can be used as follows: `reduce(greater, [1, 20, 2, -30])` yielding `20`.

3.6 Scope in Python

We discussed the scope of variables while talking about global variables and nested functions. Below is an illustration of scopes in Python (the different scopes are drawn in rectangles of different gray values):

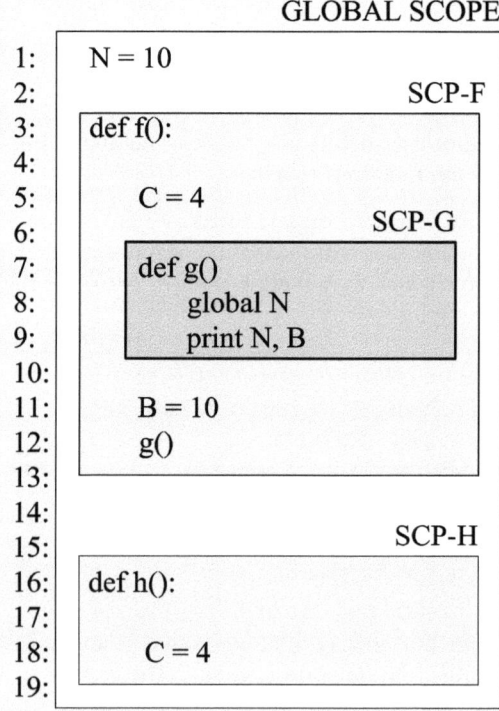

Here are the important points:

1. Any Python program has a global scope and all the other scopes (defined through functions) are *inner* scopes of the global scope. In the case of nested functions, the nested function becomes an inner scope of the outer function. For example, SCP-G is an inner scope of SCP-F, which is, in turn, an inner scope of the global scope.
2. An inner scope can access what is defined in an encapsulating scope. For example, the scope SCP-G can access what is defined in SCP-F as well as the global scope (provided that the `global` keyword is used). For example, function `g()` can call function `h()` since it is defined in the global scope.
3. A scope cannot access what is defined in an inner scope. For example, although function `f()` can call function `g()`, it cannot access what is defined in SCP-G.
4. Functions `f()` and `h()` can call each other since they are defined in the same scope. However, function `h()` cannot call function `g()` since they are defined in different scopes and function `g()` is not defined in an encapsulating scope of function `h()`.
5. Function `f()` can call function `h()` because they are defined in the same scope; however, function `f()` cannot access the local variables of `h()` since they are defined in a different scope (SCP-H) which is not including the scope of function `f()`.

 For readability and maintainability, it is a good programming practice to avoid using same names for two different variables that are in two different scopes one of which contain the other one.

3.7 Keywords

The important concepts that we would like our readers to understand in this chapter are indicated by the following keywords:

Church–Rosser Property	Dijktra's Shunting-Yard Algorithm
Side Effect	Binary & Unary & N-ary Operators
Expression Evaluation	Precedence & Associativity of Operators
Call by Value	Call by Reference
Call by Sharing	Scope&Extent

3.8 Further Reading

For more information on the topics discussed in this chapter, you can check out the sources below:

- *Turing Machine:*
  - http://en.wikipedia.org/wiki/Universal_Turing_machine
  - http://planetmath.org/encyclopedia/DeterministicTuringMachine.html
  - http://en.wikipedia.org/wiki/Non-deterministic_Turing_machine
- *Church–Rosser Property:*
  - http://mathworld.wolfram.com/Church-RosserProperty.html
  - Alonzo Church and J. Barkley Rosser. "Some properties of conversion". Transactions of the American Mathematical Society, vol. 39, No. 3 (May 1936), pp. 472–482.
- *Dijktra's Shunting-Yard Algorithm:*
  - http://en.wikipedia.org/wiki/Shunting-yard_algorithm
  - Original description of the Shunting-Yard algorithm:
    http://www.cs.utexas.edu/~EWD/MCReps/MR35.PDF
  - http://en.wikipedia.org/wiki/Edsger_Dijkstra
- *Infix, Postfix and Prefix Notations:*
  - http://en.wikipedia.org/wiki/Infix_notation
  - http://en.wikipedia.org/wiki/Postfix_notation
  - http://en.wikipedia.org/wiki/Polish_notation
- *String Formatting in Python:*
  - http://docs.python.org/library/stdtypes.html#string-formatting
  - http://docs.python.org/tutorial/inputoutput.html
- *Commenting in Python:*
  - http://en.wikibooks.org/wiki/Python_Programming/Source_Documentation_and_Comments
- *Call-by-value:*
  - http://www.linuxtopia.org/online_books/programming_books/python_programming/python_ch10s03.html
  - http://sandersn.com/blog//index.php/2009/02/19/call_by_value_in_python_and_c_and_scheme

3.9 Exercises

1. What are the values of the following expressions?

   - `2 - 3 ** 4 / 8 + 2 * 4 ** 5 * 1 ** 8`
   - `4 + 2 - 10 / 2 * 4 ** 2`
   - `3 / 3 ** 3 * 3`

2. Show the interpretation of the following expressions with parentheses (Example: The interpretation of the expression `2 + 4 * 3` can be shown with parentheses as: `2 + (4 * 3)`).

   (a) a - 3 * +a + -b ** -c
   (b) a < b < c + d == d ** -f
   (c) f ** -g + h
   (d) a == b <= c == d
   (e) not a == b + d < not e
3. Assuming that a is True, b True and c False, what would be the values of
   the following expressions?
   (a) not a == b + d < not a
   (b) a == b <= c == True
   (c) True <= False == b + c
   (d) c / a / b
4. What is the output of the following Python code?

```
1  a = 10
2  b = a
3  if a <= b :
4              print "A"
5              if a / 10 != 1 :
6                          print "B"
7              else:
8                          print "C"
9  if b >= a:
10             print "C"
```

5. What is the output of the following Python code?

```
1  a = 10
2  b = a+1
3  c = b+1
4  if a <= b <= c:
5              print "A"
6              if c > b > a:
7                          print "B"
8                          if (c > b) > a
9                                      print "C"
10                         if (c > a) or (c == a)
11                                     print "D"
12             else:
13                         print "E"
```

6. What is the output of calling function h() after the following Python code?

```
1 N = 10
2 def f(N):
```

```
 3                   N = N * N
 4                   def h ():
 5                           global N
 6                           print "N = ", N
 7                   print "N = ", N
 8
 9 def g ():
10                   N = 0
11                   print "N = ", N
12
13 def h ():
14                   global N
15                   f (N)
16                   g ()
```

7. Write a piece of Python code that obtains a string from the user and performs the following:

   • If the string contains only one character, your code should display the type of the character: Letter, Number, Whitespace, Operator, Other.
   • If it is not a letter, it should display whether it is a numerical value.
   • Otherwise, it should gracefully display the string back to the user.

8. Write a piece of Python code that gets a duration in terms of milliseconds and displays back to the user whether that duration is bigger than:

   • a minute (but less than an hour)
   • an hour (but less than a day)
   • a day (but less than a week)
   • a week (but less than a month)
   • a month (but less than a year)
   • a year.

9. The Euclidean distance between two points (a, b) and (c, d) is defined as $\sqrt{(a - c)^2 + (b - d)^2}$. Write a function distance () that takes a, b, c and d and computes the Euclidean distance. Your function should take (c, d) as $(0, 0)$ if left empty.

10. Modify the distance () function in exercise-9 to take two lists of arbitrary length and compute the Euclidean distance between them. In other words, we want the following Euclidean distance:

$$distance(L1, L2) = \sqrt{\sum_{i=0}^{N} (L1[i] - L2[i])^2}.$$

You can assume that the two lists have the same number of elements of the same type.

11. Write a piece of Python code that removes lists in a list. For example, for a list [1, 2, [4, 5]], the output should be [1, 2].
12. Write a piece of Python code that forms a string out of the elements of a list. For example, [1, 2, 3, 4] should be transformed into '1234'. You can assume that the lists are not nested.
13. Write a piece of Python code that changes the case of a string (*i.e.*, if a character in the string is lowercase, it should be made uppercase and vice versa). For example, if the string is boOK, the output should be BOok.
14. Write a piece of Python code that finds the acronym of a set of words, which are supplied as elements of a list. For example, the list ["Middle", "East", "Technical", "University"] should yield 'METU'.
15. Using the functional tools of Python, find the greatest divisor of a number. Note that a divisor of a number n is another number k which is less than n and which satisfies $n = k * x$ for a number $x < k$. (Hint: range().)
16. Write a descriptive length function desc_length() that calculates the length of a list in a different way: The length of a list is the sum of the number of characters and digits that are possessed by the elements of the list. For example, the list [12, 0, "ab"] has the length 5 since 12 has two digits, 0 has one digit and "ab" has two characters.
17. Write a Python function that computes the factorial of a number. (Hint: What you have learned in this chapter is sufficient for you to implement such a function without iterations or recursion.)
18. Write a piece of Python code that inputs an equation of the form $ax + b$, where a and b are numerical constants, and a value for x, call it x_i, and displays the result $ax_i + b$. For example, if the user supplies the string "3x+4" and the value 8 for the variable x, your Python code should display the evaluation of the following expression: 3*8+4.

Chapter 4
Managing the Size of a Problem

As explained in Chap. 3, programming is all about world problems. Sometimes, a programmer needs to deal with program demands for

- converting Celsius degree to Fahrenheit degree for the expected temperature in Paris tomorrow,
- solving a quadratic equation for an unknown x,
- calculating the edge lengths of a rectangle given the coordinates of the lower-left and upper-right corners.

These tasks are 'tiny' in the sense that the required programming is merely about calculation of a few expressions.

However, there are times when the demand is somehow different. For example, consider the case that the degree conversion is about all the cities in the world for each month of the year for the past 20 years. This now is a different case which requires a large amount of computation to be undertaken.

In contrast to 'tiny', we call such problems 'bulky'; these are problems where you can talk about the 'size' of the problem. Keeping the nature the same but changing the size, the problem varies from 'tiny' to 'bulky'.

We tackle such problems with two techniques: 'recursion', the most powerful weapon of the functional programming paradigm and the 'iteration' construct of the imperative paradigm. Interestingly, recursion is elegant, easier to understand but more difficult to build up. On the other hand, iteration is quick and dirty, easier to construct but more difficult to understand within an already written code. After having introduced both techniques, we will discuss and compare both techniques.

4.1 An Action Wizard: Recursion

The recursive-oriented approach is somewhat awkward for human understanding since we usually do not handle daily problems in a recursive manner. For example, it is quite hard to find a person who would define a postman's work as a job carried out on a bag of letters, as follows:

G. Üçoluk, S. Kalkan, *Introduction to Programming Concepts with Case Studies in Python*, DOI 10.1007/978-3-7091-1343-1_4, © Springer-Verlag Wien 2012

Job(bag_of_letters) is defined as

1. If the bag is empty, do nothing.
2. else take out and deliver the first letter in the bag.
3. Do Job(bag_with_one_letter_less)

However, this type of approach is very helpful in functional programming. Therefore, we had better take a closer look at it. Consider the common definition of *factorial*. Literally, it is defined as:

Except for zero, the factorial of a natural number is defined as the number obtained by multiplying all the natural numbers (greater than zero) less than or equal to it. The factorial of zero is defined as 1.

In mathematical notation, this can be written as in Eq. 4.1 (denoting the factorial with the postfix operator (!)):

$$N! = 1 \times 2 \times \cdots \times (N-1) \times N \quad N \in \mathbf{N}, N > 0$$
$$0! = 1 \tag{4.1}$$

Equation 4.1 can be neatly put into pseudo-code as:

define *factorial(n)*
   acum ← 1
  while $n > 0$ **do**
       acum ← *acum* × *n*
       $n \leftarrow n - 1$
  return *acum*

When we investigate the mathematical definition (Eq. 4.1) closer, we recognize that the first $N - 1$ terms in the multiplication are nothing else but the $(N - 1)!$ itself:

$$N! = \underbrace{1 \times 2 \times \cdots \times (N-1)}_{(N-1)!} \times N \quad N \in \mathbf{N}, N > 0$$

Therefore, as an alternative to the previous definition, we could define the factorial as in Eq. 4.2:

$$N! = (N-1)! \times N \quad N \in \mathbf{N}, N > 0$$
$$0! = 1 \tag{4.2}$$

There is a very fundamental and important difference between the two mathematical definitions (Eqs. 4.1 and 4.2). The later makes use of the 'defined term' (the factorial function) in the definition itself (on the right hand side of the definition) whereas the former does not.

Unless such a relation (as in the second definition in Eq. 4.2) boils down to a tautology and maintains its logical consistency, it is valid. Such relations are called *recurrence relations* and algorithms which rely on them are called *recursive algorithms*.

Now, let us have a look at the recursive algorithm (written down in pseudo code) which evaluates the factorial of a natural number:

define *factorial(n)*

  if $n \stackrel{?}{=} 0$ **then**

    return 1

  else

    return $n \times factorial(n - 1)$

Notice the similarity to the mathematical definition (Eq. 4.2) and the elegance of the algorithm.

Recurrence can occur in more complex forms. For example, the evenness and oddness of natural numbers could be recursively defined as:

- 0 is even.
- 1 is odd.
- A number is even if one less of the number is odd.
- A number is odd if one less of the number is even.

This definition is recursive since we made use of the concept which is being defined in the definition. Such definitions are called *mutually recursive*.

Are all problems suitable to be solved by a recursive approach? Certainly not. The problems that are more suitable for recursion have the following properties:

- 'Scalable problems' are good candidates to be solved by recursion. The term 'scalable' means that the problem has a dimension in which we are able to talk about a 'size'. For example, a problem of calculating the grades of a class with 10 students is 'smaller' in 'size' compared to a problem of calculating the grades of a class with 350 students. Presumably, the reader has already recognized that the 'size' mentioned above has nothing to do with the 'programming effort'. In this context, 'size' is merely a concept of the 'computational effort'. For example, assume that you are asked to calculate the grade of a *single* student, which is obtained through a very complicated algorithmic expression, and that this algorithmic expression will cost you a great deal of 'programming effort'. Now, if the algorithmic expression were not so complicated, you would spend less 'programming effort'; however, this does *not* imply that this problem is suitable for recursive programming.
- A second property of a recursively solvable problem is that whether any instance of the problem is 'downsizable' as far as the 'sizable' dimension is concerned. This needs some explanation: By removing some entities from the data that represents the sizable dimension of the problem, can we obtain a 'smaller' problem of exactly the same type?
- The third property is strongly related to the second one. It should be possible to 'construct' the solution to the problem from the solution(s) of the 'downsized' problem. The 'downsized' problem is generated by removing some data from the 'sizable dimension' of the original problem and obtaining (at least) one sub-part, which is still of the sizeable dimension's data type, but now smaller.

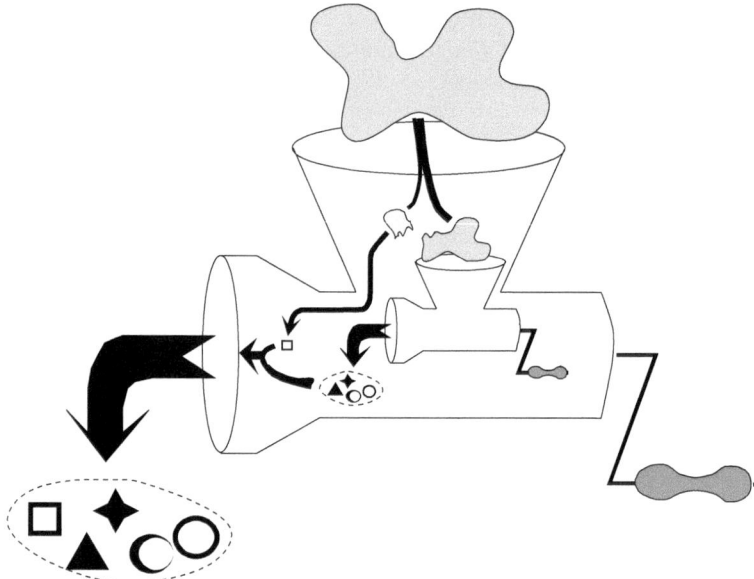

Fig. 4.1 The Recursive machine

Figure 4.1 shows a pictorial representation of recursion. Here, the mincing machine represents a recursive function. In this simplified example, the input to the machine corresponds to the argument, and the outcome from the machine corresponds to the result of the function. The transparent view of the internal structure represents the body of the function. The input which is 'partitionable' is split into a 'small' and a 'large' piece. The large piece is of the same type with the original argument. The arrows internal to the machine represent any operation the data undergoes. Therefore, the small part on its way to the output is processed and turned into the square-box □. The large piece is thrown into the mincing machine in a recursive manner. The wonderful aspect of this process is that nobody has to worry about what is going on in the internally activated mince machine. *We just assume it produces the correct result, namely* . Then, the 'correctly produced' result for the large part and the value (the square-box) for the small part is merged (through a process) to form the result of the original input.

In this described process, one point is missing. Namely, what will happen when there is no more input and the handle of the mincing machine keeps turning with the hope of producing a result? This has to be checked and a value has to be produced; a value which is manifestly agreed upon. This value entirely depends on the specific problem. It can be a representation for the end of the data; a numerical value or sometimes even nothing! Hence, our 'revised' machine looks like the one in Fig. 4.2.

What is new? Now, the machine has a *sensor* which detects the 'no meat' case and triggers the immediate output of (✦). Therefore, no further recursion is done when there is no more meat.

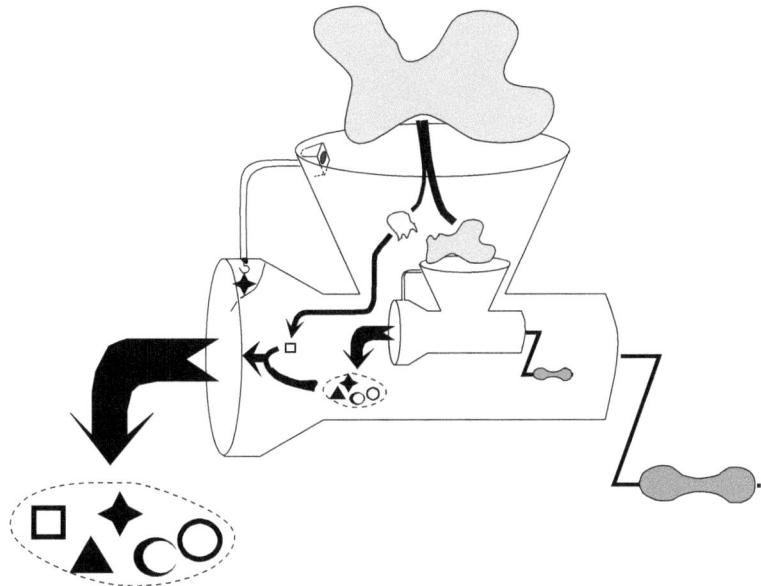

Fig. 4.2 The revised recursive machine

Now the machinery in action: In this particular case, it will mimic the recursive calculation of the factorial. To be more precise, if 'the recursive factorial machine' is to calculate 5!, the mincing machine looks like Fig. 4.3.

4.1.1 Four Golden Rules for Brewing Recursive Definitions

RULE I

> Look at the (data) content of the problem and decide on a suitable data representation. The chosen data representation should allow easy shrinking and expansion with the change in the problem's data.

For example, if the scalable dimension of the problem is about *age*, then naturally you would decide to use *integer* as the data type. If it is about a set of human names, then any container of strings would be acceptable. If it is about a sparse graph problem, then maybe a list structure of edge informations would be the best choice. Here, the main principle is to choose a data structure which is easy to shrink in relation to the downscaling. The *string* data type is, for example, easy to shrink or grow. On the other hand, *arrays* are more troublesome. Usually, if an array is chosen for the data representation, the shrinking is not carried out directly on the representation. The preferred technique is to keep and update the start and end indexes (integer values) that refer to the actual array.

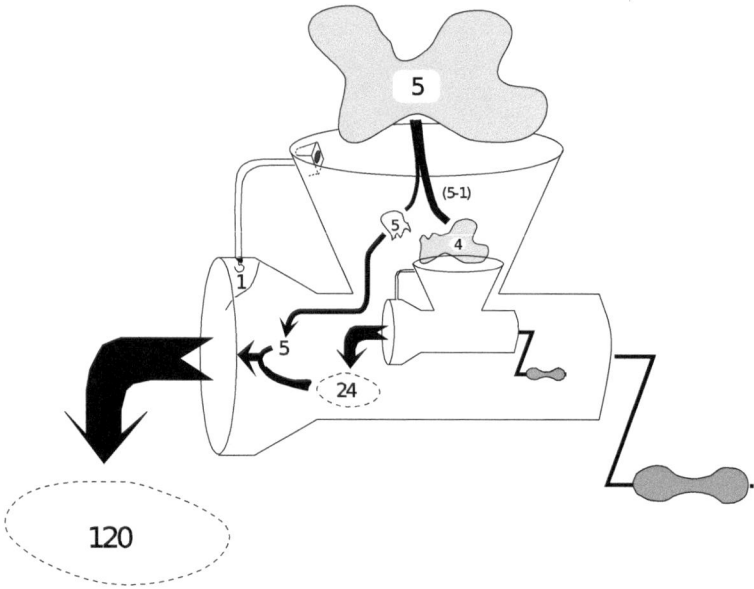

Fig. 4.3 The recursive factorial machine

Generally speaking, dynamic data structures (*e.g.* lists, trees, which we will talk about in detail in Chap. 6) are the most suitable data structures as far as 'shrinking' is concerned.

RULE II

Start with the *terminating (or, minimal) condition*. Here, you check whether the input data to the function cannot be shrunk any further. If it is the case, perform what the function is expected to do for this situation (Depending on what the function is devised for, either you return an appropriate value or you take an appropriate action).

The recursive definition canonically will start with a test for this condition. If the test succeeds, the function ceases by returning the result for the minimal case or carries out a finishing action (if the function is devised not to return a value but perform some actions).

RULE III

Handle the non-terminating condition of the input data. At this step, you have to imagine that you partition the input data. The key idea of this partitioning is that *at least* one of the pieces should be of the scalable type of the partitioned data. *You have the right (without any cause) to assume that a further call of the same function with the piece(s) that have remained as being of the same scalable type will return/do the correct result/action.* It might be possible to carry out the partitioning in different ways.

It is quite often the case that alternatives exist for this stage. The alternatives vary depending on the problem and the data structure chosen. In addition, the implementation and handling of the data structures also differ from language to language. Whereas some languages provide the user with built-in dynamic data structures (lists, trees, dynamic arrays) and operators on them, some don't. Hence, the decision preferences of this stage are somewhat language and data structure dependent. However, with time, the necessary experience builds up, so you can make the correct order of choice.

The parts obtained after the partitioning may

1. all be of the scalable type, or
2. have non-scalable pieces in addition to some (at least one) scalable type pieces.

In practice, both cases occur frequently. In both cases, you have the right to assume that any recursive call on any scalable type pieces will return the correct result (or, if it is a non-value returning task, carry out the correct action).

RULE IV

Having in one hand the correct resulting values returned or the actions performed for the pieces that were still scalable, and in the other hand, the pieces themselves which have not conserved the type (if any), we need to find the answer to the following question:

How can I construct the desired value/action for the original input data?
The answer to the question should includes the action(s) that checks whether the scalable parameter is in the terminating, or minimal, condition and the action(s) for the non-terminating condition.

If you cannot figure out a solution, consider the other partitioning alternatives (if any) that surfaced with the application of RULE III.

This is the point where 'human intelligence' takes its turn. If the data representation and the partitioning are implemented correctly, this step should not be complicated: Normally, it is just a few lines of code. Unfortunately, it is also possible that all your efforts turn out to be in vain, and there is no recursive solution that can be possibly defined.

4.1.2   Applying the Golden Rules: An Example with Factorial

Now, we now consider the factorial problem for which we seek a recursive solution by applying the *golden rules*.

Application of RULE I
   First question: What data type shall we use?
   The subject to the factorial operation is a *natural number* and the result is again a *natural number*. Therefore, the suitable data type for representing the input data is the *integer* type; but, due to the nature of the problem, we will restrict the integers only to be natural numbers.

Second question: Is this data type partitionable in the terms explained above?
Yes, indeed. There exist operations like *subtraction* and *division* defined over
the *integers* which produce *smaller* pieces (in this case, all of the integer types
as well).

Application of RULE II
Having decided on the data type (integer in this case), now we need to determine the terminating condition. We know that the smallest integer the factorial function would allow as an argument is 0, and the value to be returned
for this input value is 1. Therefore, we have the following terminating condition:

define *factorial*(n)
  if $n \overset{?}{=} 0$ **then**
    return 1
  else
      . . .

Application of RULE III
The question is: *How can we partition the argument (in this case n), so that at
least one of the pieces remains an integer?*
Actually, there are many ways to do it. Before presenting the result, here we
state some first thoughts (some of which will turn out to be useless).

Partitionings where all the pieces are of the same type

- For example, we can partition our number n in half; namely into two
  nearly equal pieces n_1 and n_2 so that either $n_1 = n_2$ or $n_1 = n_2 + 1$. Certainly, it is true that each of the 'pieces' n_1 and n_2 is 'smaller' than n,
  the actual argument. Furthermore, each of the pieces remain as the same
  type of n; in other words, they are all of an *integer* type and hence, it is
  possible to pass them to the factorial function (actually, RULE II says that
  it is sufficient if *one* of the pieces is an *integer* type; here, we have all of
  them satisfying this property).
- Alternatively, for example, it is possible to partition n into its additive constituents so that $n = n_1 + n_2 + \cdots + n_k$. There are many ways to make this
  partition and as it was for the factors above, each n_i will remain smaller
  than n and each one will satisfy the property of being an *integer*. Therefore, it is possible to pass them to the factorial function as an argument.

Partitionings with one 'small' piece and a 'large' piece
For example,

- n can be additively split into a large piece: $n - 1$ and a small piece: 1.
- n can be additively split into a large piece: $n - 2$ and a small piece: 2 (This
  will require $n \geq 2$).

- $\vdots$

Due to the nature of the results of those integer operations, *all* the pieces
(including the small ones) will possess the property of 'being the same type

as the argument of the factorial function', namely the *integer* type, but in fact, this is not our concern: we require this condition to be met only for the large pieces.

Application of RULE IV

Now, we have various ways of partitioning the input data n and of course, the input argument n itself. For every partitioning scheme, we have the right to make the very important assumption that

A further call of the factorial function with the 'pieces' that preserved the type (i.e., positive integer*) will produce the correct result.*

Certainly, we will not trace all the thought experimentations related to every way of partitioning. However, as an example, consider the $n = n_1 + n_2$ partition where n_1 differs from n_2 by 1 at the most. Due to the 'right of assumption' (stated above), we can assume that $n_1!$ and $n_2!$ are both known. The question that follows is:

Given $n, n_1, n_2, n_1!, n_2!$ can we compute $n!$ in an easy manner?

Take your time, think about it; but, you will discover that there is no easy way to obtain $n!$ from these constituents. Except for one of the partitions, all will turn out to be useless. The only useful one is the additive partitioning of n as $n - 1$ and 1. Considering also the 'right of assumption', we have at hand

- n
- 1
- $n - 1$
- 1!
- $(n - 1)!$

It is, as a human being, your duty to discover (or know) the fact that

$$n! = n \times (n - 1)!$$

And, there you have the solution. *(Some readers may wonder why we have not used all that we have at hand. It is true that we have not and there is nothing wrong with that. Those are the* possible *ingredients that you are able to use. To have the ability to use them does not necessarily mean that you have to use them all. In this case, the use of n and $(n - 1)!$ suffices.)*

For the sake of completeness, let us write the complete algorithm:

define *factorial(n)*
  if $n \overset{?}{=} 0$ **then**
    return 1
  else
    return $n \times factorial(n - 1)$

4.1.3 Applying the Golden Rules: An Example with List Reversal

The second example that we will consider is the problem of reversing a given list. If the desired function is named *reverse*, we expect to obtain the result $[y, n, n, u, f]$ from calling *reverse*$([f, u, n, n, y])$.

We assume that *head* and *tail* operations are defined for lists which respectively correspond to the first item of the list and all items but the first item of the list; in other words, *head*$([f, u, n, n, y]) = f$ and *tail*$([f, u, n, n, y]) = [u, n, n, y]$. Moreover, we assume that we have a tool which does the inverse of this operation (*i.e.*, given the head and the tail of a list, it combines them into one list). Therefore, it seems to be quite logical to put the list (in our example $[f, u, n, n, y]$) into two pieces; namely, its head: f and tail: $[u, n, n, y]$. Is GOLDEN RULE III satisfied? Yes, indeed. The tail is still of the *list type*. The same rule says that if we have satisfied this criterion, then we have the right to assume that a recursive call with the tail as argument will yield the correct result. Therefore, we have the right to assume that the recursive call *reverse*$(tail([f, u, n, n, y]))$ will return the correct result $[y, n, n, u]$. Now, let us look at what we have in our inventory:

- $[f, u, n, n, y]$ *the argument*
- f *the head of the argument*
- $[u, n, n, y]$ *the tail of the argument*
- $[y, n, n, u]$ *result of a recursive call with the tail as argument*

GOLDEN RULE IV says that we should look for an easy way that will generate the correct result using the entities in the inventory. We observe that the desired outcome of $[y, n, n, u, f]$ is *easily* obtained by the operation

$$\underbrace{[u, n, n, y]}_{tail([f,u,n,n,y])} \quad \cdot \quad [\underbrace{f}_{head([f,u,n,n,y])}]$$

also taking into account the trivial case of an empty set (which fulfills the requirement of RULE II), we are able to write the full definition ($\oplus$ denotes list concatenation):

define *reverse*(S)
   if $S \overset{?}{=} \emptyset$ **then**
      return $\emptyset$
   else
      return *reverse*$(tail(S)) \oplus [head(S)]$

4.1.4 A Word of Caution About Recursion

Recursive solutions are so elegant that sometimes we can miss unnecessary invocations of recursion and can re-compute what have already been computed.

Consider the recursive definition of fibonacci numbers as an example:

$$fib_{1,2} = 1$$
$$fib_n = fib_{n-1} + fib_{n-2} \ni n > 2$$

Based on this definition, if we devise a recursive algorithm that calculates the nth fibonacci number, we may end up with:

define *fibonacci(n)*
  if $n < 3$ **then**
    return 1
  else
    return *fibonacci(n − 1) + fibonacci(n − 2)*

This definition will work in the sense that it will produce correct results. However, each single invocation of the function with an argument bigger than 2 will invoke two recursive calls of *fibonacci()*. Like the explosion of an atomic bomb, a computation of *fibonacci(n)* will trigger approximately *fibonacci$_n$* many invocations of the function (take a pencil and paper, and draw a tree of this triggering for, let's say, *fibonacci(6)*, and then count the function calls). Being exponential in n, this is a terrible situation. The problem actually lies in the fact that the *fibonacci(n − 1)* computation requires the computation of *fibonacci(n − 2)*, which is computed (recursively) and then its use in the computation of *fibonacci(n − 1)* is simply forgotten. The computation of the second additive term of *fibonacci(n − 2)*, which was required for computing *fibonacci(n)*, does not know anything about this forgotten result. Recursively, this value is recomputed.

It is possible to fix this mistake. The solution is to save the intermediate results and hence, prevent them from being forgotten. We do this by defining a modified version of the fibonacci calculating function. This modified version, which we will call *mammothfibonacci(n)* takes the same argument as *fibonacci(n)* but returns a list of *fibonacci$_n$* and *fibonacci$_{n-1}$*:

$$[fibonacci_n, fibonacci_{n-1}]$$

Let us have a look at the definition:

define *mammothfibonacci(n)*
  if $n < 3$ **then**
    return $[1, 1]$
  else
    return *calculatenext(mammothfibonacci(n − 1))*

define *calculatenext(s)*
  return $[s[0] + s[1], s[0]]$

define *fibonacci(n)*
  return *(mammothfibonacci(n))*$[0]$

If local variables can be used, then the functionality of *calculatenext(s)* can be incorporated into the definition of *mammothfibonacci(n)*:

define *mammothfibonacci(n)*
  local *s*
  if *n* < 3 **then**
    return [1, 1]
  else
    s ← *mammothfibonacci(n − 1)*
    return [*s*[0] + *s*[1], *s*[0]]

It is possible to calculate the time that will be spent by a recursive function. The result will be a function in terms of the scalable parameter's size. Consider the first definition of the fibonacci function. If the time that will be spent to compute *fibonacci_n* is *Time(n)*, then, looking at the definition, we can say that this value is (in Chap. 5, we will talk more about measuring running time of algorithms):

$$Time(n) = Time(n - 1) + Time(n - 2) + 1$$
$$Time(1) = Time(2) = 1$$

As mentioned before, these type of equations are called *recurrence relations*. In particular, the +1 term is for the addition operation (which is assumed to be of one unit time-cost). Similarly, returning the base values for *n* < 2 is also assumed to be one unit time-cost. There are various mathematical techniques that can be applied to solve this type of recurrence relations; however, they fall under the subject known as 'algorithm analysis' are out of the scope of this book. Nevertheless, we will display a rough solution.

A feeling (you can call it experience) tells us that the solution is exponential, so we assume the general form of a^n. These types of 'educated guesses' are called *ansatz*. Substituting the 'ansatz' in our recurrence relation we obtain

$$a^n = a^{n-1} + a^{n-2} + 1.$$

Now dividing by a^{n-2}

$$a^2 = a + 1 + \frac{1}{a^{n-2}}.$$

For large *n* values, the last term can be ignored, so we have

$$a^2 = a + 1.$$

The feasible solution to this quadratic equation is

$$a = \frac{1 + \sqrt{5}}{2} \approx 1.6.$$

Therefore, the result is

$$Time(n) \propto (1.6)^n.$$

A similar analysis for the corrected form (the one with *mammothfibonacci*) yields

$$Time(n) \propto n.$$

4.1.5 Recursion in Python

In Python, you can implement recursive functions. Since there is no syntactic or semantic difference to calling a different function, we will just illustrate recursion in Python with several examples.

– Factorial of a Number

Similar to writing a "Hello World" program at the beginning of learning a new programming language, it is common to illustrate recursion using the factorial of a number. Remember that $n!$ equals $n \times (n-1) \times (n-2) \times \cdots \times 1$, which can be re-written as $n \times (n-1)!$. Below is the corresponding recursive definition in Python:

```
1  def fact(N):
2          if N < 1:
3                  return 1
4          return N * fact(N-1)
```

where the terminating condition is checked on the 2nd and the 3rd lines, and the recursive call is initiated on the last line.

– Greatest Common Divisor

Another popular example of recursion is greatest common divisor (GCD). The greatest common divisor of two integers A, B is the biggest number C such that $A \bmod C$ and $B \bmod C$ are both zero. A recursive method for finding the GCD of two numbers, a and b, can be formally defined as follows:

$$gcd(a, b) = \begin{cases} a & \text{if } b = 0, \\ gcd(b, a \bmod b) & \text{otherwise.} \end{cases}$$

which is illustrated below:

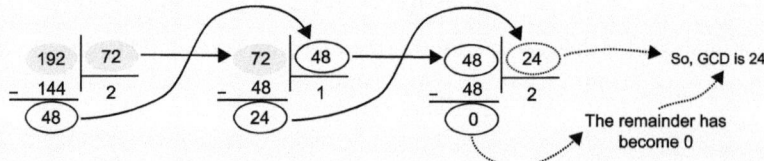

In Python, we can implement the aforementioned formal definition of GCD as follows:

```
1  def  gcd(A,  B):
2            if  B  ==  0:
3                       return  A
4            return  gcd(B,  A % B)
```

– Searching for an Item in a Set of Items

One of the clearest illustrations of recursion can be seen in searching for an item in a set of items. If we have a set of items $s : [x_1, \ldots, x_n]$, we can recursively search for an item e in s as follows:

$$search(e, s) = \begin{cases} \text{False} & \text{if } s = \emptyset, \\ \text{True} & \text{if } e = head(s), \\ search(e, tail(s)) & \text{otherwise.} \end{cases}$$

where $head(s)$ and $tail(s)$ are as follows (for $s = \{x_1, \ldots, x_n\}$):

$$head(s) = \begin{cases} \text{Undefined} & \text{if } s = \emptyset, \\ x_1 & \text{otherwise.} \end{cases}$$

$$tail(s) = \begin{cases} \text{Undefined} & \text{if } s = \emptyset, \\ \{x_2, \ldots, x_n\} & \text{otherwise.} \end{cases}$$

Below is an implementation of this formal definition:

```
1  def  search(A,  B):
2            if  len(B)  ==  0:  # B  is  empty
3                       return  False
4            if  A  ==  B[0]:  # The  first  item  of  B
5                                  # matches  A
6                       return  True
```

```
7            else:   # Continue  searching  in  the  tail
8                    #  of  B
9                       return  search(A, B[1:])
```

– Intersection of Two Sets

The intersection of two sets, A and B, is denoted formally as $A \cap B$ and defined as: $(A \cap B) = \{e \mid e \in A \text{ and } e \in B\}$. To find the intersection of two sets A and B, we can make use of the following formal description ($\oplus$ *concatenates* two sets):

$$intersect(A, B) = \begin{cases} \emptyset & \text{if } A = \emptyset, \\ \{head(A)\} \oplus intersect(tail(A), B) & \text{if } head(A) \in B, \\ intersect(tail(A), B) & \text{otherwise.} \end{cases}$$

which can be implemented in Python as follows:

```
1 def intersect(A, B):
2            if len(A) == 0:
3                    return []
4            if A[0] in B:
5                    return [A[0]] + intersect(A[1:], B)
6            else:
7                    return intersect(A[1:], B)
```

– Union of Two Sets

The union of two sets, A and B, is denoted formally as $A \cup B$ and defined as: $(A \cup B) = \{e \mid e \in A \text{ or } e \in B\}$. To find the union of the two sets, A and B, we can make use of the following formal description:

$$union(A, B) = \begin{cases} B & \text{if } A = \emptyset, \\ \{head(A)\} \oplus union(tail(A), B) & \text{if } head(A) \notin B, \\ union(tail(A), B) & \text{otherwise.} \end{cases}$$

which can be implemented in Python as follows:

```
1 def union(A, B):
2         if len(A) == 0:
3                 return B
4         if A[0] not in B:
5                 return [A[0]] + union(A[1:], B)
6         else:
7                 return union(A[1:], B)
```

– Removing an Item from a Set

Another suitable example for recursion is the removal of an item e from a set of items s:

$$remove(e, s) = \begin{cases} \emptyset & \text{if } s = \emptyset, \\ remove(e, tail(s)) & \text{if } e = head(s), \\ head(s) \oplus remove(e, tail(s)) & \text{otherwise.} \end{cases}$$

which can be implemented in Python as follows:

```
1 def remove(e, s):
2         if len(s) == 0:
3                 return []
4         if e == s[0]:
5                 return remove(e, s[1:])
6         else:
7                 return [s[0]] + remove(e, s[1:])
```

– Power Set of a Set

The power set of a set s is the set of all subsets of s; *i.e.*, $power(s) = e \mid e \subset s$. The recursive definition can be illustrated on an example set $\{a, b, c\}$. The power set of $\{a, b, c\}$ is $\{\emptyset, \{a\}, \{b\}, \{c\}, \{a, b\}, \{a, c\}, \{b, c\}, \{a, b, c\}\}$. If we look at the power set of $\{b, c\}$, which is $\{\emptyset, \{b\}, \{c\}, \{b, c\}\}$, we see that it is a subset of the power set of $\{a, b, c\}$. In fact, the power set of $\{a, b, c\}$ is the union of the power set $\{b, c\}$ and its member-wise union with $\{a\}$. In other words,

$$power(\{a, b, c\}) = \{a \cup X \mid X \in power(\{b, c\})\} \cup power(\{b, c\})$$

With this intuition, we can formally define a recursive power set as follows:

$$power(s) = \begin{cases} \{\emptyset\} & \text{if } s = \emptyset, \\ \{head(s) \cup X \mid X \in power(tail(s))\} \cup power(tail(s)) & \text{otherwise.} \end{cases}$$

and implement it in Python as follows:

```
1 def powerset(s):
2         if len(s) == 0:
3                 return [[]]
4
5         sub_power_set = powerset(s[1:])
6         return sub_power_set + \
7                 [[s[0]] + x for x in sub_power_set]
```

4.2 Step by Step Striving Towards a Solution: Iteration

Iteration is based on the repetition of a sequence of instructions for a known number of times or until a certain criterion is met.

The idea in iterative programming is to have a set of instructions which make use of an *environment* while being executed. This environment is mostly the alterable data part of the program (variables, containers, *etc.*) and the external world (files and devices connected to the computer) that can be affected by the program.

A typical iteration starts with instructions where some initializations on the environment, if any, are made. This is followed by other instructions which will be repeated multiple times. These instructions are called the *body* of the iteration. After executing the body, the flow of execution is so that the body is executed again and again.

In almost all uses of this programming technique, the repetition terminates by some controlled means. There are three alternatives to perform a test on the environment to terminate the repetition (also know as *looping*):

1. Perform a test at the beginning of the body.
2. Perform a test at the end of the body.
3. Perform a test in the body (sometimes at several places).

Each item in this list has pros and cons.

Naturally, iteration only works if the body performs changes on the environment; *i.e.*, changes which are detectable. Otherwise, the looping would run forever, which is very rarely a desired action. Therefore, some instructions perform some changes on the environment, some of which are tested to continue repetition or not.

The logic behind iterative programming combined with the experience built up over many years boils down to some good coding practice. It is a recognized fact that

• the test for stopping the repetition, as well as
• the environment modifications that are tested for

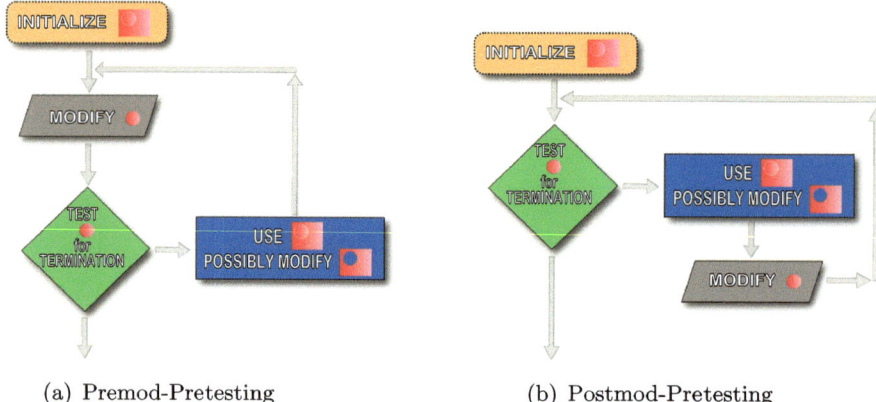

(a) Premod-Pretesting   (b) Postmod-Pretesting

Fig. 4.4 Pre-testing

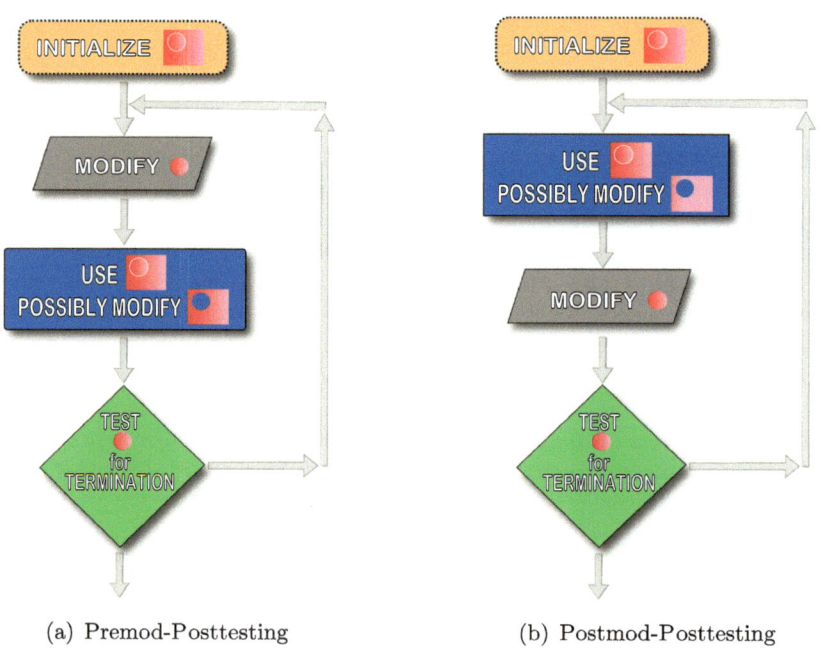

(a) Premod-Posttesting   (b) Postmod-Posttesting

Fig. 4.5 Post-testing

should be restricted to a single locality (not scattered over the iteration code). Accordingly, four common patterns in the layout of the iterations have surfaced. A very high percentage of iterations exhibit one of the patterns displayed in Figs. 4.4 and 4.5.

In the Figures,

- represents the whole environment that is used and/or modified in the iteration.
- represents the part of the environment that is modified and used in testing for termination.
- represents all used and/or modified parts of the environment which are not used in testing for termination.

In addition to these four patterns, there is a fifth one, which is seldom used: A body where termination tests are performed at multiple points.

From the four patterns displayed, the least preferable one is the premod-posttesting (Fig. 4.5(a)) because it does not prevent undesired (due to some unanticipated ingredient) modifications from being used.

The conditional, as stated previously, has to be present in all programming languages. Therefore, to implement these four iterative patterns, it is sufficient that the language provides a branching instruction; imperative languages have branching instruction whereas pure functional languages do not. However, due to the overwhelming use of these patterns plus the anti-propaganda by the structured programmers against the use of branching instructions, many imperative languages provide a syntax for those patterns of iteration. The idea is to decouple the test and the body. Many languages provide a syntax that serve to implement pre-testing patterns and in addition, some provide a syntax for post-testing. The one for pre-testing is known as the *while* construct and in many languages, it has the structure of:

while *test* do *some_action(s)*

The syntax for post-testing is known as the *repeat... until* construct and usually has the structure:

repeat *some_action(s)* until *test*

In this case, *test* is a termination condition (the looping continues until the *test* evaluates to TRUE). Sometimes, a variant of repeat exists where the *test* is for continuation (not for termination):

do *some_action(s)* while *test*

Some languages take it even further and provide syntax with dedicated slots for the *initialization*, *test*, *execution* and *modification* (or some of them).

In the Python part of this section, you will find extensive examples and information about what Python supports in terms of those patterns and constructs.[1]

As we have mentioned earlier, the structured programming style denounces the explicit use of branching instructions (gotos). For this reason, to fulfill the need of ending the looping (almost always based on a decision) while the body is being executed, some languages implement the break and continue constructs. A break

---

[1]Interestingly, you will observe that Python does not support the post-testing with a syntax, at all.

causes the termination of the body execution as well as the iteration itself and performs an immediate jump to the next action that follows the iteration. A `continue` skips over the rest of the actions to be executed and performs an immediate jump to the test.[2]

Additional syntax exists for some combined needs for the modification and testing parts. Many iterative applications have needs that:

(a) Systematically explore all cases, or
(b) Systematically consider some or all cases by jumping from one case to another as a function of the previous case.

Below are some examples of these types of requirements:

- For each student in a class, compute the letter grade.
  [*example to type* (a)]
- Given a road map, for each city, display the neighboring cities.
  [*example to type* (b)]
- Given a road map, find the shortest path from a given city to another.
  [*example to type* (b)]
- For all the rows in a matrix, compute the mean.
  [*example to type* (a)]
- Find all the even numbers in the range [100000, 250000].
  [*example to type* (a)]
- For all coordinates, compute the electromagnetic flux.
  [*example to type* (a)]
- Find the root of a given function using the Newton–Raphson method.
  [*example to type* (b)]
- Compute the total value of all the white pieces in a stage of a chess game.
  [*example to type* (a)]
- Compute all the possible positions to which a knight can move in three moves (in a chess game).
  [*example to type* (b)]
- For all the pixels in a digital image, compute the light intensity.
  [*example to type* (a)]
- Knowing the position of a white pixel, find the white area this pixel belongs to, which is bound by non-white boundary.
  [*example to type* (b)]

Especially regarding the (a) type of needs, many imperative languages provide the programmer with two kinds of iterators. In Computer Science, an *iterator* is a construct that allows a programmer to traverse through all the elements of

- a container, or
- a range of numbers.

---

[2]Minor variations among languages can occur about the location to which the actual jump is made.

The first kind of iterators, namely iteration over the members of a container, usually have the following syntax:

foreach *variable* in *container* do *some_action(s)*

Certainly, keywords may vary from language to language.

The second kind of iterators, namely iteration over a range of numbers, appear in programming languages as:

for *variable* in *start_value* to *end_value* step *increment* do *some_action(s)*

Here too, the keywords may vary. It is also possible that the order and even the syntax is different. However, despite all these minor syntactic variations, the semantic and the ingredients for this semantic remains common.

4.2.1 Tips for Creating Iterative Solutions

1. Work with a case example. Pay attention to the fact that the case should cover the problem domain (*i.e.*, the case is not a specific example of a subtype of the problem).
2. Contrary to recursion, do not start by concentrating on the initial or terminal conditions. Start with a case example where the iteration has gone through several cycles and partially built the solution.
3. If you take the pre-mod approach:
   Determine what is going to change and what is going to remain the same in this cycle. Perform the changes that are doable.
   If you take the post-mod approach:
   Determine what must have been changed (from the previous cycle) and must not be incorporated in the solution and what will remain the same in this cycle.
4. Having the half-completed solution to hand, determine the way you should modify it to incorporate the 'incremental' changes that were performed in the period prior to this point (those changes subject to (3) that were performed and have not yet been incorporated in the solution).
5. Determine the termination criteria. Make sure that the looping will terminate for all possible task cases.
6. For each variable whose value is used throughout the iteration, look for a proper value being assigned to it, *prior* to the first use. The initialization part is exactly for this purpose. Those variables, used without having had a proper value assigned, should be initialized here. The initialization values are, of course, task-dependent.
7. Consider the termination situation. If the task is going to produce a value, determine this value, secure it if necessary, and if the iteration is wrapped in a function, then do not forget to properly return that value.
8. If you have to do some post processing (*e.g.* memory cleaning up, device disconnection, *etc.*), consider them at this step. If you have written a function, do not forget that these actions must go before the return action.

4.2.2 Iterative Statements/Structures in Python

Python basically provides two types of iterative statements: namely, `for` and `while` statements, which are basically pre-testing types of loops with post-modification. As we mentioned before, Python does not provide statements for iterations with post-testing.

– Using `for` Statements in Python

`for` statements have very similar syntax to the *List Comprehension* that we have seen in Sect. 3.5:

```
1  for  <var>  in  <list>  :
2              <statements>
```

where, similar to `if` statements or statements to be executed in a function, the statements to be executed in a `for` loop have to be indented. Similar to the *List Comprehension* usage, `<var>` is set to each element of the list `<list>` one by one, and for each value of `<var>` in `<list>`, the `<statements>` are executed.

Below is a simple example:

```
1  for  x  in  [2,  4,  −10,  "c"]:
2              print  x,  "@"
```

for which, we would obtain the following output:

```
2 @
4 @
-10 @
c @
```

– Using `while` Statements in Python

`while` statements are different from `for` statements in that the iterations are not restricted to a set of values that a variable can take. Instead, a set of statements are executed *while* a condition is true:

```
1  while  <condition>  :
2              <statements>
```

where `<condition>` is a `bool` expression. Note again that `<statements>` have to be indented.

```
1 L = [2, 4, -10, "c"]
2 i = 0
3 while i < len(L) :
4         print L[i], "@"
5         i += 1
```

which would produce the same output as in the previous section.

– Using Functional Programming Tools

In Sect. 3.5, we have introduced the concept of *List Comprehension*, *filtering*, *mapping* and *reduction* that allows the application of an operation or a function on a list of entities. These tools can be considered *iterative* although the iteration is implicit.

– Nested Loops in Python

In Python, like most other programming languages, you can put loops within other loops. There is no limit on the level of nesting (*i.e.*, the number of loops you can nest within other loops); however, indentation becomes a difficult issue when the level of nesting increases. Below is a simple example:

```
1 for i in range(1,10):
2         print i, ":",
3         for j in range(1,i):
4                 print j, "-",
5         print ""
```

which would produce the following output:

```
1 :
2 : 1 -
3 : 1 - 2 -
4 : 1 - 2 - 3 -
5 : 1 - 2 - 3 - 4 -
6 : 1 - 2 - 3 - 4 - 5 -
7 : 1 - 2 - 3 - 4 - 5 - 6 -
8 : 1 - 2 - 3 - 4 - 5 - 6 - 7 -
9 : 1 - 2 - 3 - 4 - 5 - 6 - 7 - 8 -
```

> If you do not want the `print` function to
> put a newline after printing its arguments,
> end the list of arguments with a comma.

– More Control over Iterations in Python

Like most other programming languages, Python provides the following statements:

- `break`
  If you want to terminate a loop prematurely, you can use the `break` statement. When you use the `break` statement, the execution of the loop finishes and the execution continues with the next statement after the loop. The following example illustrates what the `break` statement does (Note that this is just an illustration of the semantics and there are several ways of combining a `break` with other statements (especially with `if` statements) in a loop):

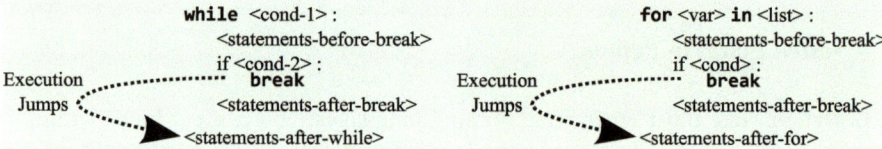

For example, we can use the `break` statement as follows:

```
1 x = 4
2 List = [1, 4, -2, 3, 8]
3 for m in List:
4         print m
5         if m == x:
6                 print "I have found a match"
7                 break
```

which would produce the following output:

```
1
4
I have found a match
```

If the `break` statement is executed in a loop which is nested within other loops, only the loop that executes the `break` statement exits.

- `continue`
  The `continue` statement is used for skipping the rest of the remaining statements in an iteration and continuing with the next iteration. The follow-

ing example illustrates what the `continue` statement does (Note that this is just an illustration of the semantics and there are several ways for combining a `continue` with other statements (especially with `if` statements) in a loop):

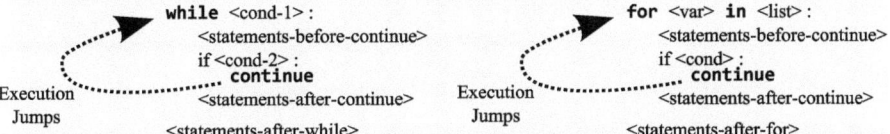

We can use the `continue` statement as follows:

```
1 List = [1, 4, −2, 3, 8]
2 i = 0
3 while i < len(List):
4         if List[i] < 0:
5                 i += 1
6                 continue
7         print List[i]
8         i += 1
```

which would produce the following output:

```
1
4
3
8
```

– Loops with `else` Statements in Python

In Python, all loops can have an `else` statement as shown below (the same holds for `for` statements) which is used for post-loop handling:

```
1 while <cond >:
2         <statements >
3 else :
4         <else −statements >
```

The statements in the `else` part are executed when the loop exits (*i.e.*, when the test condition becomes `False` in a `while` loop, or the list is exhausted in the `for` loop) normally; it means that when the loop exists with a `break` statement, the statements in the `else` part are not executed.

Fig. 4.6 Domain relations of recursive and iterative algorithms

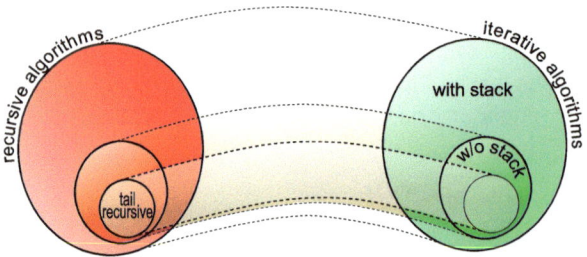

4.3 Recursion Versus Iteration

Numerous comparisons of these two techniques exist. A simple "recursion vs. it-eration" search on Google returns over 40,000 matches and the comparisons seem to be far from being coherent. The main reason is that the comparison is multidi-mensional and every individual has its own weighting on these dimensions. We will consider each dimensi on individually.

4.3.1 Computational Equivalence

This can be expressed as a simple question

> Disregarding the computational resources, does there exist a single problem which can be solved by one of the two techniques and not by the other?

The answer is a pure *no*. Furthermore, it can be proven that every iterative algorithm can be converted into a recursive one and any recursive algorithm can be converted into an iterative one that makes use of stack data structure.

The need for a stack is sometimes unnecessary. In other words, the algorithm can be re-engineered to get rid of the stack. For 'tail recursion', a certain type of recursion where the recursive call is the very last action in the definition, there exist a proven transformation that removes the recursion. This transformation is called 'tail recursion removal' and is sometimes automatically performed by compilers. Recursion removal is not confined to 'tail recursion'. This is still a hot topic in computer science and various scientists propose techniques to convert some of the recursive algorithms into iterative ones without using a stack.

Figure 4.6 depicts the equivalence relations of the two classes of algorithms and their subclasses.

4.3.2 Resource-Wise Efficiency

In contrary to the built-in facilities for arithmetical calculations and conditional con-trol of the execution flow, processors are not designed to natively support user de-

Table 4.1 Overhead costs for recursive and iterative calls

Function call	Time overhead cost	Memory overhead cost
Recursive	n unit	$(k_1 \times n)$ bytes
Iterative (w/o stack)	1 unit	k_1 bytes
Iterative (with stack)	1 unit	$(k_1 + k_2 \times n)$ bytes

$k_{1,2}$ are constants and $k_1 > k_2$

fined function calls. High-level languages provide this facility by a series of precisely implemented instructions and a stack-based short-term data structure (technically named as *activation records* on a *call stack*). Therefore, when a function call is made, the processor has lots of additional instructions to execute (in addition to the instructions of the function), which means time. Furthermore, each call has some spatial cost in the memory, *i.e.*, storage cost. Even for the 'intelligently' rewritten recursive *Fibonacci(n)* function, which fires only one recursion per call, this processing time and memory space overhead will grow in proportion to the value of n. On the other hand, a non-recursive definition of Fibonacci that does not need a stack will not suffer from any n proportional call costs. Of course, one should not confuse this cost with the cost of the algorithmic computation: Both the recursive and the non-recursive versions of Fibonacci consume additional time for adding n numbers, which is proportional to n.

We can summarize the resource cost for a function call with the sizable dimension parameter as n in Table 4.1. What is the bottom line then?

- Resource wise the best is to have an algorithm which is iterative and is not needing a stack.
- Resource wise the second best is an iterative algorithm that requires a stack.
- A Recursive algorithm is resource wise the worst.

4.3.3 From the Coder's Viewpoint

- Since it is not an inherit technique of the human mind, 'recursion', at the first sight, is easy to understand but not easy to construct. Therefore, the novice programmer's first reaction is to avoid recursion and stick to 'iteration'. As the programmer masters recursion, the shyness fades away and recursion gets frequently preferred over iteration. This is so because, for experienced programmers, recursive solutions are more apparent than imperative ones.
- Recursive solutions are more elegant, clean and easy to understand. They need fewer lines in coding compared to iterative ones. When clean code is more important than fast code, especially in the development phase, professionals will prefer a recursive solution and consider it for iterative optimization at a later stage, if necessary.

- Recursive code is more likely to either function properly or do not function at all. Compared to recursive an iterative code is more cripple prone. That makes recursive codes more difficult to trace and debug. On the other hand iterative coding is more error prone which results in an increased need for tracing and debugging.

4.4 Keywords

The important concepts that we would like our readers to understand in this chapter are indicated by the following keywords:

Bulkiness	Recurrence Relation
Recursion	Iteration
Loop	Tail Recursion

4.5 Further Reading

For more information on the topics discussed in this chapter, you can check out the sources below:

- *Recursion:*
  - http://en.wikipedia.org/wiki/Recursion
  - http://en.wikipedia.org/wiki/Recursion_%28computer_science%29
- *Tail-recursion & its Removal:*
  - http://en.wikipedia.org/wiki/Tail_recursion
- *Iteration:*
  - http://en.wikipedia.org/wiki/Iteration
  - http://en.wikipedia.org/wiki/While_loop
  - http://en.wikipedia.org/wiki/Do_while_loop
  - http://en.wikipedia.org/wiki/For_loop
  - http://en.wikipedia.org/wiki/Foreach
- *Recursion to Iteration:*
  - Y.A. Liu, S.D. Stoller, "From recursion to iteration: what are the optimizations?" Proceedings of the 2000 ACM SIGPLAN workshop on Partial evaluation and semantics-based program manipulation, 1999.

4.6 Exercises

1. What do you think the following Python code does? What happens when you call the function like as follows: f(0)? How about f(-2)?

```
1 def f(B):
2         if B:
3                 f(B−1)
```

2. Write a recursive version of the Python code that checks whether a string is palindrome.
3. Write a recursive match function that checks whether two containers are identical (content-wise and type-wise) without using Python's == operator.
4. Implement the following Ackermann function with and without using recursion:

$$A(m, n) = \begin{cases} n + 1 & \text{if } m = 0, \\ A(m - 1, 1) & \text{if } m > 0 \text{ and } n = 0, \\ A(m - 1, A(m, n - 1)) & \text{if } m > 0 \text{ and } n > 0. \end{cases}$$

5. What does the variable c hold after executing the following Python code?

```
1 c = list("address")
2 for i in range(0,6):
3         if c[i]==c[i+1]:
4                 for j in range(i, 6):
5                         c[j]=c[j+1]
```

6. How many times does # get printed after executing the following Python code?

```
1 i = j = 0
2 while i < 10:
3         print "#",
4         j = i
5         while j < 10:
6                 print "#",
7                 i += 1
```

7. Implement a recursive function for computing the factorial of a number *without* using a return statement. (Hint: Use a mutable data type as a parameter.)
8. Write a piece of Python code that eliminates the duplicates in a list. For example, the code that you are to write should transform the list [1 25 a a 38 38 c] into [1 25 a 38 c].
9. Write a piece of Python code that *flattens* a list if the list itself includes lists. For example, the code that you are to write should transform the list [1 25 [a [a b]] 38 38 c] into [1 25 a a b 38 38 c].
10. Given a three digit number (whose digits are all different and are non-zero):

(a) We can derive two new three-digit numbers by sorting the three digits. Let us use A to denote the new number whose digits are in increasing order and B the number whose digits are in decreasing order. For example, for 392, A and B would respectively be 239 and 932.

(b) Subtracting A from B, we get a new number C (*i.e.*, $C = |B - A|$).

(c) If the result C has less than three digits, pad it from left with zeros; *i.e.*, if C is 63 for example, make it 063.

(d) If C is not 1, continue from (a) with C as the three-digit number.

It turns out that, for three-digit numbers, C eventually becomes 495 and never changes. This procedure outlined above is called the *Kaprekar's process* and the number 495 is known as the Kaprekar's constant for three digits.

Write a piece of Python code that finds the Kaprekar's constant for four digit numbers.

11. Write an iterative version of the recursive greatest-common-divisor function that we have provided in the chapter. Which version is easier for you to write and understand?

12. Write an iterative version of the recursive power-set function that we have provided in the chapter. Which version is easier for you to write and understand?

13. Some integers, called self numbers, have the property that they can be generated by taking smaller integers and adding their digits together. For example, 21 can be generated by summing up 15 with the digits of 15; *i.e.*, $21 = 15 + 1 + 5$. On the other hand, 20 is a self number since it cannot be generated from a smaller integer (*i.e.*, for any two digit number $ab < 20$, the equation $20 = ab + a + b$ does not hold; or, more formally, $\forall ab \ (ab < 20) \Rightarrow (20 \neq ab + a + b)$). Write a piece of Python code for finding self numbers between 0 and 1000.

14. Write a piece of Python code to check whether the following function converges to a constant n value (Hint: It does).

$$f(n) = \begin{cases} f(n/2) & \text{if } n \bmod 2 = 0, \\ f(3n + 1) & \text{if } n \bmod 2 = 1. \end{cases}$$

Chapter 5
A Measure for 'Solution Hardness': Complexity

Up to this point, we have described the basic ingredients to build an algorithm and thereafter to implement it as a program. Soon, one discovers that usually there are multiple ways in constructing an algorithm that serves a particular purpose. How can we choose between the alternatives? It would be good to have an assertion that says "take whatever approach you like, since they will all do the same job with the same efficiency". This is unfortunately not the case. "All roads lead to Rome!" but "some roads are shorter!". How can we make an assertion about the efficiency of an algorithm? To answer this question, we need to define the aspects in which we seek efficiency:

R1. Time required by the computer to run the algorithm and perform the task.
R2. Size of the memory required to store data to carry out the task.
R3. Count of instructions and the code complexity of the algorithm.

As you can see, it is all about resources: those required to run the algorithm and the human resources to implement the algorithm. The latter, interestingly, is not often emphasized when choosing an algorithm. This aspect is called *algorithmic complexity* (also known as the *Kolmogorov complexity*) and is investigated merely of academic interest. It starts with the assertion that all output can be expressed in the form of a string, and then proceeds by investigating the content of the string. For a string ξ, the Kolmogorov complexity $C(\xi)$ is the length of the shortest binary program that generate it. Though of much academic interest, aspect (R3) is less important compared to R1 and R2, since they are much more influential on practical applications because they are about the run-time observables.

5.1 Time and Memory Complexity

To understand the time and memory efficiency of an algorithm, let us start with time and immediately consider an example.

G. Üçoluk, S. Kalkan, *Introduction to Programming Concepts with Case Studies in Python*, DOI 10.1007/978-3-7091-1343-1_5, © Springer-Verlag Wien 2012

5.1.1 Time Function, Complexity and Time Complexity

Let us assume that you are given a collection of words in a sorted order. You have the whole collection in a container that is indexable such that accessing any item in the collection takes constant time (apparently it is an array structure). The problem, for example as a subtask of writing a spell checker, is to check whether a given word exists in the sorted collection. We display two alternative algorithms, *exists*1 and *exists*2, which serve the same purpose. Our first algorithm is this:

define *exists*1(*word, collection*)
   pivot ← 0
   countofwords ← *length*(*collection*)
   while *pivot* < *countofwords* **do**
     if *word* $\overset{?}{=}$ *collection*[*pivot*] **then**
       return TRUE
     else if *word* < *collection*[*pivot*] **then**
       return FALSE
     else
       pivot = *pivot* + 1
   return FALSE

Our second algorithm is:

define *exists*2(*word, collection*)
   start ← 0
   end ← *length*(*collection*) − 1
   while *start* < *end* **do**
     pivot ← (*start* + *end*)/2
     if *word* ≤ *collection*[*pivot*] **then**
       end = *pivot*
     else
       start = *pivot* + 1
     if *word* $\overset{?}{=}$ *collection*[*pivot*] **then**
       return TRUE
     else
       return FALSE

Let us try to estimate the time that will be spent for each algorithm for a collection that has *n* elements:

- *Time required for exists1:*
  First, we consider the *exists*1 algorithm. As a shorthand notation, we will represent

$$Time\big(exists1(word, anthology)\big) \ni |anthology| = n.$$

  as *Time*(*exists*1(*n*)).

The time spent by *exists*1, *i.e.*, *Time*(*exists*1(*n*)), is the sum of time spent on two different parts: T_{prior}, the time prior to the **while** and T_{while}, the time spent in the **while**:

$$Time\bigl(exists1(n)\bigr) = T_{prior} + T_{while}.$$

T_{prior} has two ingredients: the first is an assignment of a constant value to a variable, the second is a function call and the assignment of the result of the function call to a variable.

Though we cannot know the exact running-time value of the first assignment (*i.e.*, "*pivot* ← 0"), we do know that it is a fixed value. In other words, it is independent of the *n* value (*i.e.*, the length of the collection). We will denote the time spent on the assignment of this constant value with c_0.

The second time element (*i.e.*, "*countofwords* ← *length*(*collection*)"), on the other hand, is a function call, the time cost of which is unknown. There are two possibilities about how the *length*() function is implemented:

- The language that provides the container also keeps, as a part of the internal container information, the element count of the container; therefore, providing the length information is just the retrieval of a stored value with a constant time cost, or,
- the implementation of the container does not keep the count of elements, which means that it has to be 'measured' (by counting all the elements), which will have a time cost that will increase proportional to the length of the container, in our case *n*.

We denote this time as T_{length}:

$$T_{length} = \begin{cases} \text{either} & c_1 \\ \text{or} & c_2 + c_3 \cdot n \end{cases}$$

A close investigation of the body of the while loop reveals that in the worst case, the loop will iterate *n* times and at every iteration, a constant time (let us call c_4) will be spent on the body of the while loop. Therefore, $T_{while} = c_4 \cdot n$. Putting all the time-consuming elements together:

$$Time\bigl(exists1(n)\bigr) = c_0 + \begin{cases} \text{either} & c_1 \\ \text{or} & c_2 + c_3 \cdot n \end{cases} + c_4 \cdot n.$$

But, either way, the equation above can be combined into a linear equation:

$$Time\bigl(exists1(n)\bigr) = \begin{cases} \text{either} & a_1 + a_2 \cdot n \\ \text{or} & b_1 + b_2 \cdot n \end{cases}$$

where $a_{1,2}$ and $b_{1,2}$ are some constant values.

- *Time required for exists2*:

A similar analysis for *exists2* can be performed. With a similar naming, the T_{prior} value boils down to:

$$T_{prior} = c_0 + \begin{cases} \text{either} & c_1 \\ \text{or} & c_2 + c_3 \cdot n \end{cases}$$

The while loop of *exists2* is somewhat trickier than that of *exists1*. The control of the while loop is performed over the values of *start* and *end*. At each cycle, either *start* or *end* are moved towards each other by the half distance between them. In other words, the distance between *start* and *end* is halved at each iteration. For the algorithm to terminate, this distance has to be reduced to one (then, in the next cycle, they will become equal). What is the cycle count required to achieve this value?

$$n \cdot \left(\frac{1}{2}\right)^{Cyclecount} = 1$$

It is straightforward that this yields:

$$Cyclecount = \log_2(n).$$

Hence, the time spent in the while loop of *exists2* is:

$$T_{while} = c_5 \cdot Cyclecount = c_5 \cdot \log_2(n).$$

Here, c_5 is a new constant because the time spent during a single cycle is not necessarily the same as in the *exists1*(n), namely c_4. Putting all of these together, we have:

$$Time\big(exists2(n)\big) = c_0 + \begin{cases} \text{either} & c_1 \\ \text{or} & c_2 + c_3 \cdot n \end{cases} + c_5 \cdot \log_2(n),$$

which, by the redefinition of constants, is:

$$Time\big(exists2(n)\big) = \begin{cases} \text{either} & a_1 + c_5 \cdot \log_2(n) \\ \text{or} & b_1 + b_3 \cdot n + c_5 \cdot \log_2(n) \end{cases}$$

In computer science, what interests us is the way the time cost is affected when the size of the problem *n* is increased for really large values of *n*. The big question is:

What type of functional dependency to *n* exhibits the time function of the algorithm for considerably larger *n* values?

Here, the emphasis is on two concepts:

1. The dependency on the size of the problem *n* and nothing else.
2. The asymptotic behavior of this dependency (for $n \to \infty$).

At the end of the 19th century, Bachmann, a number theorist introduced a concept to describe the limiting behavior of functions. Soon after, the famous mathematician, Edmund Landau, adding notation used and popularized Bachmann's concept. This notation is now referred to as the Bachmann–Landau notation. In 1976, Donald Knuth, the well-known computer scientist, imported the concept into the analysis of algorithms. The formal definition of the notation reads as follows:

Let n take values on a subset of real numbers for a given function f(n) and a function g(n). It is said that:

$$f(n) \quad is \quad \Theta\big(g(n)\big),$$

if there exists some positive c_1, c_2 values such that for all $n > n_0$ values:

$$c_1 \cdot \big|g(n)\big| \leq \big|f(n)\big| \leq c_2 \cdot \big|g(n)\big|. \tag{5.1}$$

Formally speaking, "$f(n)$ is $\Theta(g(n))$" means "$f(n)$ is bounded both above and below by $g(n)$ asymptotically".[1]

Now reconsider our *exist*1 algorithm which we discovered to have a time function

$$Time\big(exists1(n)\big) = a \cdot n + b,$$

where a and b are constants. Now in Eq. 5.1, set $c_1 = a$ and $c_2 = 1.001 \cdot a$ and take $g(n) = n$. We can claim that the function (n) is a bound both from above and below on $(a \cdot n + b)$ since

$$a \cdot |n| \leq |a \cdot n + b| \leq 1.001 \cdot a \cdot |n|$$

is satisfied for $n \to \infty$. Hence, we can write:

$$Time\big(exists1(n)\big) \quad is \quad \Theta(n)$$

Interestingly, we could have taken $g(n) = 7 \cdot n$ (nothing special about the 7. It is just a constant, any other number would do as well). Redefining $c_1 = a/7$ and $c_2 = a/7$, we can insert our new $g(n)$ into the defining inequality and get:

$$\frac{a}{7} \cdot |7 \cdot n| \leq |a \cdot n + b| \leq \frac{a}{7} \cdot |7 \cdot n|$$

So, this would give us the right to write:

---

[1]For historical reasons, especially among mathematicians (and also among some computer scientists), the denotation uses an equal sign (=) in the place of `is`. Others prefer to use the membership operator ($\in$). Certainly this asymmetric overloading of the equality sign is a misuse of denotation. It very easily leads to the incorrect assumption that if $A = B$ then $B = A$ which is not so in this case. Computer scientists have less of a problem with the equal sign, presumably due to the $(i = i + 1)$ practice. The use of the membership operator is correct but implies a set theoretical view, which is not exactly what (and how) we are focusing on here.

To be on the safe side, we introduce the denotation "`is`" which is certainly asymmetric. For example, (human `is` mammal) does not mean (mammal `is` human) (plural forms are omitted for the sake of simplicity).

$$Time\big(exists1(n)\big) \quad is \quad \Theta(7 \cdot n)$$

Worse than that, we could add into the definition of $g(n) = n$ any function that would remain less than n. For example, $\sqrt{(n)}$ would do the job. We could have defined

$$g(n) = n + \sqrt{(n)}$$

Setting

$$c_1 = \frac{a}{2}, \qquad c_2 = a$$

we have

$$\frac{a}{2} \cdot \big|n + \sqrt{(n)}\big| \le |a \cdot n + b| \le a \cdot \big|n + \sqrt{(n)}\big|$$

The inequality holds. We have a huge family (actually with infinitely many members) of functions that we can plug in as $g(n)$, adjust the coefficients c_1 and c_2 and make the inequality hold. Will these all be valid to be used in big-theta (Θ)? The answer is yes, but it would be useless to do this. It would serve no purpose. This would be as silly as saying "a function asymptotically behaves as itself". So what? Our sole purpose was to reveal the main actor in the n dependency while striving towards ∞. Among these infinite numbers of functions, some are more simple and we will strive to find them.

Without bothering with the proof, we will state some of the properties of the Θ operation.[2] In practice, these properties are used to reduce the subject function to the simplest form.

In order not to clutter up the notation, below, we will skip the argument (n) from $f(n)$, $g(n)$, $h(n)$, $p(n)$ and use f, g, h, p respectively. The reader should bear in mind that these three are explicit functions of n. Furthermore, assume that all 'if' conditions expressed below hold for all $n > n_0$ values, where n_0 is a constant that we are free to set.

- $\boxed{g + h \ is \ \Theta(g)}$ if $g > h$

- $\boxed{\Theta(g + h) \ can \ be \ reduced \ to \ \Theta(g)}$ if $g > h$

- $\boxed{C \cdot g \ is \ \Theta(g)}$ if C is independent of n (i.e. is constant) and non zero.

- $\boxed{\Theta(C \cdot g) \ can \ be \ reduced \ to \ \Theta(g)}$ if C is independent of n (i.e. is constant) and non-zero.

- $\boxed{C \ is \ \Theta(1)}$ if C is constant

- $\boxed{\Theta(C) \ can \ be \ reduced \ to \ \Theta(1)}$ if C is constant

---

[2]The reader should note that Θ is not a function. It defines an infinite set of functions for each argument it is given. Some authors, misusing the mathematical notation, treat Θ as A function and make it subject to functional composition, such as $F(\Theta(g(n)))$ (e.g. $e^{\Theta(n^m)}$, $(\log(n))^{\Theta(1)}$). unless the meaning is defined explicitly, such a use is incorrect.

- f is $\Theta(h)$ if f is $\Theta(g)$ and g is $\Theta(h)$
- $f \cdot h$ is $\Theta(g \cdot p)$ provided f is $\Theta(g)$ and h is $\Theta(p)$
- $\log f$ is $\Theta(\log g)$ if f is $\Theta(g)$ provided $\lg g \geq 1$ and $f \geq 1$

> When we perform an asymptotic complexity analysis of a function $f(n)$, we seek to find the simplest function $g(n)$ where $f(n)$ is $\Theta(g(n))$.

Now, applying all these rules, we can conclude that the *exists1* algorithm has $\Theta(n)$ complexity. What about *exists2*? If the internal implementation of the *length* function had a time cost proportional to n, then it would be:

$$b_1 + b_3 \cdot n + c_5 \cdot \log_2(n).$$

On the contrary, if that time cost were constant, then we would have:

$$a_1 + c_5 \cdot \log_2(n).$$

This gives us two different asymptotic complexities, namely $\Theta(n)$ and $\Theta(\log n)$, respectively. The first case is interesting in that an algorithm which implements a more clever technique than *exists1* cannot get a reduction in complexity just because of a time consuming internal function (the *length* function). This is a case which happens from time to time. If you observe an unexpected complexity behavior, the first thing you should investigate is the possibility of such hidden complexities.

How do the basic ingredients of complexity compare? The graph in Fig. 5.1 displays the most common functions that appear in complexity analysis. Note that the y-axis is logarithmically scaled (that is why the function n is not drawn as a line).

Some common complexity names used in computer science:

Naming	Meaning	Explanation
Constant	$\Theta(1)$	Independent of size n
Logarithmic	$\Theta(\log n)$	
Polylogarithmic	$\Theta((\log n)^k)$	$k > 1$
Fractional power	$\Theta(n^c)$	$0 < c < 1$
Linear	$\Theta(n)$	
"n-log-n"	$\Theta(n \log n)$	
Linearithmic	$\Theta(n(\log n)^k)$	
Quadratic	$\Theta(n^2)$	
Cubic	$\Theta(n^4)$	
Polynomial	$\Theta(n^m)$	
Quasi-polynomial	$\Theta(2^{\sum_i (\log(n))^{h_i(n)}})$	$h_i(n)$ is $\Theta(1)$
Exponential	$\Theta(2^{\sum_i n^{h_i(n)}})$	$h_i(n)$ is $\Theta(1)$
Factorial	$\Theta(n!)$	

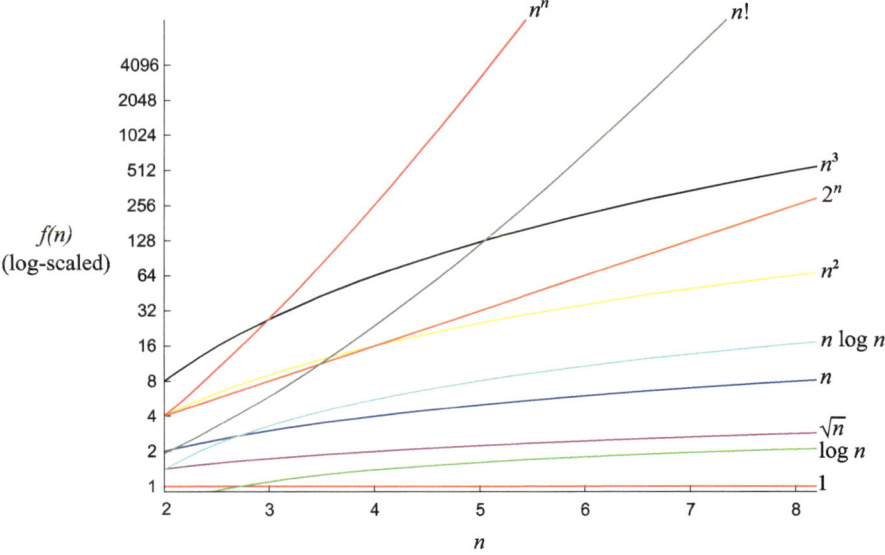

Fig. 5.1 Common complexities (The *y-axis* is logarithmically scaled)

5.1.2 Memory Complexity

Very similar to our interest in the analysis of the time aspects of an algorithm, we should also be attentive to the memory requirements of an algorithm because memory is another delicate resource we have to keep an eye on. The memory that is subject to complexity analysis is about data: as with 'time', in memory complexity analysis, the algorithm is inspected for the size of the 'memory' it requires as a function of the size n of the 'sizable' input of the algorithm.

Similar to the case with the time resource, it is possible that two algorithms serving exactly the same purpose can vary in their memory requirements. For example, let us compare three well-known array sorting algorithms for their time and auxiliary memory[3] complexity:

Algorithm	Time complexity	Auxiliary memory complexity
Selection sort	$\Theta(n^2)$	$\Theta(1)$
Heapsort	$\Theta(n \log n)$	$\Theta(1)$
Mergesort	$\Theta(n \log n)$	$\Theta(n)$

The assumption that memory requirements are inversely related to the time requirement is not always true (as seen above), though, sometimes, this is the case. This is

---

[3] Auxiliary memory, in this context, is the additional memory other than that required to hold the input.

due to the structure of the Von Neumann machine. The time cost to access any place (given an address) in the memory is constant (*i.e.*, a time complexity of $\Theta(1)$). If we give up this random accessibility due to memory space consumption and replace it by a search in the memory, then depending on the search, a time complexity is introduced which varies form logarithmic to linear.

5.1.3 A Note on Some Discrepancies in the Use of Big-Oh

In addition to Θ, there are five more definitions courtesy of Bachmann–Landau. Below is a list of their verbal definitions (we include Θ as well, for completeness):[4]

Notation	Naming	Meaning
$f(n)$ *is* $O(g(n))$	• Big Omicron • Big O • Big Oh	f is bounded *above* by g (up to constant factor, as it was with Θ) asymptotically
$f(n)$ *is* $\Omega(g(n))$	• Big Omega	f is bounded *below* by g (up to constant factor, as it was with Θ) asymptotically
$f(n)$ *is* $\Theta(g(n))$	• Big Theta	f is bounded *both above and below* by g (up to constant factors) asymptotically
$f(n)$ *is* $o(g(n))$	• Small Omicron • Small O • Small Oh	f is dominated by g asymptotically
$f(n)$ *is* $\omega(g(n))$ $f(n) \sim \omega(g(n))$	• Small Omega • on the order of • twiddles	f dominates g asymptotically f is equal to g asymptotically

The most popular one is Big-Oh. Given a function $f(n)$, Big-Oh defines the set of all the functions that remain above $f(n)$ when n approaches infinity. If $f(n) = n$ for example, it is perfectly legitimate to say '$f(n)$ *is* $O(n^2)$', or '$f(n)$ *is* $O(n^n)$'. Of course, it is also legitimate to say '$f(n)$ *is* $O(n)$'. Remember that we had a similar problem with Big-Theta where we were allowed to have any multiplicative constant factor plus any function that remained smaller. Now, with Big-Oh, this freedom extends to the use of any function asymptotically greater than $f(n)$. Please note that Big-Oh is the super set of Big-Theta. According to the similar reasoning we made for Big-Theta, we seek the *simplest* (and yet the smallest) function that is still Big-Oh of $f(n)$. With this implicit desire, the outcome of the task of seeking Big-Oh of a function becomes the same as that of Big-Theta. So, commonly, when we are expressing the Big-Oh of a linear time dependency, we say that it is $O(n)$. Some well-known authors, such as Cormen and Knuth, pinpoint this misuse of Big-Oh (*i.e.* Using Big-Oh with the intention of meaning a 'tight asymptotic bound'

---

[4]The table is adapted from Wikipedia.

which should actually be expressed as Big-Theta). Unfortunately, this is extremely wide-spread and almost all scientific works use Big-Oh instead of Big-Theta.

5.2 Keywords

The important concepts that we would like our readers to understand in this chapter are indicated by the following keywords:

Complexity	Time Complexity
Θ Notation	Code Complexity
O Notation	Space Complexity
Best-, Worst- and Average-Case Complexity	

5.3 Further Reading

For more information on the topics discussed in this chapter, you can check out the sources below:

- *Algorithm Analysis:*
  - http://en.wikipedia.org/wiki/Analysis_of_algorithms
- *Computational Complexity:*
  - http://en.wikipedia.org/wiki/Computational_complexity_theory
  - L. Fortnow, S. Homer, "A Short History of Computational Complexity", Bulletin of the EATCS 80: 95–133, 2003.
- *Time Complexity:*
  - http://en.wikipedia.org/wiki/Time_complexity
- *Big-Theta and Big-Oh Notations:*
  - http://en.wikipedia.org/wiki/Big_Theta_notation
  - http://en.wikipedia.org/wiki/Asymptotic_analysis
- *Best-, Worst- and Average-Case Analysis:*
  - http://en.wikipedia.org/wiki/Best,_worst_and_average_case

5.4 Exercises

1. Find the Big-Theta and Big-Oh complexities of the following functions:
   (a) $f(n) = 3n + n^2 + n\log(n)/3$.
   (b) $f(n) = \frac{n^2}{1+n^2}$.
   (c) $f(n) = n\sqrt{n} + n\log(n) + n^2/90000000000000$.
   (d) $f(n) = n/\sqrt{n} + n/\log(n) + 1/n$.

(e) $f(n) = g(n) + 3n + n^3 \log(n)$, where $g(n)$ is $\Theta(n^3)$.

(f) $f(n) = g(n) + 3n + n^3 \log(n)$, where $g(n)$ is $\Theta(\log^4(n))$.

(g) $f(n) = g(n)h(n) + g(n) + h^2(n)$, where $g(n)$ is $\Theta(\log^4(n))$ and $h(n)$ is $\Theta(n^3/\log(n))$.

2. What is the running time complexity of the following Python function? Use both the Big-Theta and the Big-Oh notations.

```
1 def f(L):
2    if L == []:
3       return 0
4    return (f(L[0]) if type(L[0]) == list else 1)\
5                                          + f(L[1:])
```

3. What is the running time complexity of the following Python function? Use both the Big-Theta and the Big-Oh notations.

```
1 def f(N):
2    return N if N == 0 or N == 1 else \
3               (True if not f(N-1) else False)
```

4. What is the running time complexity of function h() defined below? Use both the Big-Theta and the Big-Oh notations.

```
1  def f(L):
2     if L == []:
3        return 0
4     return (f(L[0]) if type(L[0]) == list else 1)\
5                                           + f(L[1:])
6  def g(N):
7     return N if N == 0 or N == 1 else \
8                (True if not f(N-1) else False)
9
10 def h(L):
11    while L != []:
12       if g(len(L)):
13          L.pop()
14       L.pop()
```

5. What is the running time complexity of function f defined below? Use both the Big-Theta and the Big-Oh notations.

```
1 def count(L):
2    cnt = 0
```

```
3    if L != []:
4       for x in L:
5          cnt = cnt +1
6    return cnt
7
8 def f(L):
9    i = 0
10   while i < count(L)-1:
11          if L[i] > L[i+1]:
12                  return False
13   return True
```

6. What is the running time complexity of function f defined below? Use both the Big-Theta and the Big-Oh notations.

```
1 def count(L):
2    cnt = 0
3    if L != []:
4       for x in L:
5          cnt = cnt +1
6    return cnt
7
8 def f(L):
9    i = 0
10   while i < count(L)-1:
11          j = 0
12          while j < i:
13                  if L[j] > L[i] and i != j:
14                          return True
15   return False
```

7. Consider the following two sorting algorithms in Python. Compare their auxiliary memory complexities.

```
1 def f1(List):
2    for i in range(1, len(List)):
3       save = List[i]
4       j = i
5       while j > 0 and List[j - 1] > save:
6          List[j] = List[j - 1]
7          j -= 1
8          List[j] = save
9
10 def f2(List):
```

```
11    List2 = []
12    for i in range(0, len(List)):
13      save = List[i]
14      j = 0
15      while j < i and List2[j] < save:
16        pass
17        j += 1
18      List2.insert(j, save)
19    List[:] = List2[:]
```

8. Consider the following two implementations in Python. Compare their auxiliary memory complexities.

```
1  def cop_catan1(boys, girls):
2
3      # mixed = cartesian product of boys and girls.
4      mixed = [(b, g) for b in boys for g in girls]
5      allowed = []
6
7      for couple in mixed:
8        if couple[0][1] + couple[1][1] < 60:
9          allowed.append(couple)
10
11     return allowed
12
13 def cop_catan2(boys, girls):
14
15     allowed = []
16     for b in boys:
17       for g in girls:
18         if b[1]+g[1] < 60:
19           allowed.append((b, g));
20
21     return allowed
22
23 # Example run:
24 #boys =[("Ali", 20), ("Veli", 30),
25 #("Deli", 40)]
26 #girls =[("Ayse",50), ("Fatma",40),
27 #("Hayriye",30)]
28 #cop_catan1(boys, girls)
29 #cop_catan2(boys, girls)
```

Chapter 6
Organizing Data

While implementing computer solutions to real world problems, you will very soon discover that you frequently encounter certain types of data such as: numbers, strings, 'yes'/'no' type of information. Moreover, you will encounter the need to group some certain information together. For example, whenever we are asked to undertake some programming related to spatial data (programming about geographical positions, flight simulators, first-person-shooter games, architectural design, *etc.*), a desperate need for representing 'coordinates' emerges. Alternatively, in any e-government or e-commerce applications, there is the concept of 'private data' (like name, surname, address, *etc.*).

In computer science,

- identifying a data kind and its organization in the memory, and
- identifying operations that can be performed on that kind of data (and its organization)

are named as defining a *data type*.

Computer languages provide home-brew solutions for some data types, which we glimpsed in Chap. 2—"Data: The First Ingredient of a Program". These were the basic or primitive data types and were provided by almost all decent high level programming language.

While implementing computer solutions to real world problems, we come across points where we decide about how we are going to organize the data in the memory. Sometimes a simple container suffices, but sometimes the nature of the problem domain or a subpart of the problem, combined with the programming demands related to the data enforces more sophisticated data organizations. There is a collection of patterns of use of such data organizations, which occur so frequently in a wide spectrum of problems that obviously the specific data domain needs to personalize. Those patterns of use of the data organization and their properties form a kind of abstraction, which is independent of what the data actually is, what domain it comes form, what it is used for *etc.* These patterns of use represented as a bundle of certain operations is called *Abstract Data Type*, commonly abbreviated to *ADT*.

G. Üçoluk, S. Kalkan, *Introduction to Programming Concepts with Case Studies in Python*, DOI 10.1007/978-3-7091-1343-1_6, © Springer-Verlag Wien 2012

6.1 Primitive and Composite Data Types

We have covered primitive and composite data types already in Chap. 2. Please go back and review them in order to make most from the current chapter.

6.2 Abstract Data Types

An ADT is abstract in the sense of being away from their program wise implementation and having a formal, rigorous definition. This definition is a description about 'what' and not about 'how'. Although imperative alternatives exist, the preferred denotation in the literature is functional. This will be our choice as well and whenever possible, we will give a functional description of an ADT.

There are mainly two types of functions contained in those descriptions:

(1) Those that construct or modify the abstract entity, and
(2) those that return values inferred or obtained from the abstract entity.

It is a necessity of the functional approach to return a value and have all effects represented in the value (in other words refrain from side effects). Therefore, in this denotational approach, actions on the abstract entity which both modify the entity and return a value (other than the entity itself) is handled. Functions of type (1) return the modified abstract entity whereas type (2) functions return all the other type of obtainables.

For ease of understanding, we will use an infix notation for the constructor function and a symbol for the minimal form of the abstract entity (for example, the empty stack, queue or priority queue).

If a function is defined in more than one line, implicitly a top to down matching is assumed. We stop at the matching line, which is decided based solely on the arguments.[1]

6.2.1 Stack

Verbal definition: A collection of items in which the next item to be removed is the item most recently stored and no other items can be removed or investigated. The most recently stored item is called the *top* of the stack.

A stack is also known as a *push-down-list* or as a *Last-in-First-out* (LIFO) structure.

There are two operations that modify the stack: *push* adds a new item to the stack and *pop* removes the topmost item. Some imperative approaches overload

---

[1] If none of the lines matches in such a multi-line function definition and the argument is legitimate, that is a clear indication of wrong function definition.

the pop operation with two tasks: (1) modify the stack by removing the top item, (2) return the removed item as the value of the function. As stated above, this is something we dislike in a functional approach so we will separate these two tasks: Task 1 will be implemented by the *popoff* function, and task 2 by the *top* function.

In addition, there are two other functions: *new* creates a stack and *isempty* checks whether the stack is empty or not.

Formal definition: We represent the *push(item, stack)* function, which returns a stack with the pushed item on top, by the infix operation

$$item \odot stack$$

and an empty stack with $\emptyset$. S represents a stack, ξ represents an item that can be placed on that stack.

- $new() \to \emptyset$
- $popoff(\xi \odot S) \to S$
- $top(\xi \odot S) \to \xi$
- $isempty(\emptyset) \to \text{TRUE}$
- $isempty(\xi \odot S) \to \text{FALSE}$

Usage: Stacks are used whenever we have to remember the trace we have followed in the course of carrying out a computation. The first to remember is the most recent visited.

Certainly the most widespread usage is the 'call stack'. As stated in previous chapters, CPUs do not provide a built-in facility for function calls. This very handy feature is implemented by a complicated series of actions. It is quite possible that a function calls another function (that is what we call 'functional composition'). The mechanism that performs the evaluation of a function has to know where to return when the evaluation of the innermost function is completed. A stack is used for this purpose.

Another usage is when, for a kind of systematic exploration or search in a high-dimensional space (*e.g.*, searching for the list of moves leading to a check-mate from the current board configuration in a chess game), an alternative solution is sought. This is technically called 'backtracking'.

Reversing or matching up related pairs of entities (such as palindromes, and matching parentheses) are also tasks which require stack usage. Generally speaking, any task that can be solved recursively will mostly require a stack to be solved iteratively.

6.2.2 Queue

Verbal definition: A collection of items in which the next item to be removed is the item in the collection which was stored first. Apart from that item, no item can be removed or investigated. The first stored item of the queue is called the *front* of the queue.

A queue is also known as a *first-in-first-out* (FIFO) structure.

There are two operations that modify the queue: *add*, that adds a new item to the queue and *remove*, that removes the front item. As with the stack, some imperative approaches overload the *remove* operation with two tasks: (1) modify the queue by removing the front item, (2) return as value the removed item. With the same reasoning, we will separate these tasks into (1) *remove* and (2) *front*.

In addition to these, there are two other functions. *new* creates a queue and *isempty* checks whether the queue is empty or not.

Formal definition: We represent the *add*(*item*, *queue*) function, which returns a queue with the added item to the end of the queue, by the infix operation

$$item \boxplus queue$$

and an empty queue with $\varnothing$. Q represents a queue, ξ represents an item that can be added to that queue.

- $new() \rightarrow \varnothing$
- $front(\xi \boxplus \varnothing) \rightarrow \xi$
- $front(\xi \boxplus Q) \rightarrow front(Q)$
- $remove(\xi \boxplus \varnothing) \rightarrow \varnothing$
- $remove(\xi \boxplus Q) \rightarrow \xi \boxplus remove(Q)$
- $isempty(\varnothing) \rightarrow$ TRUE
- $isempty(\xi \boxplus Q) \rightarrow$ FALSE

Usage: In the world of programming, queues are used

- when there is a limitation on the resources; all processes that require the resources have to wait for turn before execution.
- when a real life simulation is to be performed (*e.g.* simulation of any sort of vehicle traffic, production or service line simulation *etc.*).
- where a decision/exploration/search process needs to keep an order of first-in-first-out (*e.g.* Breadth-first search in graphs, $A^\star$ path finding).

6.2.3 Priority Queue (PQ)

Verbal definition: PQ is a collection of items such that

- each item is assigned a value, which is named priority, that is binary comparable for ordering;
- the collection provides efficient access to the highest-priority-item.

There are two operations that modify the PQ: *insert*, that inserts a new item into the priority queue and *deletehighest*, that removes the highest-priority-item from it. As with the previous ADTs, we consider the tasks of providing the highest-priority-item and deleting it to be different tasks, though some approaches combine them into a single action (a single 'delete' action that returns a value as well as causes a side-effect). Then, we will have a separate highest-priority-item returning function that we call *highest*.

In addition to these, there are two other functions. As usual, *new* creates an empty PQ and *isempty* tells whether a PQ is empty or not.

Formal definition: We represent the *insert(item, PQ)* function, which returns the PQ with the *item* inserted, by the infix operation

$$item \frown PQ$$

and an empty PQ with $\lozenge$. *PQ* represents a priority queue, ξ represents an item that can be inserted into that priority queue, *priority* is a function, given an item, provides its assigned priority.[2] $>$ is a comparison operator capable of comparing two priority values for ordering.

- $new() \rightarrow \lozenge$
- $highest(\xi \frown \lozenge) \rightarrow \xi$
- $highest(\xi \frown PQ) \rightarrow$
  if $priority(\xi) > priority(highest(PQ))$ **then** ξ **else** $highest(PQ)$
- $deletehighest(\xi \frown \lozenge) \rightarrow \lozenge$
- $deletehighest(\xi \frown PQ) \rightarrow$
  if $priority(\xi) > priority(highest(PQ))$ **then** PQ
  else $\xi \frown deletehighest(PQ)$
- $isempty(\lozenge) \rightarrow$ TRUE
- $isempty(\xi \frown PQ) \rightarrow$ FALSE

If the problem requires the lowest-priority-item, all the definitions can be rewritten with the substitution of *highest* by *lowest* and '$>$' by '$<$'.

Usage: Priority queues are used in somewhat similar places to queues: it is mostly about managing limited resources. However, this time it is not fairness that counts, it is favoritism. Due to task-oriented rationalism, there is a priority value assigned to each item that enters the (priority) queue. When the 'next' item is called, the one with the highest priority exits the (priority) queue. One would choose a PQ for

- managing deadlines for homeworks or paying bills.
- job scheduling where many processes are waiting to be executed.
- handling the printing of files which vary in sizes (*e.g.* smaller the size higher the priority).
- managing the bandwidth on a transmission line of a computer network (*e.g.* real-time video streaming would have higher priority than (FTP) file transfer).
- sorting unsorted items by first inserting all of them into a PQ, then removing them one by one.

---

[2]The item is assumed to contain its priority information.

The best implementation of a PQ is by means of a heap, a special binary tree where every node has a priority value greater than its children. When we introduce the tree ADT, we will describe this in detail.

6.2.4 Bag

Verbal definition: An unordered collection of items that may have duplicates.
Bag is also known as *multiset*.

There are two operations that modify the bag: *add* and *remove*, both of which have the exact meaning their names imply. *remove* will remove only one instance of an item from the bag.

The single query function *count* tells how many copies of an item are in the bag. If the item is not in the bag then a *count* value of zero is returned.

Formal Definition: We represent the *add*(*item*, *bag*) function, which returns the bag with the *item* inserted, by the infix operation

$$item \looparrowright bag$$

and an empty bag with $\bowtie$. B represents a bag, ξ, η represent two different items that can be added to the bag.

- $new() \to \bowtie$
- $count(\xi, \bowtie) \to 0$
- $count(\xi, \xi \looparrowright B) \to 1 + count(\xi, B)$
- $count(\xi, \eta \looparrowright B) \to count(\xi, B)$
- $remove(\xi, \bowtie) \to \bowtie$
- $remove(\xi, \xi \looparrowright B) \to B$
- $remove(\xi, \eta \looparrowright B) \to \eta \looparrowright remove(\xi, B)$
- $isempty(\bowtie) \to$ TRUE
- $isempty(\xi \looparrowright B) \to$ FALSE

6.2.5 Set

Verbal definition: An unordered collection of items where each item occurs at most once. A set is defined over a *universe*. The universe is made up of all the elements allowed to be a member of the set. Having the universe to hand, an item is either in the set (is a member of the set) or not.

A set has two modifier functions: *add* adds a member to the set. *remove* removes a member. *member* is a predicate function that tells whether an item is a member or not.

Formal Definition: We represent the *add*(*item*, *set*) function, which returns the set with the *item* inserted, by the infix operation

$$item \uplus set$$

and an empty bag with $\emptyset$. *S* represents a set, ξ, η represent two different items that can be added to the set.

- *new*() $\rightarrow$ $\emptyset$
- *remove*(ξ, $\emptyset$) $\rightarrow$ $\emptyset$
- *remove*(ξ, $\xi \uplus S$) $\rightarrow$ *S*
- *remove*(ξ, $\eta \uplus S$) $\rightarrow$ $\eta \uplus$ *remove*(ξ, *S*)
- *member*(ξ, $\emptyset$) $\rightarrow$ FALSE
- *member*(ξ, $\xi \uplus S$) $\rightarrow$ TRUE
- *member*(ξ, $\eta \uplus S$) $\rightarrow$ *member*(ξ, *S*)
- *isempty*($\emptyset$) $\rightarrow$ TRUE
- *isempty*($\xi \uplus S$) $\rightarrow$ FALSE

Some definitions also add the *complement* operation with respect to the universal set. If that is the case the definitions have to be extended by an additional argument which will carry the universal set.

6.2.6 List

A collection of items accessible one after another. The list begins at the head.

Verbal definition: A collection of items accessible one after another beginning at the head and ending at the tail.
A list has three modifier functions: *cons*, that inserts an item into the list so it becomes the head; *head*, a function that provides the first (head) item of the list; *tail*, a function that returns a list with its first item removed.
Formal Definition: We represent the *cons(item, list)* function, which returns the set with the *item* inserted, by the infix operation

$$item \mathbin{.} set$$

and an empty list with []. This list is also commonly referred to as *nil*. *L* represents a list, ξ an item that can be inserted into the list.

- *new*() $\rightarrow$ []
- *head*($\xi \mathbin{.} L$) $\rightarrow$ ξ
- *tail*($\xi \mathbin{.} L$) $\rightarrow$ *L*
- *isempty*([]) $\rightarrow$ TRUE
- *isempty*($\xi \mathbin{.} L$) $\rightarrow$ FALSE

6.2.7 Map

Verbal definition: Map is a collection of items where each item is (efficiently) accessible by a *key*. The key can be any arbitrary type. So, the relation between keys and the items is exactly a *function*.

A map is also known as an *associative array/container* or *dictionary*.

Map has two modifiers, namely *store* and *clear*: *store* performs the association of the key to the item, *clear*, removes the association of a key to an item. The *fetch* function returns the item stored under the association of a key.

Formal Definition: We denote an empty list with ♯. M represents a map, ξ is an item that can be inserted into the map. $\varkappa$ and κ are two distinct keys.

- $new() \rightarrow \sharp$
- $fetch(store(M, \varkappa, \xi), \varkappa) \rightarrow \xi$
- $fetch(store(M, \varkappa, \xi), \kappa) \rightarrow fetch(M, \kappa)$
- $clear(store(M, \varkappa, \xi), \varkappa) \rightarrow M$
- $clear(store(M, \varkappa, \xi), \kappa) \rightarrow store(clear(M, \kappa), \varkappa, \xi)$

Usage and implementation: Maps are used when you have to associate some piece of information with some data (mostly a string) which has a very sparse domain. Let us take a concrete problem as an example and a solution as a map implementation:

Consider the names of all the citizens in a country with a population of 40 million. We want to store and retrieve some information about each citizen given his/her name. Actually, if the citizens had unique sequential integers as names, life would have been fantastic. In this case, an array of 10 million elements would suffice. Each element of the array could even hold all the information of an individual citizen as a whole if the total information for a citizen were about a couple of hundred bytes. However, this is not the case. So, it would be good to find a way to map any name to an integer in constant time. The best would be a case where have exactly the same amount of array elements as the count of citizens and a 'perfect' function that would generate a unique number just by looking at the name string. This is, of course, almost impossible, so we have to compromise to achieve a feasible solution: if the size of the population is N, we can have an array of N/k elements. So, if we have a good function that maps all the names to integers in the range of $[1, N/k]$ without making any positive/negative discrimination, we will have more or less k citizens that map to the same integer. This is not a bad compromise since it is independent of N. Therefore, with a single computation, we can determine the integer for a given name and then jump to the array element holding the information for that citizen in constant time. In the location pointed to by that integer, a linked list of at most k citizens is stored, and we can make a linear search over the names in the linked list to locate the record for the sought citizen. That means, we access an element in $\Theta(1)$ time. Such a 'good' function is called a *hash function*. There are various types of hash functions as well as techniques to store items that map to the same integer. The idea, though, is the same: based on the data that makes up the item (in the case above, the 'name string'), compute an integer value which has an even distribution over the domain of that data, and then using that integer as an index to an array to access the related information in constant time.

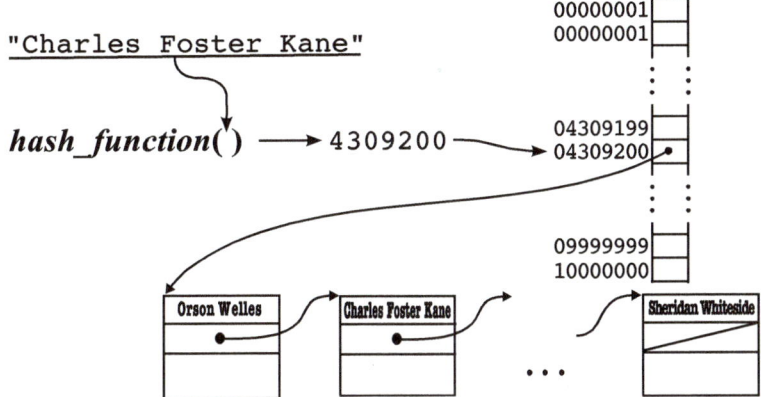

Fig. 6.1 A map implementation

Fig. 6.2 A General Tree

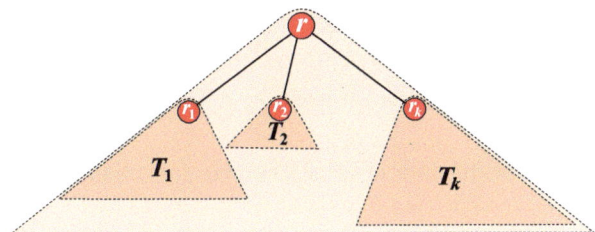

Hashes are the best implementations of the map ADT (see Fig. 6.1).

6.2.8 Tree

Verbal definition: A tree is a collection of nodes where each tree has a distinguished node r, called the root, and zero or more nonempty (sub)trees $T_1, T_2, \ldots, T_k$, each of which root is connected by a directed edge from r. The root of each of those subtrees (T_i) is called a *child* of r, and r is the *parent* of each subtree root (see Fig. 6.2).

Here is some terminology on trees.

- Nodes may have any type of data items attached, which are called the *datum*.
- Nodes with no children are called *leaves* or *terminals*.
- Nodes that have the same parent are called *siblings*.
- A *path* from a start node n_1 to an end node n_k is defined as a sequence of nodes $n_1, n_2, \ldots, n_k$ such that for all $1 \le i < k$, n_{i+1} is a child of n_i (see Fig. 6.3).
- The length of a path is one less the cardinality of the path, in other words, it is the number of edges on the path, namely $k - 1$.

Fig. 6.3 Path from root to
node **K**

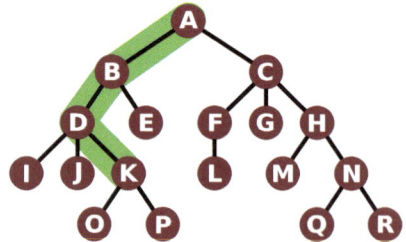

Fig. 6.4 Level numbering in
a tree

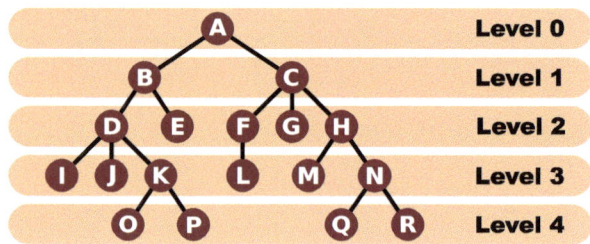

- The depth or level of a node is the length of the unique path from the root to the node (see Fig. 6.4).
- The *height of a node* is the length of the longest path from the node to a leaf.
- The sibling nodes, or siblings, are the immediate children of the same node (see Fig. 6.5(a)).
- The *height of a tree* is defined as the height of the root.
- If there is a path from α to β, then α is an *ancestor* of β, and β is a *descendant* of α. Furthermore, if $\alpha \neq \beta$, then the ancestor and descendant are called the *proper ancestor* and *proper descendant*, respectively (see Fig. 6.5(b)).

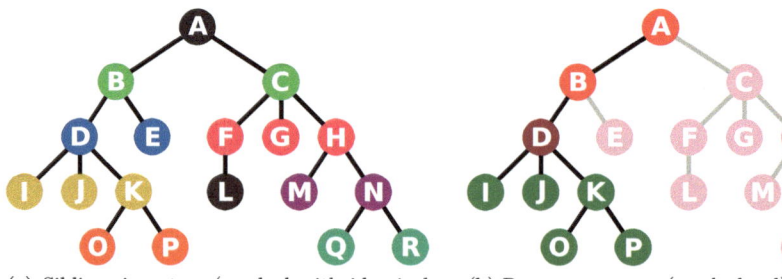

(a) Siblings in a tree (marked with identical colors)

(b) Proper ancestors (marked red) of node **D** and its proper decendants (marked green)

Fig. 6.5 'Family relations' in a tree

A tree has two modifiers: The first is *makenode(item)* that creates a tree (consisting of a single node) having the item attached as datum to the node.[3] The second is *addchild* which admits only trees and insert a new child at the top node. The child becomes the 'first' child. *datum* and *haschild* act as their names imply. *firstchild* is a function, given a tree returns the subtree which is the 'first' child of the top node. *remchild* returns a tree with the 'first' child (subtree) removed. Some common operations on trees are:

Visiting all the nodes: This is also called *tree traversal* or *walking a tree*. The question is: Which node is visited first and which is the next one? This systematic is important and names the traversal. When we arrive at a node there are two tasks to be carried out:

- Process the information at the node (the datum),
- Visit the children (yes that was a recursive definition).

Therefore, for all kind of trees there are two possibilities:

- First process the datum then visit the children, or,
- first visit the children and then process the datum.

These two recursively definable alternatives are called *pre-order-traversal* and *post-order-traversal*. If the tree is a binary tree (a tree with two-and-only-two children), then there is also a third possibility: Visit the left child, process the datum, visit the right child. This is called *in-order-traversal*.

Altering a tree: Quite often there is a need to make a change in the tree. Common changes are:

- Insert a new child at any position. This can be a single node as well as a huge, new subtree. Inserting a subtree is called *grafting*.
- Delete a child at any position. If the child has children, in other words if it is interior node, then the removal is called *pruning*

Searching a tree: Trees are powerful tools for organizing data for searching. The trivial search is, of course, to visit all the nodes. But, it is possible to organize the data so that,

(1) Start at the root.
(2) Consider the datum, is it what you are looking for? Otherwise depending on the datum, make a decision to which child to descend to.
(3) Descend to the child.
(4) Go to step (2).

The trick here is to have the data organized in such a way that, at any node, the search is continued by descending to a single child only. The datum at that node will direct the way to proceed.

---

[3] Different then some other definitions we do *not* consider the emptyset as an instance of a tree. Though denotationally it looks attractive, having an empty set as a tree clutters the subtree definition. That way a dangling edge to a subtree, a child, which does not exist at all, becomes possible.

We will return to this topic when we consider the usages of the trees.

Formal Definition: T , t represents two distinct trees, δ is an item that can be attached (as datum) to a node of tree.

- *datum(makenode(δ))* → *δ*
- *datum(addchild(T, t))* → *datum(T)*
- *firstchild(addchild(T, t))* → *t*
- *remchild(addchild(T, t))* → *T*
- *haschild(addchild(T, t))* → TRUE
- *haschild(makenode(δ))* → FALSE

Usage: Trees have a broad range of uses. The main uses can be classified as below:

- *Representing a hierarchical relational structure*: When any world knowledge which has a hierarchy in itself has to be represented as structured data, it is the 'tree' ADT that we select as the data type. Moreover, most ontological[4] information can be represented as trees. Figures 6.6 and 6.7 display examples of such hierarchical structures from the real world.
- *Representing an action logic*: Sometimes depending on the answer to a particular question, a certain action (from a set of possible actions) is carried out. Thereafter, a new question will be answered, and as a function of the answer, another action (from another set of possible actions) is carried out. This ... *question-answer-action-question...* sequence continues until a termination criteria is met. Trees are also convenient in representing such action logics. Trees of this kind are called *decision trees*, and they can be constructed automatically (using different inference mechanisms) or manually (by a human). Decision trees fall into the *classification algorithms* category of computer intelligence and are widely used.

  In Fig. 6.8, you can see two examples of decision trees, which are self explanatory.

  And-Or trees are a variant of decision trees. In a decision tree, upon the answer, we proceed to the next question by descending to one of the children, whereas in an and-or tree, each node is either a conjunction (and) or disjunction (or) of the children. The children are either further conjunctions/disjunctions or simple questions that can be answered with true or false. And-or trees are heavily used by inference and proof systems.

  Figure 6.9 displays a paranoid logic rule system expressed as an and-or tree. Nodes that have an angle arc on their links to their children are conjunctions (and nodes), others are disjunctions (or nodes).

  Another group of trees are concerned with encoding and decoding actions. In this field, a set of atomic information, called the alphabet, is coded into

---

[4]Wikipedia: In computer science and information science, an *ontology* is a formal representation of knowledge as a set of concepts within a domain, and the relationships between those concepts. It is used to reason about the entities within that domain, and may be used to describe the domain.

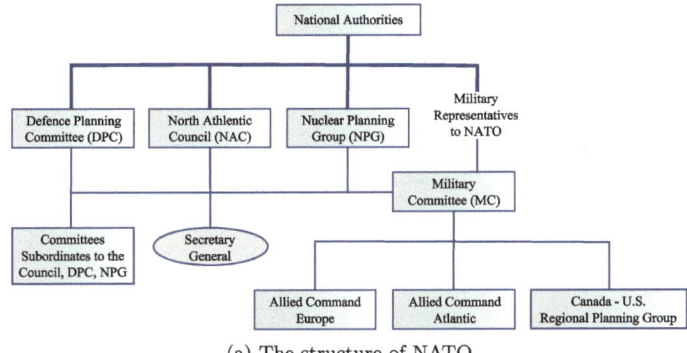

(a) The structure of NATO

(b) Organizational chart of a company

Fig. 6.6 Trees representing various hierarchical relational structures—I

a sequence of bits. Encoding can be undertaken for various reasons such as confidentiality or compression (reducing the size of the information).

Morse code is used to transmit texts as a sequence of dits (a short tone represented by a dot: '.') and dahs (a longer tone represented by a dash: '-'). A sequence terminates with a period of silence. The alphabet was designed by Samuel F.B. Morse, an American artist, in 1836 and reflects artistic intelligence more than engineering intelligence. Decoding of a Morse code can be expressed as a tree, a *dichotomic* decision tree (see Fig. 6.10). Upon the reception of a dot or a dash, you follow the green link or red link, respectively. Hopping down from node to node will stop when a period of silence is observed. If the reception is correct, you must have landed at a node with a alphanumerical data in it.

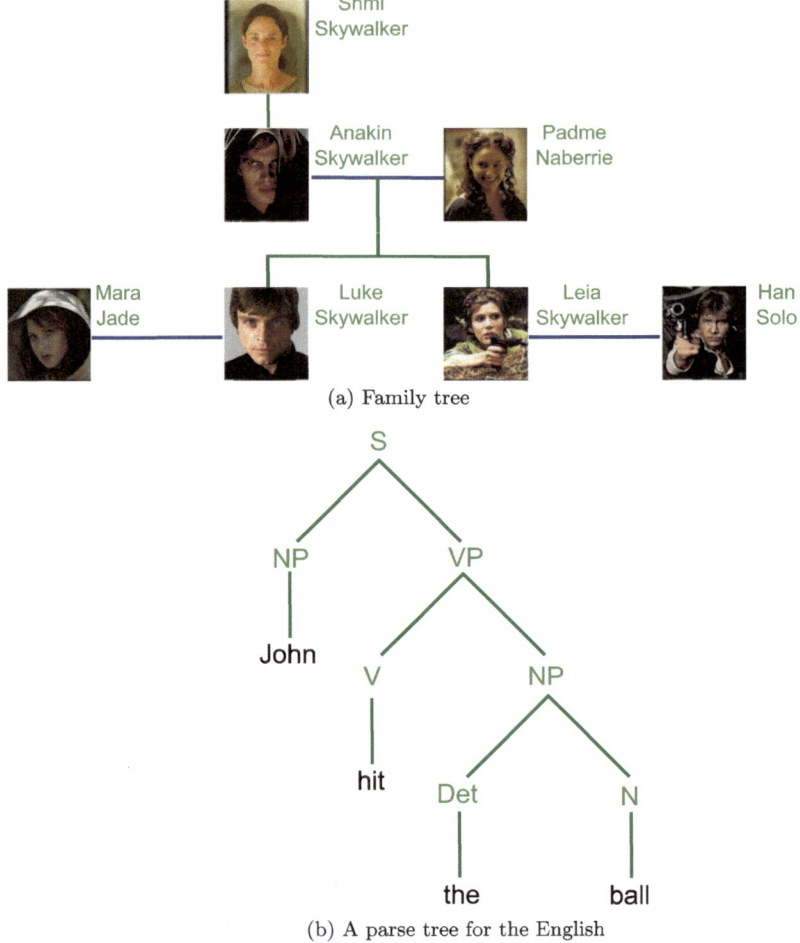

(a) Family tree

(b) A parse tree for the English

Fig. 6.7 Trees representing various hierarchical relational structures—II

Another encoding, this time for a different purpose, namely compression, is
Huffman coding. The idea behind Huffman coding is to assign each member of the alphabet a unique binary code depending on the use frequency of
the members of the alphabet in a given text. The assignment is such that frequently used members of the alphabet get shorter binary codes whereas less
frequently used ones get longer codes. There is a well-defined optimal algorithm that constructs the coding as a tree. Assume that we are to encode the
string[5]

---

[5]The example is taken from the book *Algorithms* by Sedgewick.

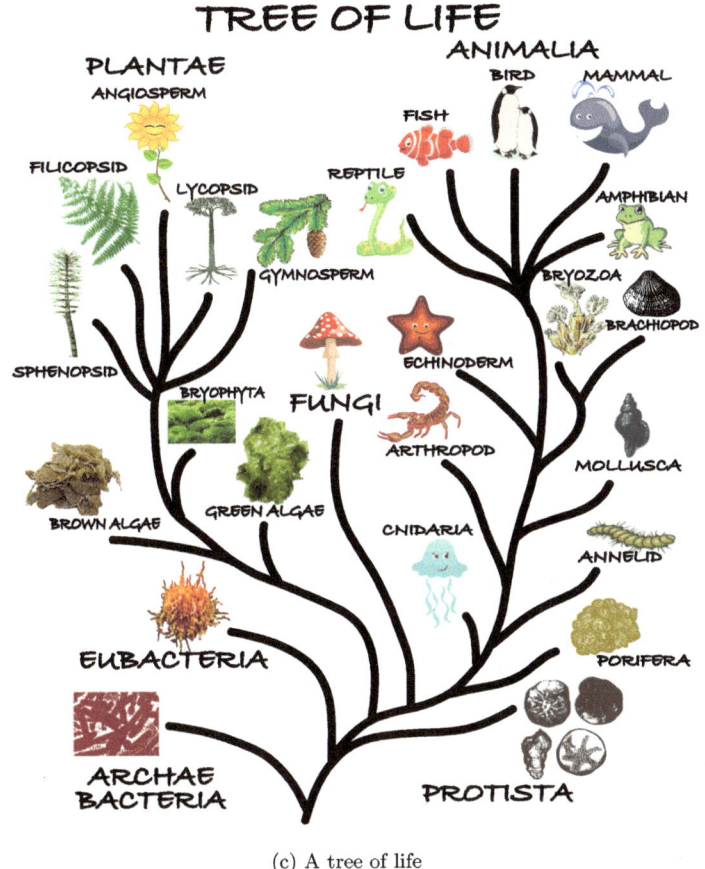

(c) A tree of life

Fig. 6.7 (*Continued*)

A-SIMPLE-STRING-TO-BE-ENCODED-USING-A-MINIMAL-NUMBER-
OF-BITS

There are eleven dashes, three A's, three B's, *etc.* The frequency table for this
string is shown below:

A	B	C	D	E	F	G	I	L	M	N	O	P	R	S	T	U	–
3	3	1	2	5	1	2	6	2	4	5	3	1	2	4	3	2	11

The Huffman coding algorithm would construct the tree in Fig. 6.11.
The small numbers at the nodes are only for information: any such number
depicts the frequency sum of the subtrees of that node. Now encoding a letter
is achieved by traversing the path form the root to that letter and recording
'0' for a left branching and '1' for a right branching. For example, the letter
'A', starting from the root, is reached by a "left, right, right, left" move which

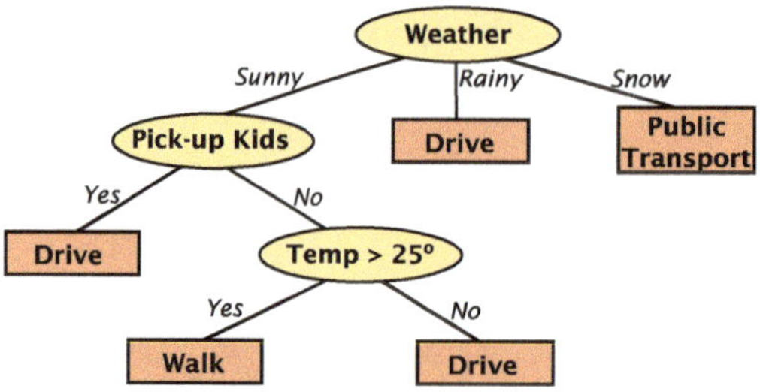

(a) Decision to walk or drive

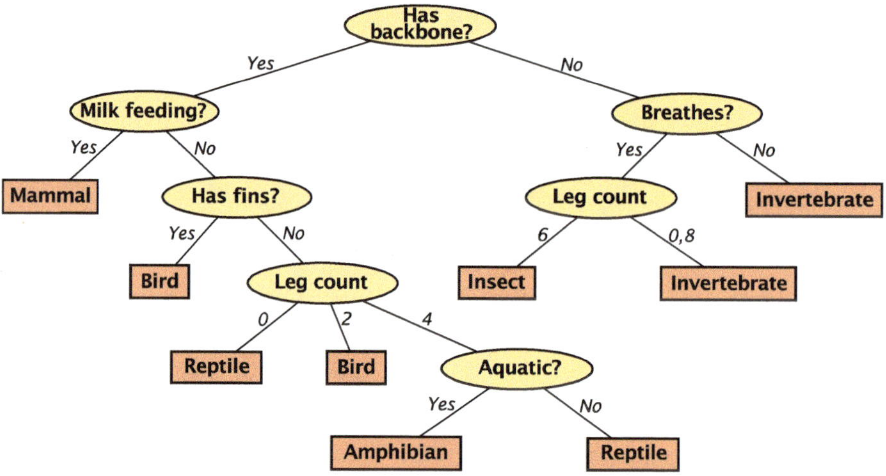

(b) What kind of an animal?

Fig. 6.8 Decision trees

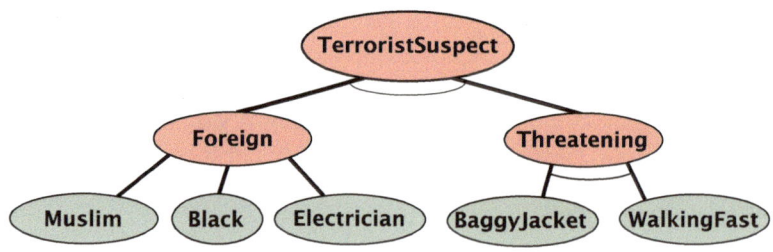

Fig. 6.9 And-or tree of a paranoid logic rule system

therefore can be encoded as 0110. For the reader curious about the result, the final encoding would be:

```
0110111100100110101101011000111001111001110111011101110
0100001111111101101001110101110011111000000110100011
0010110110010110111100001001001000011111110110110110
```

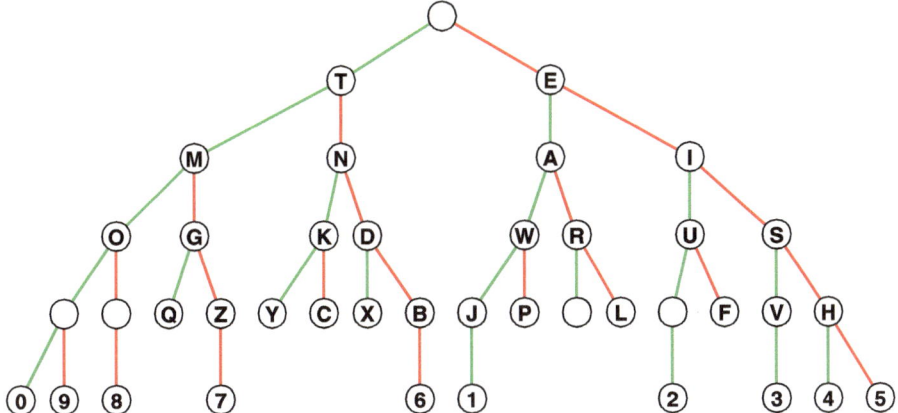

Fig. 6.10 Morse code (punctuation marks are omitted intentionally)

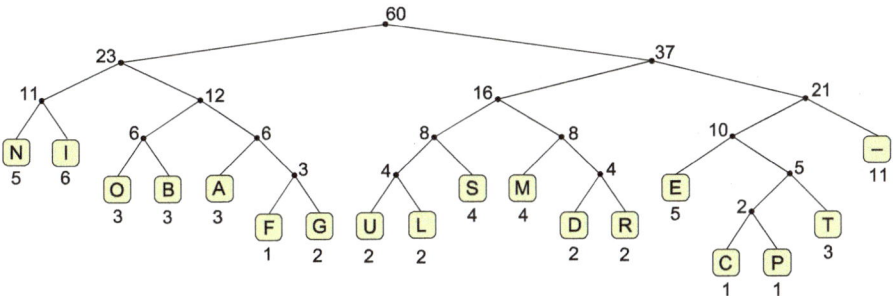

Fig. 6.11 Huffman code tree for: "A-SIMPLE-STRING-TO-BE-ENCODED-USING-A-MINIMAL-
NUMBER-OF-BITS"

```
10001000001101001101000111100010000101001011110001011
111101000111011101010011110111001
```

That is a binary code of 236 bits. We started with a string of 44 characters from an 18 character alphabet which, uncompressed, would require
$60 \times \lceil \log_2 18 \rceil$ bits. That is 300 bits. So we obtained a compression ratio of
$(300 - 236)/300 = 21\%$

- *Organizing data for a quick search*: Trees are a convenient way of organizing
  data in such a way that a search for any data item can be performed by making
  a decision at the root and then, if necessary, descend to one of the children to
  continue the search by making a decision at that child node. The benefit here
  is that if the tree is such that the depth of all leaves are more or less equal, then
  at every descent, the number of elements in the subtree is reduced by a factor
  of $1/n$, where n is the count of branching at the node. So, if at every level a
  branching into n children occurs and there are N data items in the tree, then to
  reach a leaf will take $\log_n(N)$ descents. If the tree keeps data items at interior

nodes as well as leaves, it is quite possible that the search will terminate even earlier.

Though theoretically the branching count n can be any number in search trees, using 2 is very common in practice. The reason for this is simple: the time complexity of such a search is $\Theta(\log N)$ because $\log_n(N)$ is proportional to $\log N$ by a constant factor. So, why not chose the simplest one, $n = 2$? This will also ease the coding of the branching condition by having a single conditional (if statement). Based on this idea, various binary search trees have been developed:

– Red-Black tree
– AVL tree
– Splay tree
– T-tree
– AA tree
– Scapegoat tree

These are all binary search trees, having at worst as average, $\Theta(\log N)$ search/insertion/deletion time complexities. Red-black and AVL trees are the most preferred ones. Having all leaves more or less at the same depth is called the *balance* of the tree. A binary tree, even if it starts out balanced, has to keep its balance against insertion and deletions. There are different algorithmic approaches in 'keeping the balance', which is why we have so many different binary search trees.

One type of binary tree, which is actually not a search tree, is outstanding in its simplicity but still useful. A *heap* is a binary tree where each node holds a data item which is larger than any of its children's. The root, in this case, holds the largest data item in the tree. This is exactly the aspect that a heap is used for: to provide the largest item among a set of data. However, this is what we actually expect from the priority queue (PQ) ADT. Therefore, heaps are very convenient for implementing PQs.

Heaps are used extensively for sorting. The idea is to (i) extract the largest (the root) element out of the heap and store it and append it to the sequence (which will finally become the sorted data), then (ii) update the heap and continue the process until no elements are left on the heap. The update phase is extremely cheap in time complexity (costs only $\Theta(\log N)$). So, the whole sorting has a complexity of $\Theta(N \log N)$.

What is even more interesting is that it is possible to have a tree view on an array, an $\Theta(1)$ indexable container which usually holds the data during sorting. So, there is even no need to have an additional heap structure. The method is as follows:

(1) We start with the array holding the unsorted data.
(2) The array content is made into a heap (this is called *heapification*).
(3) The root element of the heap is placed in the first position of the array (that element is in its final location according to its value).
(4) The remaining elements are heapified.

(5) Now the next largest is the root, and is moved to the place just after the last placed (largest) one in the array.

(6) If there are still unsorted elements we continue from (4).

Consider an array of 10 elements:

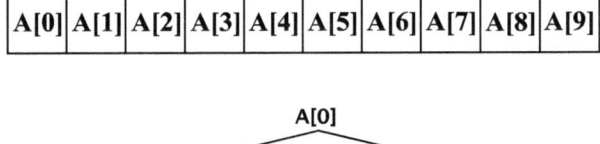

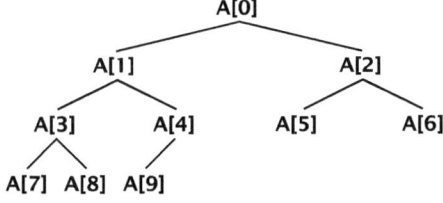

The tree view of the array is:

As you can easily observe, the rule is simple: For any array element $A[k]$, the left child is $A[2k+1]$ and the right child[6] is $A[2k+2]$, provided that it exists.

6.3 Abstract Data Types in Python

6.3.1 Associative Data (Dictionaries) in Python

Python provides a `dict` data type, which is mutable (*i.e.*, it can be modified) and sequenced (*i.e.*, container data type such as strings, tuples and lists). Essentially, a `dict` type corresponds to the map ADT described above. It is an unordered set (or, sequence) of *key-value* pairs, which follows the syntax given below:

`{key_1:value_1, key_2:value_2, ..., key_N:value_N}`.

where the keys are unique (*i.e.*, they are all different from each other). Note the curly braces (*i.e.*, `{}`) and the columns (*i.e.*, `:`) between *key-value pairs*. The keys in a dictionary can be any immutable data type; *i.e.*, strings, tuples, numbers and boolean values.

---

[6]If the indexing started at [1] instead of [0], the left child would have been $A[2k]$ and the right child would have been $A[2k+1]$.

 A dict type can use any immutable data type (*e.g.*, strings, tuples, numbers, boolean values) as a key. However, if a tuple contains a member of a mutable data type, it cannot be used as a key. Moreover, the keys have to be different since they are used for indexing the dictionary.

– Accessing Elements of a Dictionary

The items in a dictionary can be accessed using a key value within brackets. For example, `person = {'age': 20, 'name':'Mike'}` is a dict type whose items can be accessed like `person['age']` and it can be updated like `person['age'] = 30`. If the key does not exist in the dictionary, Python gives an error unless it is an assignment:

```
>>> person = {'age': 30, 'name':'Mike'}
>>> person
{'age': 30, 'name': 'Mike'}
>>> person['ssn']
Traceback (most recent call last):
  File "<stdin>", line 1, in <module>
KeyError: 'ssn'
>>> person['ssn'] = 124
>>> person
{'age': 30, 'name': 'Mike', 'ssn': 124}
```

The list of keys and values in a dictionary can be accessed using the `keys()` and the `values()` functions:

```
>>> person
{'age': 30, 'name': 'Mike', 'ssn': 124}
>>> person.keys()
['age', 'name', 'ssn']
>>> person.values()
[30, 'Mike', 124]
```

– Creating Dictionaries

One can create a dictionary using either of the following ways:

- Enclosing a set of *key-value* pairs within curly braces, like `{'age':10,
  'name':'Tom'}`.
- Supplying as argument to the `dict()` function a nested list or a
  nested tuple of items where each item has two items. For example,
  `dict([[20, 30], [30, 40], [40, 50]])` creates the dictionary
  `{40: 50, 20: 30, 30: 40}`.
- Using the `input()` function as follows:

```
>>> d = input('Give me a dict:')
Give me a dict:{'age':20}
>>> d
{'age': 20}
```

– Modifying Dictionaries

A value in a dictionary can be updated using `Dict['key']` =
`<new_value>`. If the key `'key'` does not exist in `Dict` already, it is created and assigned the value `<new_value>`.

To remove a *key-pair* from a dictionary, the `del` statement can be used:

```
>>> person = {'age':20, 'name':'Tom'}
>>> del person['age']
>>> person
{'name': 'Tom'}
```

– Useful Operations on Dictionaries

- Membership of a key in a dictionary can be tested using the `in` operator:

```
>>> person
{'name': 'Tom'}
>>> 'age' in person
False
>>> 'name' in person
True
>>> 'Tom' in person
False
```

Note that only the membership of keys can be tested with the `in` operator. If you need to check the membership of a certain value, you can use
`value in Dict.values()`.
- The assignment of one dictionary to another uses sharing. If you do
  not want one data to be shared by different variables, use `Dict2 =
  Dict1.copy()`.

- The elements of a dictionary can be erased using the `Dict.clear()` function.

6.3.2 Stacks in Python

In Python, lists can be used for implementing a stack. As you can see above, the stack ADT should provide the following operations:

- $new() \rightarrow \emptyset$: An empty stack is created. A function returning `[]` can be used for the functionality of the *new()* operation; *i.e.*, `S = []`.
- $popoff(\xi \odot S) \rightarrow S$: The item at the top of the stack is removed. The `pop()` function of lists satisfy the *popoff()* operation; *i.e.*, `S.pop()`.
- *push(item)*: The *item* is put at the top of the stack. In Python, lists provide the `append(item)` function that achieves what is required by the *push()* operation; *i.e.*, `S.append(item)`.
- $top(\xi \odot S) \rightarrow \xi$: The top item is returned without the stack being modified. The *top()* operation can be easily implemented in Python by `List[-1]`; *i.e.*, `S[-1]`.
- *isempty(S)*: Checks whether the stack is empty or not. In Python, `S == []` can be used.

Below is an example of the use of a stack in Python. The function accepts a postfix expression as a string and evaluates it:

```
 1  def postfix_eval(String):
 2      ''' Example String: 3 4 + 5 6 * + '''
 3      Stack = []
 4      for token in String.split():
 5          if '0' <= token <= '9': # Operand
 6              Stack.append(token) # Push operation
 7          else: # Operator
 8              operand2 = Stack.pop()
 9              operand1 = Stack.pop()
10              result = eval(operand1 + token + operand2)
11              Stack.append(str(result)) # Push operation
12      return Stack[0]
```

For example, the result of the function call `postfix_eval('3 4 + 5 6 * +')` is `'37'`.

Since the formal definitions of ADTs do not talk about implementations, we avoided talking about the complexities of different operations that ADTs offer. Since we are talking about the implementations of ADTs in Python, now we can talk about the complexities of different operations. The following table lists the complexities of the operations for the Stack implementation mentioned above:

Operation	Complexity	Explanation
new	O(1)	Creating an empty list requires constant time.
popoff	O(1)	The last item of the list is removed. Although removing an item from the list requires O(n), removing the last item is O(1).
push	O(1)	The item is put at the end. Although inserting an item at an arbitrary position in a list requires O(n), putting an item at the end is O(1).
top	O(1)	Accessing an element in a list is O(1)
isempty	O(1)	A simple comparison against the empty list, which requires constant time.

 Note that the complexities of operations for the Stack implementation listed above may change depending on the Python version and implementation that you use.

6.3.3 Queues in Python

In Python, lists can be used for the implementing a queue. As we have seen above, the queue ADT should provide the following operations:

- *new*() → ∅: Returns an empty queue; Q = [].
- *front*(Q): Returns the element at the front; Q[0].
- *add*(*item*, Q): Adds the element (at the end); Q.append(item).
- *remove*(Q): Removes the element at the front; Q.pop(0).
- *isempty*(Q): Checks whether the queue is empty; Q == [].

Below is a hypothetical example of a queue at a bank:

```
1  def bank_queue ():
2      Queue = []
3
4      while True:
5              if a_new_customer_arrived :
6                      new_customer = get_customer ()
7                      Queue . append ( new_customer )
```

```
8
9            customer_to_be_served = Queue.pop(0)
10           serve_customer(customer_to_be_served)
```

The following table lists the complexities of the operations for the Queue implementation mentioned above:

Operation	Complexity	Explanation
new	O(1)	Creating an empty list requires constant time.
front	O(1)	Accessing an element in a list is O(1)
add	O(1)	The item is put at the end. Although inserting an item at an arbitrary position in a list requires O(n), putting an item at the end is O(1).
remove	O(n)	Removing the first element requires shifting the remaining elements in the list.
isempty	O(1)	A simple comparison against the empty list, which requires constant time.

6.3.4 Priority Queues in Python

The priority queue (PQ) ADT (described above) can be implemented in Python using lists, like the previous ADTs.

There are two options for representing PQs in Python (and most other PLs):

- *Keeping the queue sorted*
- *Finding the maximum when needed*

The latter is described here and the former is left as an exercise. Below we describe how the operations on a PQ can be implemented in Python:

- *new()* → ∅: `PQ = [].`
- *insert(item, priority)*: `PQ.append((item, priority)).`
- *highest(PQ)*:
  `PQ[[y for (x,y) in PQ].index(max([y for (x,y) in PQ]))][0]`
- *deletehighest(PQ)*:
  `del PQ[[y for (x,y) in PQ].index(max([y for (x,y) in PQ]))].`
- *isempty(PQ)*: `PQ == [].`

The following table lists the complexities of the operations for the Priority Queue implementation mentioned above:

Operation	Complexity	Explanation
new	O(1)	Creating an empty list requires constant time.
insert	O(1)	Adding an element at the end is O(1).
highest	O(n)	The item with the highest priority is sought, which requires O(n) comparisons.
deletehighest	O(n)	Finding and removing the item with the highest priority requires O(n) comparisons and shifts.
isempty	O(1)	A simple comparison against the empty list, which requires constant time.

Note that these complexities only apply for the implementation discussed above.

6.3.5 Trees in Python

Until the next chapter, we will use lists, nested lists or nested dictionaries to implement the tree ADT (described above) in Python. Below is an example tree:

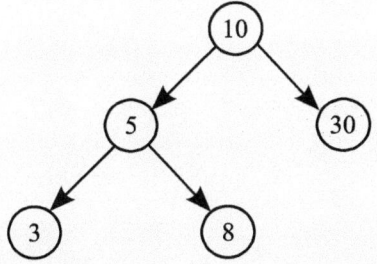

- *Representing Trees with Lists*:
  We can represent a tree using a list where the items in the list correspond to the nodes of a tree, and the parent-child relationships in the tree are determined based on their positions in the list. In binary trees, the children of a node which is at the nth position (where n starts from 0) in the list are at positions $2 \times n + 1$ and $2 \times n + 2$. For the example tree above, the list representation would look like: [10, 5, 30, 3, 8].
- *Representing Trees with Nested Lists*:
  Using nested lists, a tree node is equivalent to a list [Value, Left_Tree, Right_Tree], where Value is the value that is stored at the node, and Left_Tree and Right_Tree are respectively the left and the right branches emanating from that node. For non-existing branches, an empty list or a symbol that cannot be a value in any part of the tree can

be used. For leaf nodes, either one-item lists (*i.e.*, [3]) or a list with empty branches (*e.g.*, [3, [], []]) could be used.

The example tree in the above figure can be implemented with lists in any of the following ways:

- [10, [5, [3, [], []], [8, [], []]], [30, [], []]].
- [10, [5, [3, '#', '#'], [8, '#', '#']], [30, '#', '#']], where the empty branches are marked with '#'.
- [10, [5, [3], [8]], [30]].

If your tree does not require modifications (*i.e.*, insertions or deletions of nodes), then tuples can be used as well. When using lists, one can, of course, start with an empty tree and then insert nodes and branches one by one.

- *Representing Trees with Dictionaries*:

Alternatively, you can use the dict type in Python, where each node is equivalent to a dictionary like: {'value': <node_value>, 'LeftTree': <Left_Tree>, 'RightTree':<Right_Tree>}

Using the dict type, we can represent the example tree (from above) as follows:

```
Tree = \
   { 'value' : 10, \
     'left' : {'value': 5, \
               'left': {'value': 3, \
                        'left': {}, \
                        'right': {}},\
               'right': {'value': 8, \
                         'left': {}, \
                         'right': {}}}, \
     'right' : {'value': 30, \
                'left': {}, \
                'right': {}}\
   }
```

When using dictionaries, you can, of course, start with an empty tree and then insert nodes and branches one by one.

– Traversing Trees in Python

Assuming that the trees are represented using lists with empty lists as empty branches (the case with dictionaries are left as an exercise), we will see different ways of visiting every node in a tree in Python. Since each of these traversals visit each node once, the overall complexities of these traversals is O(n).

- *Pre-order Traversal*:
  In pre-order traversal, the node is visited (or processed) before its left and right branches:

```
1 def preorder_traverse(Tree):
2         if Tree == []:
3                 return
4         value = Tree[0]
5         print value
6         preorder_traverse(Tree[1])
7         preorder_traverse(Tree[2])
```

For the example tree `[10, [5, [3, [], []], [8, [], []]], [30, [], []]]`, the `preorder_traverse` would print: 10 5 3 8 30.

- *In-order Traversal*:
  In in-order traversal, the node is visited (or processed) after its left branch but before its right branch:

```
1 def inorder_traverse(Tree):
2         if Tree == []:
3                 return
4         value = Tree[0]
5         inorder_traverse(Tree[1])
6         print value
7         inorder_traverse(Tree[2])
```

For the example tree `[10, [5, [3, [], []], [8, [], []]], [30, [], []]]`, the `inorder_traverse` would print: 3 5 8 10 30.

- *Post-order Traversal*:
  In post-order traversal, the node is visited (or processed) after its left branch and right branches:

```
1 def postorder_traverse(Tree):
2         if Tree == []:
3                 return
4         value = Tree[0]
5         postorder_traverse(Tree[1])
6         postorder_traverse(Tree[2])
7         print value
```

For the example tree `[10, [5, [3, [], []], [8, [], []]], [30, [], []]]`, the `postorder_traverse` would print: 3 8 5 30 10.

6.4 Keywords

The important concepts that we would like our readers to understand in this chapter are indicated by the following keywords:

ADT   Stacks
Queues   Priority Queues
Trees   Tree Traversal
Pre-order, In-order, Post-order Traversal   Binary Tree
Binary-search Tree   Huffman coding

6.5 Further Reading

For more information on the topics discussed in this chapter, you can check out the sources below:

- *ADT:*
  – http://en.wikipedia.org/wiki/Abstract_data_type
- *Stack:*
  – http://en.wikipedia.org/wiki/Stack_%28data_structure%29
- *Queue:*
  – http://en.wikipedia.org/wiki/Queue_%28data_structure%29
- *Priority Queue:*
  – http://en.wikipedia.org/wiki/Priority_queue
- *Last-in First-out (LIFO):*
  – http://en.wikipedia.org/wiki/LIFO_%28computing%29
- *First-in First-out (FIFO):*
  – http://en.wikipedia.org/wiki/FIFO_%28computing%29
- *Tree:*
  – http://en.wikipedia.org/wiki/Tree_%28data_structure%29
  – http://xlinux.nist.gov/dads//HTML/tree.html
- *Hufman Coding:*
  – http://en.wikipedia.org/wiki/Huffman_coding

6.6 Exercises

1. Add a *length*() operation to the formal definition of the stack ADT. Note that the length of an empty stack is zero. Hint: You can use a recursive rule.
2. Add a *reverse*() operation to the formal definition of the queue ADT.
3. Is it possible to implement a stack using a queue? If not, why not? If yes, how? Assume that you can add new operations to the queue ADT.

4. Implement a priority queue ADT in Python by keeping the data sorted in such a way that each *front* operation can be performed by one access to the list.
5. What is the difference between a bag, a set and a list?
6. Consider an *add*(*item*, *DQ*) function, which returns a DQ with the added item to the DQ by the infix operation

$$item \circ DQ$$

An empty DQ is represented with ∅. ξ and η represent items that can be added to that *DQ*. There is a second constructive operation on a DQ which can be formalized as:

- $inject(\xi, \emptyset) \rightarrow \xi \circ \emptyset$
- $inject(\xi, \eta \circ DQ) \rightarrow \eta \circ inject(\xi, DQ)$

Other operations on a DQ are defined as follows:

- $new() \rightarrow \emptyset$
- $pilot(\xi \circ DQ) \rightarrow \xi$
- $remove(\xi \circ DQ) \rightarrow DQ$
- $eject(\xi \circ \emptyset) \rightarrow \emptyset$
- $eject(\xi \circ DQ) \rightarrow \xi \circ eject(DQ)$
- $beaver(\xi \circ \emptyset) \rightarrow \xi$
- $beaver(\xi \circ DQ) \rightarrow beaver(DQ)$
- $len(\emptyset) \rightarrow 0$
- $len(\xi \circ DQ) \rightarrow 1 + len(DQ)$

What is the result of the functional composition below?

$remove(eject(add(1, add(1, (eject(add(0, remove(add(1, add(1, new())))))))))))$

7. What is expected to be found in the variable a after the following code executes?

   $a = add(1, add(2, new()))$
   while $len(a) < 6$
   do
       $s = beaver(a) * pilot(a) + pilot(a)\%beaver(a)$

       if $s\%2 == 0$ **then**
           $a = add(s, a)$
       else
           $a = inject(s, a)$
   done

8. Why do you think Python does not allow mutable data types as key values?
9. Re-write the three tree traversal functions (*i.e.*, `preorder_traverse`, `inorder_traverse`, `postorder_traverse`) for trees implemented with dictionaries.
10. Write a Python function `depth` that takes a tree (in nested-list representation) as an argument and returns the maximum depth in the tree. Note that the depth

of the root node is 0, and the depth of a node other than the root node is one plus the depth of its parent node.

11. Write a Python function `duplicates` that takes a tree (in nested-list representation) as an argument and returns the list of duplicate nodes (*i.e.*, nodes that have the same values).

12. Write a Python function `flip` that takes a tree (in nested-list representation) as an argument and returns the horizontally flipped version of the tree; in other words, the mirror image of the tree along a vertical axis is returned as a result of the flipping operation.

13. Write a Python function that prints the values of the nodes such that a node x gets printed before another node y only if the level of node x is less than or equal to the level of node y.

Chapter 7
Objects: Reunion of Data and Action

In Chap. 2—"Data: The First Ingredient of a Program", we described how a world problem can be solved using a computer, and we stated that we had to separate data from the actions on the data, which might have sounded unintuitive. This separation is necessary due to the nature of the technology on which we build computers; though both the data and the actions are stored in the memory in a Von Neumann architecture, the CPU makes a clear distinction in *interpreting* the information stored in the memory; for the CPU, a content in the memory is either a data or an instruction. Prior to accessing the memory, the CPU *knows* exactly what type of information it is accessing.[1]

Unfortunately, the world (and the universe we live in), which has to be partially or fully 'modeled' for almost all computational problems, is made of 'entities', also known as 'objects'. They vary from 'simple' to 'complex'; a simple object is mostly merely a collection of some properties whereas a complex one also includes actions. For example, a glass object does not have more than a set of properties, *e.g.*, 'size', 'shape' and 'color', all of which are different types of data. Now, consider the modeling of a military battalion; such a complex structure can hardly be represented by a bunch of physical parameters: A battalion is an entity with many built-in complex actions; for a senior-army commander sitting in his headquarter, a battalion corresponds to a range of actions and some parameters which are fused together. Presumably, the commander will order the battalion to 'move to the geographical coordinate X', 'counter attack Y', *etc.*

Moreover, there is another interesting aspect that needs attention: A battalion consists of sub-objects such as companies and commanding officers (see Fig. 7.1). Some of these sub-objects further include other military sub-objects, forming a hierarchical structure. Such hierarchical structures are usually common for any complex entity in life. Furthermore, when there is a hierarchical structure, naturally, all the

---

[1] This is certainly not the only solution to information processing. Our brain (*i.e.*, a *connectionist machine*, where every function is handled in the connections of identical self-functioning units), for example, does not make this black and white distinction; you can hardly pinpoint a neuron (nor a group of them) and claim that item stores the age of your grandmother (and nothing else).

G. Üçoluk, S. Kalkan, *Introduction to Programming Concepts with Case Studies in Python*, DOI 10.1007/978-3-7091-1343-1_7, © Springer-Verlag Wien 2012

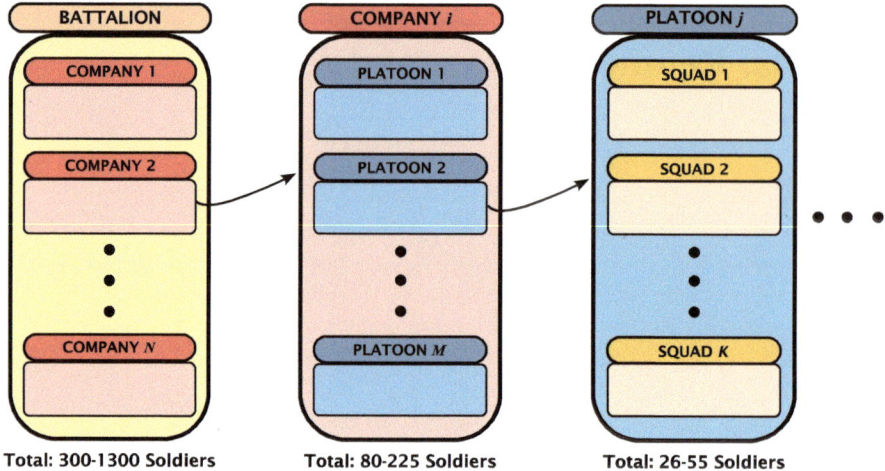

Fig. 7.1 The battalion and its sub-objects in a battalion

definitions of an entity are made in terms of the entities just one level below (technically speaking, if the entity is of a tree structure, its definition will refer to its children only (and not to any further descendants)). Therefore, a battalion can be modeled in terms of companies and some commanding officers and not in terms of jeeps and individual platoons (as shown in Fig. 7.1).

7.1 The Idea Behind the Object-Oriented Paradigm (OOP)

Let us look at the following situation:

- The real world is made up of entities (or objects), which incorporate both data and actions.
- In the real world, complex objects are defined in terms of less complex objects in a hierarchical manner.
- The computer world, which today is heavily based on the Von Neumann architecture, at the lowest level, requires a representation in which data is separated from actions.

With this motivation, some high-level languages are designed to have constructs to represent entities which have both data and action characteristics. Representations of the real-world entities are called *objects*, resembling the naming of the 'things' in the real world. Certainly, at the machine-instruction level, the data and the actions are still kept separate from each other; however, the programmer does not have to worry about this separation since the language takes care of it. So, with an OOP-supporting programming language, the programmer can look at real-word objects, focus on their composition and behaviors, and translate them one-to-one into the *objects* of the programming world.

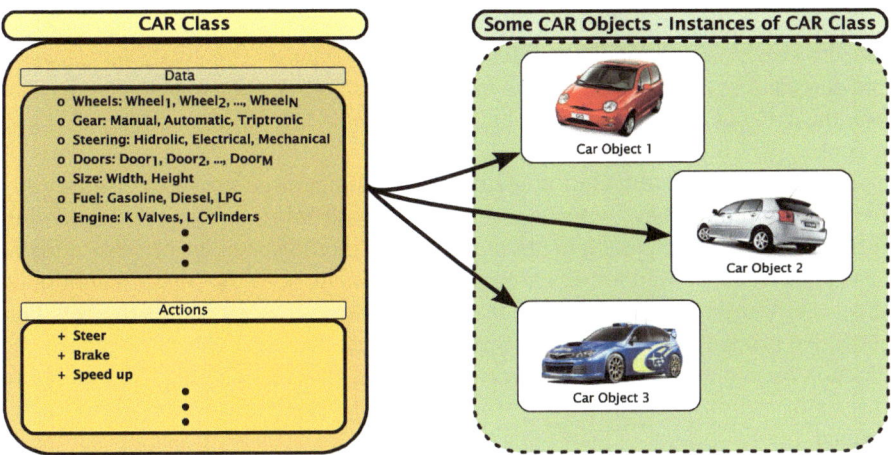

Fig. 7.2 Definition of a CAR object and a set of its instances, *i.e.*, CAR objects

This is not the first time that, at the higher levels of programming, we construct some entities which do not exist at lower levels: as introduced in the previous chapters, functions do not exist at the machine instruction level, for example, but any high-level programming language allows implementing them. Other examples include arbitrarily-sized integers, complex numbers or matrices; although they do not exist at the machine-instruction level, many high level languages provide them.

7.2 Properties of Object-Oriented Programming

The object-oriented programming life is organized around the 'object' concept. For the sake of integrity, modularity and efficiency, there are some properties imposed on the object, some of which are productive while others are restrictive. Below, we will investigate these properties in detail, But, before we proceed, there is an aspect that has to be introduced.

There is a distinction between the definition of an object and the actual creation of that object for use (see, *e.g.*, Fig. 7.2). The definition of a car object, for example, includes the properties of a car and the actions that can be performed on its properties and its sub-entities. Making such a definition of an object resembles drawing the architectural blueprint of a building. Later, when demanded, one or many buildings can be manufactured from this blueprint. It is also possible that not a single building will be constructed from the blueprint, and the blueprint will turn to dust on a shelf.

In programming, the definition of an object, *i.e.*, the blueprint of the object, is called a *class*.[2] After the class is defined, the programmer can create *instances* of that class and every instance will have its own data. As will be explained later, not only the data but even the actions of an instance may differ from another's data and actions.

As mentioned above, a class contains the definition (or description) of some data and some actions. These actions may serve a broad interest. However, according to the object-oriented paradigm, all these actions should somehow be related to the object that the class defines. In other words, for example, if the object definition is about a military battalion, it is irrelevant to have an action, as part of the battalion class, that prints the names of the poets that lived in the 18th century. Similarly, the function for a cubic equation solver, for example, has also no place in a battalion class. Any action which is a part of a class has to be related to the object being defined.

The actions defined within a class are called *methods*. Some of the methods in the class are for interacting with the object. Some others are just helper actions (methods), which are needed by the methods that handle the interactions with the object. Assume that we are to write simulation software for land forces. As a part of this task, a class is defined for military battalion. There will be several interactions with the 'battalion object's. For instance, a simple task will be to display the 'battalion' on the screen. Another will be about defending a geographical location or region, which is a complicated task. In particular, the complicated tasks will require a functional breakdown of the task into subtasks, which will be further broken down into other subtasks. Those low-level sub-tasks are absolutely internal. Here is an example; the 'battalion object' is asked to defend the 'Red mountain', and the internal algorithms of the object at some stage will decide to move platoon number '16' (a sub-component of the 'battalion object') from its former coordinates to new coordinates, involving internal actions that look like:

```
move_platoon(16,<49.307217N,118.10302W>)
```

Internal methods, like `move_platoon`, are called *private methods*.

As you will see in the next section, in the object-oriented paradigm, it is inappropriate to call an object's internal (private) methods outside the object (see Fig. 7.3). Methods, which can be called from the outside world and hence are about the interaction of the object with its external world, are called *public methods*. So, if we want the object to carry out an action, "we call its corresponding public method". An equivalent jargon is to say that "we send the corresponding *message*" to the object.

There are three main features of the object-oriented programming paradigm:

- Encapsulation.
- Inheritance.
- Polymorphism.

---

[2]To make things more complicated, some authors use the word 'object' as a synonym for the 'instance of a class'.

Fig. 7.3 Illustration of
classes. A class consists of
data and methods; methods
can be private and public,
depending on their
accessibility from outside the
class

Actually, these concepts do not have a causal connection among themselves. The fabric of programming, which claims to use the ingredients that resemble (or it is better to say, are inspired by) the objects of real life, 'naturally' brings them together.

7.2.1 Encapsulation

As far as object-oriented programming is concerned, encapsulation refers to two concepts:

- The language-wise implementation of the very basic concept of an object; namely, bringing together (or encapsulating) data and the actions on the data. In other words, it is the ability to define a 'class'.
- Hiding the internals of an object from the outer world (*i.e.*, the part of the program that will interact with the object but is not a part of the object itself).

Some scholars consider *encapsulation* as only one of these distinct concepts whereas others use it as a combination of both concepts. We prefer to take 'encapsulation' as a combination of the two concepts. The novel idea of the OOP is 'reuniting data and action', as referred to in the title of this chapter. We reunite them because: (a) we are used to dealing with objects and, (b) we have to implement 'real-world objects' into our programs and perform computations with/on them. Furthermore, our experience with real-world objects tells us that the data part of a real-world object should be kept 'private'; private to the 'action takers' of that object. As an example, consider a 'court object', or a 'high school object': It is unacceptable to have an unsupervised access to the 'records' of a 'court object' or to the 'student grades' of a 'high school object'. Therefore, we prefer to have an intermediary who would control access to those records. The programming world is not very different from the real world: many dynamics in the real world have counterparts in the programming world. Thus, it is necessary to 'hide' the internals of an 'object' from the environment and only allow specific member actions of the object deal with external requests.

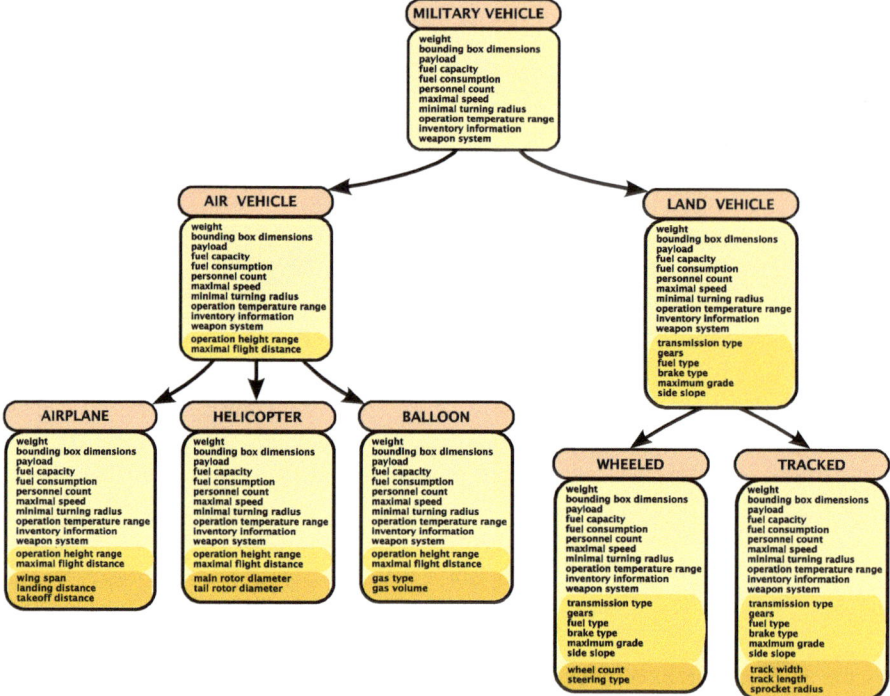

Fig. 7.4 An object (or class) hierarchy tree with the inherited items *highlighted*

7.2.2 *Inheritance*

'Inheritance' in OOP does not exactly represent the concept used in biology. In OOP, an object's definition can be based on an already defined object. *Inheritance* is the automatic copying of the data field declarations and method definitions of the 'already defined object' to the newly defined object. Presumably, the newly defined class will have also additional data fields and methods. It is also possible that some of the method definitions that were copied (inherited) are abandoned and got redefined.

In inheritance, we can speak of a class hierarchy, which can be displayed as a tree. At the root is a base class, whose children are the classes that were derived from it (it is quite possible that more than one class is derived, for which reason we talk about *children* and not a *single child*). Moreover, more new classes can be derived from the children of the root node. Therefore, we have a tree, called a *class hierarchy tree* or a *diagram*, sometimes, it is also referred to as an *inheritance tree*. Figure 7.4 displays an example inheritance tree.[3]

---

[3]The example is extremely simplified, and we excluded the amphibian subcategory.

Fig. 7.5 A part of the
Microsoft Foundation Class
that displays several
inheritance levels

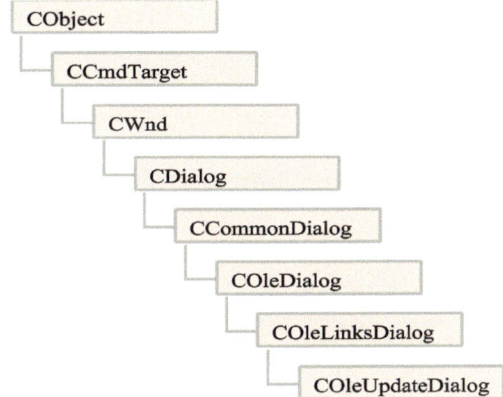

In inheritance, the idea is to go from a 'simpler' or 'more general' object to a 'more specialized' one as we descend the tree. As displayed in Fig. 7.4, a 'tracked vehicle' (a tank, for example), is a specialization of a 'land vehicle', which is itself a specialization of a 'military vehicle'. Each level of specialization adds new data fields to the class definition. Object-oriented languages provide easy syntax for automatic copying of the data fields and methods for defining a new class based on an existing one. Generally, inheritance can be achieved as simply as:

```
class tracked_vehicle:land_vehicle
// tracked_vehicle derives from land_vehicle
  {
  int wheel_count;
  int steering_type;
       ⋮

  ⟨definition of new/redefined methods⟩

       ⋮

  }
```

It is possible that a new object inherits from two or more objects, which is called *multiple inheritance*. If the inherited classes have *distinct* data fields and methods, then multiple inheritance is straightforward: the new class contains a union of all the data fields as well as all the methods. However, if the data fields or the methods are not *distinct*, the intersection of the sets of the data fields and/or the intersection of the sets of methods are not empty; then special treatment is needed: object-oriented languages have their own styles and rules to deal with such clashes. This is an aspect which object-oriented programming is much criticized for.

Another criticism of object-oriented programming is the uncontrolled growth of the inheritance tree. It is an observed phenomenon that programmers who are fond of object-oriented programming have a tendency to structure their design on a (preferably single) large tree of inheritance. Quite often, the depth of such a tree exceeds 10 levels having a couple of hundred to thousand classes. Figure 7.5 is an example from MFC (Microsoft Foundation Class), a widely-used library in soft-ware development on Microsoft's platforms. The `COleUpdateDialog` class is used when you need to setup a dialog to update embedded objects in a document. Below, you can see the path that leads to the `COleUpdateDialog` class starting from the root of the MFC inheritance tree. Following this path is known as the *yo-yo problem* of object-oriented programming, which is the problem of the programmer's need to scan the inheritance graph up and down to understand the control flow of a program.

7.2.3 Polymorphism

The word 'polymorphism' stems from the Greek meaning 'many forms'. In pro-gramming, polymorphism refers to the fact that a method may have the same name but perform different actions (*i.e.*, 'have different forms') on different object types; or, alternatively said, there are a bunch of objects but all respond to the same mes-sage (*i.e.*, method) in their own way. The first thought that comes to mind is the very reasonable question:

> Since the responses are different and the objects are different, why are the method names the same?

In a sensible use of polymorphism, the shared name will refer to same semantic. For example, consider that we are constructing a program for drawing and editing planar geometric shapes such as squares, triangles and circles. In object-oriented program-ing, these shapes will be internally represented by different objects. We will have a square object, a triangle object as well as a circle object. Needless to say, each shape on the screen will be an instance of one of these objects. Naturally, such a program will provide some common functionalities for all the shapes: Painting a shape with a color is a good example; moving them on the screen is another. The existence of polymorphism in OOP allows us to have all those different geometric objects im-plement a different painting algorithm under the same name: 'paint'. Therefore, an OOP programmer is able to send any of the objects the 'paint' message, presumably with the color information attached, and get the shape painted.

The way polymorphism is implemented in a programming language is a delicate matter since polymorphism is a broad concept and what you can expect from it depends on how the language implements this concept.

Below are some possible polymorphism expectations of a programmer (and the answers):

- *I want to define a generic class for sorted lists. For the moment, I do not want to restrict the data type of the elements. In other words, I want to implement a 'sorted list of X' object. Later, when I need a sorted list of floats, for example, I should be able to use that generic class, specifying that the undetermined type X is a* `float` *and the name of this 'sorted list of floats' class should be* `sorted_float_list`. *Parallel to this, I want to have a* `sorted_integer_list`. *Naturally, this time, X will be the* `integer` *type. With a single statement of the language, I should have a* `sorted_float_list` *available and with another statement, I should have a* `sorted_integer_list` *available. Is this possible?*

This type of polymorphism is called *parametric polymorphism* and is supported by many OOP languages, including C++, C# and Java. In parametric polymorphism, you cannot add or remove members from the classes derived from the 'generic class'. Moreover, the members cannot be redefined; the language will not allow algorithmic changes to be made in the implementations. In other words, you cannot have one sorting method implementation for the `sorted_float_list` and a different one for the `sorted_integer_list`

- *I have written a class that I call* Ah_Chuy_Kak.[4] *Then, I derived a new class* Buluc_Chabtan[5] *from this by inheritance. The former defines five methods. The later,* Buluc_Chabtan, *inherits these five methods. I also added some new methods to* Buluc_Chabtan *but I want to change (redefine) the inherited method named* war. *Is this possible?*

  Yes, it is possible. What you want to do is called *subtype polymorphism with early binding* (also called *subtype polymorphism with static binding* or *subtype polymorphism with static linkage*). You can have a 'new' definition for an 'old' method in a derived class. All the methods newly defined in the derived class (Buluc_Chabtan) will use this new definition. If it is a 'public method', then the external calls ('war' message calls to Buluc_Chabtan) will be received by this redefined 'war' method.

- *I realized that the redefinition of the 'war' method has only been made use of in the newly defined methods of* Buluc_Chabtan. *Actually, some of the five methods inherited from* Ah_Chuy_Kak *also were using the 'war' method. Although I redefined the 'war' method, the inherited methods still insist on using the former definition of 'war'. Is it possible to fix this?*

  You are actually demanding that a base class can use a method from its derived class. Since there can be more than one such derived class, at the compile-time there is an ambiguity about which one to use. This could have been solved by tracing through the code but no language processor would ever do this. Furthermore, what about the class instances created at run time? There, even tracing would fail. Therefore, the only way out is to defer the binding of the method to run-time. This is called *subtype polymorphism with late binding* (also called *subtype polymorphism with dynamic binding* or *subtype polymorphism with dynamic linkage*). In compiled languages, late binding is implemented by means of *virtual functions*, which bring some overheads (both time-wise and size-wise) but provide the programmer with increased power. In interpreted languages, since everything is performed at run-time, late-binding is congenital.

---

[4] The war god of Mayas.

[5] Another war god of Mayas.

7.3 Object-Oriented Programming in Python

Python is a multi-paradigm programming language and object-oriented programming is one of these paradigms.

7.3.1 Defining Classes in Python

The blueprint of an object, *i.e.*, a class, can be defined in Python as follows:

```
1  class <class_name >:
2     <variables  with  values > OR <function  definitions >
3     <variables  with  values > OR <function  definitions >
4     ...
5     <variables  with  values > OR <function  definitions >
```

Below is a simple example:

```
1  class Person :
2     name = " "
3     age = −1
4     def Print ( self ):
5        print "Name:" ,  self .name ,  " age:" ,  self .age
```

where name and age are *member variables* and the function Print is a *member function* of the Person class. When an instance of a class is created, the object has the member variables and the member functions defined in the class, as shown below:

```
>>> mark = Person ()
>>> mark
<__main__.Person instance at 0xb7dd0a8c>
```

With the line mark = Person(), we have created an instance of the Person class, *i.e.*, an object, which is assigned to the variable mark. Now, we can work with the member variables and the member functions:

```
>>> mark.Print ()
Name:    age: -1
>>> mark.name = "Mark"
>>> mark.age = 20
>>> mark.Print ()
Name: Mark   age: 20
```

– Member Variables & Functions in Python

Objects in Python are mutable; *i.e.*, their content can be changed after they are created. This allows classes to be defined and the objects created from them to be modified (*i.e.*, added new member variables or functions) on the run. For example, consider a modified version of the `Person` class above:

```
1  class Person2:
2            pass
```

which now does not have any members. However, we can add new members to the objects created from them on the run:

```
>>> mark = Person2()
>>> mark.age
Traceback (most recent call last):
  File "<stdin>", line 1, in <module>
AttributeError: Person2 instance has no attribute 'age'
>>> mark.age = 10
>>> mark.age
10
>>> def f():
...    print "A humble function at your service"
...
>>> mark.f = f
>>> mark.f()
A humble function at your service
>>> del mark.age
>>> mark.age
Traceback (most recent call last):
  File "<stdin>", line 1, in <module>
AttributeError: Person2 instance has no attribute 'age'
```

As shown in the above example, we can add members to an object and delete them. However, the modifications on an object are not reflected in the class itself. In other words, if we create another instance of the `Person2` class (name it `jill`), `jill` *will only have what is defined in the `Person2` class and will not be affected by the changes in `mark`.*

If you want your modifications to affect all subsequent instances of the class, you can modify the class directly (considering the empty `Person2` definition):

```
>>> Person2.age = 10
>>> Person2.name = " "
>>> mark = Person2()
>>> mark.age
10
```

```
>>> jill = Person2()
>>> jill.age
10
```

– Accessors and Modifiers in Python

In most cases, the member functions will change the member variables, make
some calculations on them or just return them. The *public* member functions
which just return the values of the member variables are called *accessors* and
the public member functions that modify the member variables (usually, by just
setting them to the parameters) are called *modifiers*. Accessors and modifiers
allow appropriate access to an object and determine what you can do with the
object.

Whether accessor or modifier, the functions that need to access the member
variables of the object need to have at least one parameter, the first of which
always points to the current object. Using this first parameter, the member variables and functions of an object can be accessed. Below is a simple example:

```
1  class Person3:
2    '''Definition of Person3:
3      _name and _age are private'''
4    _name = ""
5    _age = -1
6    def getName(self):
7      return self._name
8
9    def setName(self, new_name):
10     self._name = new_name
11
12   def getAge(self):
13     return self._age
14
15   def setAge(self, new_age):
16     self._age = new_age
17
18   def greet(self):
19     if self._age != -1:
20       print "My name is", self._name, ", and I am",\
21         self._age, "years old. Nice to meet you."
22     else:
23       print "<Uninitialized>"
```

In this definition, getName and getAge are accessors while setName
and setAge are modifiers. _name and _age member variables. Below is an

example:

```
>>> mark = Person3()
>>> mark.greet()
<Uninitialized>
>>> mark.setName("Mark")
>>> mark.setAge(20)
>>> mark.greet()
My name is Mark , and I am 20 years old. Nice to meet you.
```

 The name of the first parameter pointing to the current instance of the class can have a different name other than `self`; `self` is just a convention and not a must. However, since some code-browsing tools or integrated development environments might depend on this convention, the use of `self` as the name corresponding to the current class instance is strongly recommended.

In Python, if the name of the member variables start with an underscore, it means that they are not meant to be modified directly from outside the object (*i.e.*, they are reserved for internal usage); *i.e.*, they are *private* (as opposed to public). In the case of the `Person3` class, the variables _name and _age are private.

 Whether the member variables of objects in Python are public or private are established by a naming convention: If the name of the variable starts with an underscore, that member variable is private; otherwise, it is public. In no way Python moderates the access to any member variable.

A stricter way to make member variables private is to use two leading underscores in their names:

```
>>> class Person4:
...   __a = 10
...   def f(self):
...     print self.__a
...
>>> mark = Person4()
>>> mark.__a
Traceback (most recent call last):
  File "<stdin>", line 1, in <module>
```

```
AttributeError: Person4 instance has no attribute  '__a'
>>> mark.f()
10
>>> mark._Person4__a
10
```

where, in fact, Python transforms the name of the variables so that it is a little bit more difficult to access it.

– Initializing Member Variables in Python

In Python, __init__ function can be used to initialize the member variables of the class when an object is instantiated. Below is a simple example:

```
1  class Person4 :
2     '''Definition of Person4:
3     _name and _age are initialized upon creation'''
4
5     def __init__(self, name="", age=-1):
6        self._name = name
7        self._age = age
8
9     def greet(self):
10       if self._age != -1:
11          print "My name is", self._name, ", and I am",\
12             self._age, "years old. Nice to meet you."
13       else:
14          print "<Uninitialized>"
```

which we can use as follows:

```
>>> mark = Person4()
>>> mark
<__main__.Person4 instance at 0x0000000002D2B588>
>>> mark.greet()
<Uninitialized>
>>> tom = Person4('Tom Tommy', 20)
>>> tom.greet()
My name is Tom Tommy , and I am 20 years old. Nice to meet you.
```

As shown in the example, the __init__ function has to take a self argument and any number of additional arguments. It is a good practice to provide default values for all of the arguments other than the first one.

7.3.2 Inheritance in Python

In Python, you can use the following syntax to define new classes *inheriting* from others:

```
1  class Student(Person3):
2    '''Student Class: Child Class of Person4 Class'''
3    _grades = []
4    _year = -1
5
6    def getGrades(self):
7      return self._grades
8
9    def setGrades(self, new_grades):
10     self._grades = new_grades
11
12   def getYear(self):
13     return self._year
14
15   def setYear(self, new_year):
16     self._year = new_year
```

which can be used like below:

```
>>> tom = Student()
>>> tom.greet()
<Uninitialized>
>>> tom.setName("Tom Mot")
>>> tom.setAge(20)
>>> tom.greet()
My name is Tom Mot , and I am 20 years old. Nice to meet you.
>>> tom.setGrades([10, 20, 30])
>>> tom.getGrades()
[10, 20, 30]
```

Note that `tom` is an instance of the `Student` class that inherits the member variables and the functions from the `Person3` class.

– Virtual Functions in Python

In Python, every function is by default virtual; *i.e.*, they can be extended or overwritten by the inheriting class, as shown below:

```
1  class Father:
2    '''Parent class'''
```

```
 3
 4    def humble(self):
 5            print "In father object"
 6
 7    def mumble(self):
 8            self.crumble()
 9
10  class Child(Father):
11     '''A derived class that inherits from
12           the Father class'''
13
14    def humble(self):
15            print "In child object"
16            Father.humble(self)
17
18    def crumble(self):
19            print "I crumble"
```

In this example, humble function is extended in the Child class. The mumble function is not defined in the Child class; however, it can call a function which is defined in the inheriting class. Below is an illustration:

```
>>> c = Child()
>>> c.humble()
In child object
In father object
>>> c.mumble()
I crumble
>>> c.crumble()
I crumble
```

7.3.3 Type of Objects in Python

Consider the Person3 class (the example is valid for other classes, too):

```
>>> a = Person3()
>>> b = Person3()
>>> a == b
False
>>> c = a
>>> c == a
True
```

In other words, in Python, by default, two objects are equal to each other only if they *share* the same data. In the above example, a and b are different by default although, content-wise, they are the same. If you want to check the equality based on content, you need to define a new function (as given below) or overload the equality operator (as shown in the next section):

```
>>> def Eq(Pers1, Pers2):
...     return Pers1.getName() == Pers2.getName() \
...         and Pers1.getAge() == Pers2.getAge()
...
>>> a = Person3()
>>> b = Person3()
>>> a == b
False
>>> Eq(a, b)
True
```

7.3.4 Operator Overloading

Consider a simple example:

```
1 class Person5:
2     name = ""
3     age = 20
4
5     def __eq__(self, other):
6         return self.name == other.name\
7             and self.age == other.age
```

which is illustrated below:

```
>>> a = Person5()
>>> b = Person5()
>>> a == b
True
>>> a.name = "Tom"
>>> a == b
```

Below is a list of other operators that you can overload (Note that this list is not complete—Check the *Further Reading* section for pointers to the whole list):

Operator	Function to be overloaded
+	`__add__(self, other)`
-	`__sub__(self, other)`
*	`__mul__(self, other)`
/	`__div__(self, other)`
<	`__lt__(self, other)`
<=	`__le__(self, other)`
==	`__eq__(self, other)`
!=	`__ne__(self, other)`
>	`__gt__(self, other)`
>=	`__ge__(self, other)`

7.3.5 Example with Objects in Python: Trees

Objects in Python are very handy with self-referential structures, like Trees.
Below is a simple example:

```python
 1  class Node:
 2          '''Node definition of the tree'''
 3          def __init__(self, value=""):
 4                  self._left = None
 5                  self._right = None
 6                  self._value = value
 7
 8          # Left modifier & accessor
 9          def getLeft(self):
10                  return self._left
11          def setLeft(self, leftNode):
12                  self._left = leftNode
13          # Right modifier & accessor
14          def getRight(self):
15                  return self._right
16          def setRight(self, rightNode):
17                  self._right = rightNode
18          # Value modifier & accessor
19          def getValue(self):
20                  return self._value
21          def setValue(self, value):
22                  self._value = value
```

Given this definition of a tree, we can easily construct a tree, as follows:

```
Root = Node(10)
Root.setLeft(Node(5))
Root.setRight(Node(30))
Root.getLeft().setRight(Node(8))
Root.getLeft().setLeft(Node(3))
```

which construct the tree below:

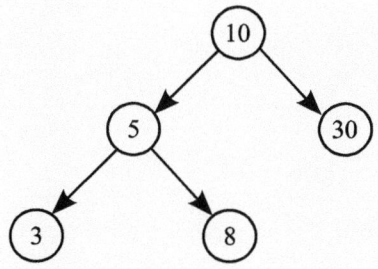

We can define a traversal of a tree as shown below:

```
1 def preorder_traverse(Tree):
2         print Tree.getValue(),
3         if Tree.getLeft() != None:
4                 preorder_traverse(Tree.getLeft())
5         if Tree.getRight() != None:
6                 preorder_traverse(Tree.getRight())
```

which would print 10 5 3 8 30 when called with preorder_traverse(Root).

7.3.6 Example with Objects in Python: Stacks

You can implement the Stack ADT in Python using objects as follows:

```
1 class Stack:
2
3         def __init__(self, items=[]):
4                 self._items = items
5         def push(self, item):
6                 self._items.append(item)
7         def pop(self):
8                 return self._items.pop()
```

```
 9              def isempty ( self ):
10                     return self._items == []
11              def printStack ( self ):
12                     print "Stack:", self._items
```

which then can be used as follows:

```
>>> st = Stack()
>>> st.push("A")
>>> st.push("10")
>>> st.push(20)
>>> print st.pop()
20
>>> st.printStack()
Stack: ['A', '10']
```

7.4 Keywords

The important concepts that we would like our readers to understand in this chapter are indicated by the following keywords:

Classes	Objects
Data Abstraction	Encapsulation
Inheritance	Polymorphism
Member Variables	Member Functions
Virtual Functions	Operator Overloading

7.5 Further Reading

For more information on the topics discussed in this chapter, you can check out the sources below:

- *Data Abstraction or Information Hiding:*
  - http://mitpress.mit.edu/sicp/full-text/sicp/book/node26.html
  - http://en.wikipedia.org/wiki/Abstraction_%28computer_science%29
    #Abstraction_in_object_oriented_programming
- *Encapsulation:*
  - http://en.wikipedia.org/wiki/Encapsulation_%28object-oriented_
    programming%29

- http://www.javaworld.com/javaworld/jw-05-2001/jw-0518-encapsulation.
  html
- *Polymorphism:*
  - http://en.wikipedia.org/wiki/Polymorphism_in_object-oriented_programming
- *Operators and functions that can be overloaded:*
  - http://docs.python.org/reference/datamodel.html#basic-customization

7.6 Exercises

1. What is the difference between data abstraction and encapsulation?
2. Is the existence of virtual functions and operator overloading sufficient to have polymorphism in an OOP language?
3. Since objects are mutable, they are affected by the *aliasing* problem. Write a member function `copy` for the `Person3` class that copies a given object to the current instance without being affected by the aliasing problem.
4. Why is it a good idea to write accessors and modifiers for an object?
5. In Python, everything is an object, and objects are mutable but some objects, such as tuples, strings, numbers are immutable. Define an object of your own which is not mutable. Hint: look up `__setattr__` and `__delattr__` methods.
6. Define a new object in Python for implementing the Queue ADT.
7. Extend the object-based Tree definition provided above such that a node can have more than two children.

Index

G. Üçoluk, S. Kalkan, *Introduction to Programming Concepts with Case Studies in Python*, DOI 10.1007/978-3-7091-1343-1, © Springer-Verlag Wien 2012